*Romantics and Modernists in British Cinema*

**Edinburgh Studies in Film**
Series editors: Martine Beugnet and John Orr

*Chinese Cinemas*
Evans Chan

*The Sense of Film Narration*
Ian Garwood

*Film and the Visual Arts*
Steven Jacobs

*Romantics and Modernists in British Cinema*
John Orr

# *Romantics and Modernists in British Cinema*

*John Orr*

EDINBURGH UNIVERSITY PRESS

For Ailsa



First published in hardback by Edinburgh University Press in 2010.

Edinburgh University Press Ltd
22 George Square, Edinburgh EH8 9LF

www.euppublishing.com

Typeset in Garamond MT Pro
by Servis Filmsetting Ltd, Stockport, Cheshire, and
printed and bound in Great Britain by
Printondemand-worldwide.com

A CIP record for this book is available from the British Library

ISBN 978 0 7486 4014 0 (hardback)
ISBN 978 0 7486 4937 2 (paperback)



Published with the support of the Edinburgh University Scholarly
Publishing Initiatives Fund.

# *Contents*


Acknowledgements vii

List of figures ix

Introduction: romantics versus modernists? 1

1. 1929: romantics and modernists on the cusp of sound 5
   The documentary legacy: *Drifters* 7
   The forging of the fugitive film: *A Cottage on Dartmoor* 11
   Transgressing triangles: *Piccadilly* and *The Manxman* 14
   *Blackmail* and transition 18
   Constructive and deconstructive: *Number Seventeen* 23

2. The running man: Hitchcock's fugitives and *The Bourne Ultimatum* 25
   Jason's Waterloo: Hitchcock, Greengrass and deepest fears 25
   The fugitive kind: pre-war, wartime, post-war 28
   British Hitchcock: from romance thriller to post-romantic fable 32
   The poetics of treachery: Dickinson and Cavalcanti 34
   The triumph of the short film: *Bon Voyage* and *Aventure malgache* 37
   Post-romantic fugitives: *Stage Fright* and *Frenzy* 40
   Epilogue: the *Frenzy* murders 42

3. Running man 2: Carol Reed and his contemporaries 44
   Fable versus romance: *The Third Man* and *They Made Me a Fugitive* 54
   Reed and subterfuge: *The Man Between* and *Our Man in Havana* 57
   Reed's successors 62

4. David Lean: the troubled romantic and the end of empire 64
   Forgotten Lean: the Ann Todd trilogy 64
   *Madeleine*: the perverse unveiled 70

*The Sound Barrier*: the faltering sublime and the end of empire 77
Enthusiast or fanatic? The paradox of Lean's 'Lawrence' 79

5. The trauma film from romantic to modern: *A Matter of Life and Death* to *Don't Look Now* 86
Prelude: Thorold Dickinson and Anton Walbrook 88
Juxtaposition: *A Matter of Life and Death* and *Dead of Night* 89
Powellian trauma: *Black Narcissus*, *The Small Back Room*, *Peeping Tom* 94
Female 'madness' and modernism: *The Innocents* and *Repulsion* 101
The trauma double bill: *Don't Look Now* and *The Wicker Man* 108
The neo-romantic turn and death in Venice: *Don't Look Now* 110
Romantic symbol and modernist edit 112

6. Joseph Losey and Michelangelo Antonioni: the expatriate eye and the parallax view 115
Losey and Pinter: the modernist moment in *The Servant* and *Accident* 119
Coda: *Providence* as Resnais's riposte to Losey 128
Antonioni's parallax view: *Blow-Up* and *The Passenger* 129
What's in a title? *The Passenger* or *Profession: Reporter* 135
Coda: the native eye in *Radio On* 139

7. Expatriate eye 2: Stanley Kubrick and Jerzy Skolimowski 141
Freedom and fate: *Barry Lyndon* 148
Skolimowski and running water: or, *Deep End* and *Cul-de-Sac* 152
Rise and fall: *The Shout*, *Moonlighting*, *Success is the Best Revenge* 156
Bringing it all back home: *Moonlighting* and *Success is the Best Revenge* 159

8. Terence Davies and Bill Douglas: the poetics of memory 164
Mimetic modernism and family mysteries: the Douglas trilogy 167
Davies: the romantic imagist and the poetry of memory 171
Floating through space and time: *The Long Day Closes* 173
The past as present: *The House of Mirth* and *The Wings of the Dove* 177

9. Conclusion: into the new century 180

Select bibliography 185

Index 189

# *Acknowledgements*

I would like to thank Joel Finler for his film stills, which are reproduced with permission, John Caughie and Duncan Petrie for their astute advice before this book was written, Dan Yaccavone, Dorota Ostrowska and Ana Salzberg for their encouragement while it was being written, and Martine Beugnet, for her wisdom at all times.

I would also like to thank the editorial staff of the online journal *senses of cinema* (http://www.sensesofcinema.com), especially Rolando Caputo, for their continued support of my writing and their publication of earlier versions of material contained in this book: 'Forgotten Lean: the Ann Todd Trilogy', 47, 2008, and 'The Trauma Film and British Romantic Cinema 1940–1960', 51, 2009.

# *List of figures*

1.1 Offscreen Corpse: Anny Ondra in *Blackmail* 20
2.1 Fear, Flight, Betrayal: Robert Donat, Peggy Ashcroft and John Laurie in *The 39 Steps* 26
3.1 Painter Meets Gunman: James Mason and Robert Newton in *Odd Man Out* 53
3.2 Lime's Last Stand: Orson Welles in *The Third Man* 57
4.1 Opium or Arsenic? Ann Todd and Ivan Desny in *Madeleine* 75
4.2 Prophet or Avenger? Peter O'Toole in *Lawrence of Arabia* 82
5.1 Through the Looking Glass: Kathleen Byron and Deborah Kerr in *Black Narcissus* 95
5.2 The Trauma Rapture: Deborah Kerr and Martin Stephens in *The Innocents* 103
5.3 Welcome to the Dollhouse: Carol Lynley in *Bunny Lake is Missing* 107
5.4 Watching My Funeral Go By: Julie Christie, Hilary Mason and Clelia Matania in *Don't Look Now* 112
5.5 Hoodlum in the Age of Pop Art: James Fox in *Performance* 113
6.1 The Townhouse as Goldfish Bowl: Dirk Bogarde, James Fox in *The Servant* 123
6.2 Thomas the Vagrant: David Hemmings in *Blow-Up* 133
6.3 Thomas the Magnifier: David Hemmings in *Blow-Up* 133
7.1 One False Eyelash, One False Move: Malcolm McDowell in *A Clockwork Orange* 145
7.2 The Rogue as Holy Fool: Ryan O'Neal in *Barry Lyndon* 150
8.1 Snug and Cosy: Alyse Owens and Leigh McCormack in *The Long Day Closes* 174
8.2 Out in the Cold: Stephen Archibald in *My Childhood* 174

# *Introduction: romantics versus modernists?*

Is there a case for seeing cinema as a contest between 'romantics' and 'modernists'? Yes and no. If there is a clash between romanticism and modernism in what is called 'British' cinema – strictly UK cinema if we include Anglo-Irish production in Northern Ireland – it is as much *internal* as external. There are clusters of romantics and modernists (external): but there are also internal struggles of the soul between romantic and modernist forms of feeling that affect nearly every important filmmaker. Romantic and modernist aesthetics are contrary impulses which inhere in most directors in varying degrees, so that no absolute division between them ever emerges. Instead the coexistence of contrary impulses can be highly fertile. Most great directors are romantics to some degree and modernists to another. There is no fixed ratio but most do come down on one side or the other. We can with some poetic licence slot great names under one of the bipolar categories as we shall now do: Hitchcock, Lean, Powell, Reed and Hamer as romantics; Losey, Polanski, Antonioni, Kubrick and Skolmowski as modernists. And following the lead of Peter Wollen, we can also speak of 'neo-romantics' like Nicholas Roeg, John Boorman, Ken Russell and Derek Jarman as a second, more self-conscious generation that grew out of 1960s modernist style and Pop Art (Wollen 1993: 43–4), but endowed it with a new romantic sensibility, a sensibility which culminated, I would argue, in the very different memory-cinema of Terence Davies at the end of the 1980s. We can also note an important point made by Thomas Elsaesser when analysing the TV-funded 'New British Cinema', of the 1980s, which many saw at the time as an 'innovative', low-budget form. Elsaesser points out that the great modernist innovation came from the 'expatriate gaze', the 'outsider-as-insider' view of the 1960s and 1970s, and this had proved much more memorable (Elsaesser 1993: 60).

These judgements feed into the second half of this book. Just as Elsaesser critiqued the 'televisual' quality of the much touted Channel 4 cinema of the 1980s, so Wollen repudiated the claims for an auteurist 'British New Wave' in the early 1960s based on films made in the industrial North. By and large both judgements, it seems to me, are right, which is why this book shows a preference for the 1940s, the decade of world war and fading Empire, as the great decade of native British romanticism, and the newly consumerist 1960s and 1970s, as the two great decades of modernism when expatriate directors played a vital role in film form. Of course, decades are arbitrary in their cut-off and less than half the story, but they do remain a necessary starting point. Much of the inspiration guiding the first part of this study comes from Raymond Durgnat's *A Mirror for England* since it remains the best general book ever written on British cinema and one that is unlikely to be surpassed. The present study is both a homage and a riposte. Much of the new film material from the 1970s onward which Durgnat did not explore is explored here and earlier film history revised accordingly. And the challenge in doing this has been to avoid overuse of two terms which for so long have been like critical lead balloons hovering over UK territory: 'gritty' and 'realism'. Orr, for example, has made a spirited attempt to revitalise the concept of 'realism' in a post-Bazinian context, but on the success or failure of this, the jury is still out (Orr 2002: 104–13; Orr 2003: 299–317). Romanticism and modernism can be equally fraught in this context of concept re-creation but this study, I hope, will provide us with new and fresh ways of seeing things often viewed with complacency.

Let us by way of passing, then, look at a film in which the romantic and the modern fluidly intersect. In Patrick Keiller's ingenious documentary fiction *London* (1994) Paul Scofield is the unseen Narrator, a ship's doctor who returns to London to help the project of his dying ex-lover, 'Robinson', now living in Vauxhall, to chronicle the essence of the city. Under an early caption of 'the romantic' the film sees the endeavour as a bold quest to 'get outside of oneself' and 'tunnel through time' to capture the city's nature; and in seeing the city anew to see oneself anew, 'to see oneself from the outside, to see oneself in a romance'. The film is both a commentary by the Narrator on Robinson's quest and a visual summation of it, a series of still-frame moving images, documentary tableaux of scenes across the city. The quest is romantic, the execution modern – a collage of images with narrative commentaries that never once include a sighting of the two main 'characters' in the film. The Narrator has a voice but no presence; Robinson has no voice and no presence except through the Narrator's where he is the ghost that governs the narrative. We could say, then, that the quest is transcendent, the execution immanent. Robinson's 'London' strives to be more than the sum of its fractured parts. But is it? Does its modernist form override its romantic impulse or vice versa? In a way the answer is open, as in any good modernist text with no resolution. The spectator has to resolve it. Is 'London' resurrected in Keiller's film as a magic organic whole, or does it fracture it into pieces?

Romantics wish through art to transcend the fractured and divisive life-world they see around them and recompose it, making their artistic mark by so doing. By contrast, modernists strive to explore the vast mosaic of the life-world's immanent nature and take it as is, a mystery in itself which makes the act of representing it equally mysterious. In film, paradoxically, the great British romantics like Hitchcock, Lean, Reed and Powell have often worked though classical 'invisible' narration and under tight censorship: the great romantic films invoke war and its aftermath or the end of Empire and frame within them the romantic ironies of personal passion. In British film romantic irony hinges to a great extent on the mismatch between public and personal passion: the great examples here would be *Black Narcissus* (1946) and *Lawrence of Arabia* (1962). In turn, the modernists challenge censorship and try to get under the skin of contemporary life, but this leads to its own puzzles and mysteries which are intrinsic to both the substance of the film and the style they seek to impose so that style and substance often separate out, a gap, a fissure opening up that can never easily be closed. In romanticism film form appears organic, in modernism fractured. In the neo-romantic revival of Roeg, Boorman and Jarman where censorship is much looser, shock is a modernist tactic often allied to pathos as a romantic form, a wager on aesthetic risk that has produced either sublime or ridiculous cinema, often within the career of the same director.

The cool modernism of the 1960s and 1970s is also a post-imperial moment and more focused on the present. The myth of patriotic war recedes into the distance and the largesse of Empire becomes a dim memory. Culturally and politically, the country appears naked, the future uncertain, the expatriate eye trained and inspired to see things the British cannot, and may not want to see. As opposed to the transcendent quest for unity and the romantic ironies its failures generate (especially strong in Hitchcock and Reed), we have a realm of perceptual ambiguity that is almost schizoid. Films like *Accident* (1967) and *Blow-Up* (1966) offer us the lure of totally opposed readings of a single set of moving images. Films like *A Clockwork Orange* (1971) are a shock but equally schizoid since we try to make fixed interpretations at our peril. And it is appropriate perhaps to end with the intertwining of memory and modernism in the work of Liverpudlian Terence Davies and Edinburgh-born Bill Douglas both of whom create film memories out of the post-war period when classical film was in the ascendant, but with artistic techniques which owe everything to the innovations of the next decade. Both directors loved classical Hollywood yet both followed in the footsteps of Ingmar Bergman.

So this is a twentieth-century history which starts at the end of the silent era in 1929, stops deliberately in the year 2000 with Davies' beautifully austere *The House of Mirth*, then starts again with a postscript in the new century. There are some notable and unfair omissions: Jarman and Greenaway, because I have already written about them (Orr 2000: 327–38) and because dozens of others have also written about them; and there is also little on Nicholas Roeg after *Don't Look Now* (1972), and Boorman and Ridley Scott because they made most of their films outside the UK. Meanwhile in the new century it is still premature to judge key directors like Lynne Ramsey, Pawel Pawlikowski and Andrea Arnold because they are still making films on which their reputation will depend. So this is a history mainly, a reflective meditation on time past and time recent, selective certainly, but totally unlike, I would hope, anything that has been written for quite some time.

CHAPTER 1

# *1929: romantics and modernists on the cusp of sound*

In the UK, we could say, the silent cinema perishes in its moment of triumph. The five landmark films of the silent era came at the instant of transition to sound in 1929. Let us list them: John Grierson's documentary of North Sea herring fleets, *Drifters*, Anthony Asquith's fugitive narrative, *A Cottage on Dartmoor*, E. A. Dupont's racial city drama, *Piccadilly*, Alfred Hitchcock's psychosexual melodrama, *The Manxman* and finally his famous transition to sound, *Blackmail*, which exists in both silent and talkie versions and whose title, plot-wise, says it all. If we call these films 'avant-garde' because they are path-breaking, which they were, let us remember they are not part of a clearly unified British avant-garde movement. They are more accurately modernistic, experimenting with the possibilities of silent film narrative in an epoch of artistic modernism. If we add a sixth title, exploring the new sound medium but with the same path-breaking panache and inventiveness, it would have to be Hitch's throwaway constructivist thriller *Number Seventeen,* made in 1931 but not released until the following year. And then we have to face the fact that three of the six pictures bear the signature of one director, generally recognised as the most talented that England has ever produced. Yet all six films are still products of their time, of a crucial moment of transition that is impersonal and folds into history. All six break new ground in complementary ways: they are followed by films that build on their legacy right through the rest of the century.

On the other hand, sound ushers in a new era for the nascent British film industry with its new studios: the mechanics of establishing sound narratives take priority. Structuring screenplays and formulating *mise-en-scène*, overcoming the restrictions that sound technologies had initially imposed on the moving image, were the main tasks. The paradox here is enormous: embryonic modernism is supplanted by embryonic classicism. Something, inevitably, was lost in translation and only with the war did the promise of 1929 start to be realised. And it was not until the 1960s that we see a full reprise of the modernist project in UK cinema, a neo-modern wave. At the same time these five silents contain the seeds of the sensibility that dominates an earlier phase of UK cinema – romanticism. They are, we might argue, romantic and modern at the same time. For history's hard-boiled evolutionists, cinema creates a problem and its own contradictions. In 1929 the romantic and the modern coexisted before the romantic triumphed: and the romantic won out because it fitted more easily with the new *classical* conventions of sound narrative, of how to structure in cinematic terms the well-made film. Divorced from modernism, romanticism thrived by getting into bed with classicism, a marriage of convenience if ever there was one. Thus a history that appeared progressive then goes circular and ends up as regressive – and all the while life, film and technology move on!

The UK *founding five plus one*, if we use this formula, made up for lost time on the new international circuit that cinema had become. The Americans had D. W. Griffith, Douglas Fairbanks and Mary Pickford, Rudolf Valentino, Charlie Chaplin (from south London, of course) and Buster Keaton. The French had Abel Gance and René Clair. The Germans had two thriving cinematic schools, both modernistic, that overlapped to great effect and entranced the world – Expressionism and the New Objectivity. The arch-modernistic Soviets had Sergei Eisenstein, Vsevolod Pudovkin, Lev Kuleshov, Dziga Vertov and Alexander Dovzhenko, all nourished on the stark realities of tempestuous revolution. The British valiantly brought up the rear and for that reason still get overlooked. But *the founding five plus one* match their international rivals and foretell much of what is to come, setting markers for what must be translated into sound narrative, where the challenge became this – to recapture the power of the image the best silents possessed, but also take forward the innovative potential shown to great effect in *Blackmail* and *Number Seventeen.* At the same time there are in these films enduring themes, themes that in the British context are repeated through to the twenty-first century. The *founding five plus one* provides the prototype. If their artistic power was vitiated by the abrupt transition to sound, the talkies were still a vital financial boost to the undeveloped British film industry. In 1925 British films had captured only 5 per cent of the home market, but by 1932, thanks to the exhibition quotas established under the Cinematographic Act 1927, this had increased to 24 per cent: as a consequence the larger companies and exhibitors were able to adjust more rapidly to sound than their European competitors (Street 1997: 18–19). That commercial success may have created the paradox of diminishing at first the quality of the product, but cinema everywhere had to adjust and rely on improved technologies. By 1936 Hitchcock had shown his mastery of the new medium in the back-to-back brilliance of *The 39 Steps* and *Sabotage*, only to leave three years later for Hollywood and the producing talents of David O. Selznick. In Hitchcock's absence it was the circumstances of the Second World War which enabled the UK, free from occupation, to establish itself as a major player in the industry and a source of artistic greatness in the medium itself.

For the founding five in 1929, there may have been no clear avant-garde in its loose modernist project but one common source for its starburst of creativity was the London Film Society, founded in 1925 to bring the best in international cinema to the metropolis. And it was a place where avant-garde aspirations were nurtured and where, some critics would say, a Bloomsbury-style film avant-garde was forged (O'Pray 2003: 36–8). Its founder, Ivor Montagu, a filmmaker and critic who was to co-edit *The Lodger* in post-production, had returned from Germany inspired by what he had seen in the industry there, as indeed had Hitchcock. He worked in Germany first as an art director, then as full director of *The Mountain Eagle* (1926) and *The Pleasure Garden* (1926) for producer Michael Balcon, one of the most influential figures in shaping the industry transition to sound. Montague, who constantly challenged British film censorship at the time, was in the process of switching his allegiance from the Americans to the Germans and the Soviets and the results showed in the Society's programme. The great events were its screenings from Weimar cinema of *Waxworks* (1924), *Raskolnikov* (1923) and *The Cabinet of Dr. Caligari* (1919) plus the films of G. W. Pabst, Walter Ruttman and Hans Richter. Its keynote lectures in 1929 were given by Pudovkin and Eisenstein. In addition to Hitch and Montague, a third regular of the Film Society was the Cambridge graduate and close friend of Montague, Angus MacPhail, who later became a key scriptwriter for Ealing Studios and for Hitchcock. A fourth enthusiast was Asquith, whose silent films such as *Shooting Stars* (1927) and *Underground* (1928) were perhaps as significant as Hitchcock's in the run-up to sound. Sexton has pointed out that in their silent features Hitch and Asquith shared a common trope, a juxtaposition of cultural Englishness against international stylisation in film form itself. In *Underground* Asquith wove the pattern of a psychological thriller with expressionist lighting in the London Underground around mundane Londoners and everyday events, while Hitchcock's *The Lodger* (1927) had contrasted the stylised expressionist framing of Ivor Novello as a menacing stranger with the plain uneventful lives of the Buntings, the defensive lower-middle-class family where he seeks lodging (Sexton 2002: 361). Moreover, although British cinema has been aligned by many critics with the genre cinemas of Hollywood, the best of 1929 shows a difference, that of the UK to continental Europe. In its inception, British cinema was distinctly European.

## THE DOCUMENTARY LEGACY: *DRIFTERS*

It is significant that one of the strong points of 1930s British film was the rise of the documentary which, relying more on music, voice-over and recorded location sound than it did on narrative dialogue and structured plotting, was able to give the camera greater freedom of movement and greater imagination in the recorded image. Yet Grierson's *Drifters* was silent cinema owing much to the stylistics of Soviet film, especially to Vertov and Eisenstein. From Vertov it takes the device of filming in, for example, its trawler shots of the disappearing headland, still landscapes from moving objects: from Eisenstein it takes the quick juxtaposition of shots and the principles of repetition and difference: returning to film the same object or figure twice while cutting away between and after to a new shot altogether, a montage principle of one step backward and two steps forward. Like *Strike* (1924), it celebrates the power and pain of the world of work and like *The Battleship Potemkin* (1925) it films the ship's crew at sea in what Grierson calls 'an epic of steam and steel'. This is the heavy duty herring fleet of the new industrial world, and there is no nostalgic paean to the sea. Where it differs from the Soviets in its sensibility, however, lies in its search for organic unity, rejecting the dialectics of class strife in favour of the resourceful community, of the fishermen in the herring fleets on the North Sea. It is a workers' romance. Not only does it celebrate the isolated community, it also celebrates that community's wider link to industrial society. The catch is a small-scale conquest of nature in the interest of mankind, or put mundanely the commercial interest of Britain. We end with stirring sequences of crated and barrelled herring transported by rail, road and sea to destinations around the country and beyond. The forging of patriotism which British filmmakers took on as their major task ten years before the onset of war is here in miniature, where the enemy is the ocean or at best other predators such as conga and dogfish which compete with the fleets for the herring shoals. But in the Griersonian world-view humans, largely speaking, are in harmony.

Grierson is thus substituting for Eisenstein's dialectic montage in which both meaning and dramatic climax are intertwined around the crystallisation of strife, an *organic* montage, a dynamic compilation of related shots into a forged meaning with a difference, an organic composition stressing communal harmony. The sparse verbal poetry lies in the intertitles: the sense of visual poetry lies in Grierson's *découpage* of the moving image. The absence of a voice-over commentary, which often defines the meaning of a sound documentary as it does, for example, in sections of *Night Mail* (1936) made seven years later, is something that *Drifters* does not need It is compiled and created as silent documentary and appears to tell its own story. Yet its style statement is inseparable from its fundamental theme. It is a romantic fable of final unity overcoming danger in the encounter between humans and nature, and division between the organic and industrial world. It is also, as a narrative, an adventure story of sorts. The trawler's journey is to find the shoals, make the catch overnight and get safely back to port through the storm-tossed waves of the North Sea. Everyone pulls their weight and plays their part. The crew's faces become familiar through repetition, especially in a mosaic of close shots, yet as in Eisenstein they remain anonymous. There are no names, no privileging of any of the figures on board through intertitles. In its own perverse way, anonymity confers equality under shared duress.

Thus while sound becomes a facilitator of narrative information and direction, it also creates a dilemma over the question of voice-over. Does commentary enhance or vitiate our response to the documentary image? In another short fishing film nine years later, which follows on from Grierson's path-breaking silent, *North Sea* (1938), directed by Harry Watt, who had worked under Grierson's leadership at the GPO (General Post Office) film unit, broke with the new convention of voice-over commentary to dramatise the plight of a deep-sea trawler in trouble during a storm that radios ashore for help. Instead of commentary he created a drama-documentary using scripted dialogue for real fishermen and simultaneously broke with the fragmented montage style of Grierson in favour of a more unified dramatic narrative in which the fishermen become characters in a crisis story. Thus Watt attempted to retain and broaden the poetry of Grierson's original through dramatic dialogue and through the SOS crisis of the boat in difficulty calling in radio help. As a result Watt's film became popular box-office docudrama, an immediate predecessor to Jennings' *Fires Were Started* (1942), the most powerful and compelling of all the wartime docudramas filmed in *cinéma vérité* style. *Fires Were Started* tells a story of blazing warehouses in the East End in the latter days of the London Blitz with dialogue but no voice-over, poetic montage and with time-compression, a day and night in the life of a local fire unit faced, unlike Grierson's herring fleets, with the destructive fall-out from enemy bombers.

Both *North Sea* and *Fires Were Started* imprint on the cinematic imagination with more power than the sound documentary Grierson earlier produced for the GPO film unit, *Night Mail* directed by Watt and brilliantly edited by Cavalcanti and Basil Wright. Yet *Night Mail* retains a haunting power and singularity. The documentary had the bonus of poetry from W. H. Auden and a score by Benjamin Britten during the closing sequences of the film as it approaches its final destination in Glasgow when Grierson's own voice-over orchestrates what is intended as an audio-visual hymn to UK unity through the mail train's poetry-in-motion. The film lasts a day and night, like *Drifters*, and employs the time-compression of the habitual trip which the film seeks to make special, if not monumental. In truth, it cannot bear the weight of the Griersonian myth, the magical harmony of the nation that it seeks to extract from the material of his film footage. For Grierson and his followers the night mail is one of the great wonders of the organic industrial world, the moving miracle of communication that has its own unity of being. Yet *Drifters* is more universal for being more specific. It was a dilemma that would not go away and with the demands and exigencies of war, it falls into clearer focus.

If we look for wartime examples of the same destructiveness at sea, and one which enhances the poetic montage of Grierson's classic, we need go no further than David Lean's inspired directing and editing in the first section of his war feature *In Which We Serve* (1942) where the destroyer HMS *Torrin* is dive-bombed and sunk off the coast of Crete at the most dangerous stage of the war for a besieged and isolated Britain. Here, of course, drama-documentary has new poetic licence and with Noël Coward's screenplay becomes substantially fictional. The film (based on a real-life incident, the sinking of Lord Mountbatten's ship HMS *Kinross* off the coast of Crete) is directed by Lean as a patriotic melodrama: but it is the action scenes at sea that signify the true forging of social solidarity. By contrast, the peacetime flashbacks that depict the social differences between officers and ordinary sailors are awkward and contrived, marred by the tone of condescension of Coward's dialogue. It is the urgency, the bewilderment, the suddenness of the attack from German dive-bombers that justifies the fast editing, the fades and superimpositions, the virtuoso montage of multiple-shot composition. Technically speaking, Lean achieves by tonal dissonance a complex structure of feeling, the contrast between impending disaster, the anxieties of the besieged crew and the calm stoicism of officer command. Grierson's trawler storm on the return to port is graphic enough, but by comparison a picnic: yet it sets the tone for the look and style of Lean's picture which perfectly integrates documentary footage with studio simulation and the use of that infallible standby, the studio water-tank.

When Lean flashes back to an earlier North Sea battle between *Torrin* and a German destroyer fought in a storm at night he films the studio replication with a photographic clarity that 'carries' the look of the location into the studio itself. The high-contrast photography with its low lighting levels and, on deck, the translucent sheen of reflected light on rain-soaked waterproofs, becomes a template for the post-war look on *terra firma* of American *film noir* and the British fugitive film. The nocturnal look clearly looks forward also to the secret assignations at Carnforth railway station in *Brief Encounter* (1945) but also has continuity with the nocturnal look of previous railway stations, in *Night Mail.* In fact, *Brief Encounter* follows *Night Mail* in just the same way that *In Which We Serve* had followed *Drifters* – a doubling, if you like, of romantic lineage. The nocturnal *mise-en-scène* of the onrushing mail train is, metaphorically speaking, an establishing shot for much to follow in post-war British cinema. The train and the fugitive both run at twilight or at night. With Cavalcanti's superlative editing on *Night Mail*, there are sounds too to match the chiaroscuro images of pale platforms and dark, glistening steel – the scream of the engine whistle, the hissing of steam, the insistent rhythm of the pistons which, as the mail train crosses the Scottish border at dawn, Auden's voice tries to match with onomatopoeic lyrics, scattergun phrasing and rhyming verse. Not only is the night mail a medium of near-mythic communication, it is also a vessel of unbridled expectation. Grierson's final voice-over proclaims rhetorically: 'None will hear the postman's knock without a quickening of the heart, for who can bear to think himself forgotten?' In Lean's classic love story the passenger train is that same vessel of rich expectation, bringing anxious lovers to their secret rendezvous. Changing the gender of the phrase to 'for who can bear to think *herself* forgotten?' would give us an entrée into the heart of Laura Jesson, hoping beyond hope that the looming train will deliver her to the craggy, handsome figure of Alec Harvey. Lean's picture trades not only on the joy of arrival but even more on the poetry of departure. The lover's departure thus seems a companion piece and a sequel but also a mournful celebration of loss that, one feels, is beyond the scope of the GPO film unit, beyond any documentary of that kind. Yet somehow, somewhere along the line, Grierson's general project has set it in motion.

## The forging of the fugitive film: *A Cottage on Dartmoor*

This silent feature by Anthony Asquith, son of the British Liberal prime minister of the early 1920s, is a key to the subsequent career of Alfred Hitchcock and the triumph of the fugitive film in the post-war years. So much that happens in that very rich and short time-span is contained in this film. Uncannily enough it also coincides with the publication of the début novel of Graham Greene, *The Man Within*, which the author started in 1926 at the age of twenty-two. Greene, who was to contribute so much to the fugitive genre in both fiction and film starts his literary career with a young man on the run who shelters from his pursuers in a remote country cottage. In Asquith's film the opening sequence shows us much the same, but Asquith's fugitive Joe (Ugo Henning) is an escaped convict from Dartmoor, and it is the police, not fellow criminals, who are pursuing him. The opening shot-composition is unforgettable: a tree with bare branches silhouetted on a stormy landscape, then a dark figure jumping into view from above the frame before a cut to him fleeing at first amidst the smoke of burnt stubble and then silhouetted against the sunset. For an encore Asquith films his fugitive's reflection in a pool of water before cutting to a child in a bath, guilty adult juxtaposed to innocent child, the wild rockpool to the domestic tub. Then repetition: once more the convict on the open landscape leaping down out of the top of the frame past the jagged silhouette of a leafless tree, then turning away to flee, or so it seems, from the camera itself. Suddenly the cottage is in sight, then another elliptical cut to the prison he has left – the shadow of warder's cap on the cell door and beyond a close-up of the forced grate on the wall beside the cell window. Asquith's visual language tells its own story: card titles appear unnecessary.

Inside the cottage where the young mother, Sally (Norah Baring), cares for her baby the scene is one of domestic tranquillity about to be disturbed. Asquith again uses offscreen space. Joe's silhouette edges into the right of the frame as Sally exits through the back door. As she sees him the camera tracks in dramatically to extreme close-up on her astonished gaze then flashes back to the hairdressing salon where they had both worked and first met. The timing of the flashback is pitch perfect, a key moment where Sally is dragged out of the ordinary into the extraordinary but also out of the present and into the past. Having begun with the dramatic flight Asquith goes back to the workaday aspect of experience, where the storyline also unravels the prehistory to its fugitive desperation. Here Asquith forges an intimate and intense visual language that charts the intertwining of jealousy and desire. Joe's desire for Sally is exacerbated and intensified by a wealthier rival, a local farmer (Hans Schlettow), who seeks all the options of the salon – haircut, shave, manicure etc. – to prolong his stay in the barber's chair. With the slightest of facial inflections, Joe's desiring gaze on Sally turns into a jealous gaze at the bulky farmer and Asquith uses a plethora of mirror shots – since this is a huge hairdresser's salon – to blend narcissism with surveillance where those watching themselves are also being watched and the camera captures everything. As Joe attends to the farmer's hair, Sally manicures his rough, stubby nails. A series of close-shots with rapid edits suggests an erotic threesome and there is an echo in the male rivalry of suppressed attraction on Joe's part for his burlier rival, a motif that is repeated by Hitchcock in the vexed love-triangle of *The Manxman*.

The barber's chair is also the site of the sharp blade that matches the everyday to the horrific – the shaving razor. The *mise-en-scène* of the farmer's wounding again displays the virtues of montage in converting the ordinary implement into the extraordinary instrument. The myth of Sweeney Todd the demon barber would no doubt have been in the mind of Asquith's audience, but the hesitating razor held near the throat becomes a sign of vacillating jealousy in which motive becomes ambiguous. In *Blackmail* and *Sabotage* Hitchcock's murders play on exactly the same register as Asquith's wounding – the nearness of the everyday implement as a weapon of death but with a knife not a razor. It is the sudden impulse of the instrument at hand, the absence of prior intent that gives the scene its structure. As if to show he wasn't fixated on knives Hitchcock later replaces them with 3-D scissors in *Dial M for Murder* (1954) and he uses the image of the open razor to great effect in the trembling hand of a traumatised Gregory Peck in *Spellbound* (1945), where he also copies from Asquith the use of the sudden subjective flash to red in extreme crisis.

The fugitive theme and psychosexual storyline are followed by a third legacy the film bequeaths, the presence of cinema within the film. The farmer takes Sarah to see a local talkie and jealous Joe stalks them, sitting furtively in the row behind. Asquith gives a fascinating cameo of cinema culture at the time, using rapid cuts and repetition in Soviet-style montage and creating a special paradox. The film appears to be a silent with an orchestra in the pits, not the talkie the couple enthuse about. And for this scene Asquith originally did record synchronised sound to give voice to the orchestra, though it was not used in the final cut. Instead the cross-cutting of audience reaction and orchestral instruments is used to create a special audio-visual tension, as if we are being asked to *imagine* the crescendo of orchestral sounds as we see extreme close shots of musicians playing (repeating images of trombone, piano and percussion); seen silently, imaginary crescendo in sound matches the reactive (visual) crescendo of spectators watching a thriller that holds them in suspense before ending in relief with the triumph, we presume, of good over evil. The big screen here is also a medium of seduction since, lit only by the screen's flicker, our couple are caught spellbound in their upward gaze: the film ends with Sarah's head leaning for the first time on the farmer's shoulder. The only viewer immune to all of this is Joe, who is watching not the screen but the couple in front of him. The couple's drama-fix is on the screen, but his is in the balcony and it is them. And if his film has an extended montage sequence set in a cinema, Asquith duly makes his own cameo appearance as an innocent spectator whom two schoolboys mistake for the star they see on the screen in front of them. Seven years later Hitchcock's make-over of Joseph Conrad's seedy London anarchist Mr Verloc in *Sabotage* also makes him a cinema proprietor in working-class London. His wife's idea of vengeance for the gruesome death of her young brother is nurtured by the kids' cartoon 'Who Killed Cock Robin?' which she watches from the side of the cramped auditorium: another cinema sequence that incites hatred and has tragic consequences.

We can see here the origin of so many things: the reflexive meditation on film that is itself cinematically experimental – cue Michael Powell's *Peeping Tom* (1960); the cinema as physical object – cue Hitchcock's *Sabotage*; the auteur's cameo walk-on – cue Hitchcock again. Again in Hitchcock's *The 39 Steps* Robert Donat as Richard Hannay arrives, pursued by police, at an isolated crofter's cottage in the Scottish Lowlands, where he charms the crofter's disaffected wife. The fugitive theme is even wider in its post-war repercussions.

Trevor Howard in *They Made Me a Fugitive* (1947) and John McCallum in *It Always Rains on Sunday* (1947) both play criminal figures who are Dartmoor fugitives on the run. In Hamer's film McCallum as Tommy Swann like Joe hides also in the bedroom of his former sweetheart: in Cavalcanti's film escaping convict Howard as black marketer Clem Morgan also confronts a lone woman in a cottage on Dartmoor. Just like Joe, James Mason as fugitive Johnny McQueen in *Odd Man Out* (1947) also dies shot by the law, in the arms of his sweetheart. In Asquith's film Joe makes his jail break at the start of his picture: fifty years later in Hitchcock's *Frenzy* (1972) wrongly convicted Jon Finch as Richard Blaney makes his break for freedom at the very end to seek out the real murderer.

## TRANSGRESSING TRIANGLES: *PICCADILLY* AND *THE MANXMAN*

Triangles only work, or fail to work, in the age that celebrates romantic love, an age which in Western cultures may now be over. A triangle in effect must work and not work at the same time – it adds what is missing in the binary relationship, but at the same time threatens to destroy it. Another way of putting it is this: it is a transitional triad stranded between dyads and is thereby doomed. It also involves mimetic rivalry in which the rivals possess a closeness that is finally difficult to bear, but also a vital difference. In *Dartmoor* Asquith had contrasted chunky farmer with fastidious barber but predicated their likeness on screen closeness to Norah Baring: all three knowingly together around the barber's chair and later unbearably close in the cinema balcony. In *The Manxman* the male rivals are boyhood friends who have grown up together and as adults may well be in love with one another. The difference lies in class, for one is a local fisherman and the other a successful lawyer. In Arnold Bennett's screenplay for *Piccadilly* the two women vying for the same man are both cabaret dancers. The difference lies in race as well as class. Shosho is not known as a dancer at all but discovered as a truculent maid washing dishes in the kitchens of the dance emporium and dancing to entertain the other kitchen staff. The other woman, Gilda Grey, is already a dance-floor celebrity. The latter is posh, white and English: the former olive-skinned, Chinese and living in Limehouse. Or to put it another way, round, in Asquith's and Hitchcock's films the woman changes her allegiance while in Dupont's film the man changes his – and breaks through the racial barrier. As implied in their respective titles the geography differs too. Asquith and Hitchcock both celebrate the remote and the regional. Dupont's film celebrates the city cabaret and the lure of metropolis. Piccadilly is not Dartmoor or the habitat of the Manxman, yet everywhere love is the usual sacrificial feast.

As a director newly arrived from Weimar Germany Dupont may be considered one of the first major exponents of the expatriate gaze in British film, the outsider who brings an unfamiliar eye to bear upon familiar territory, but also to discover new territories within which cinema up to that point had not explored. The point is moot. Versions of Piccadilly were starting to appear onscreen but versions of Limehouse were still in short supply. Taken together in the same film, the contrast is electric. From the other side of the world came Anna May Wong, Chinese-Californian, whose American accent did not need to crash through the sound barrier in a silent movie and thus destroy the illusion of Limehouse Chinese. Her version of Shosho now has iconic status. For indeed both expatriates prospered: yet when they went on to the United States – she back and he forward – both faltered. This had been a brave film for both and neither could find a niche in the Hollywood studio system of the sound era where Dupont descended into mediocrity and Wong played second fiddle to Marlene Dietrich in Josef von Sternberg's *Shanghai Express* (1932). Thus we should be thankful to British film for small mercies. Wong did not need to break the sound barrier but she did break the race barrier, albeit briefly, and dominated this picture as much as another American, Louise Brooks, had triumphed the same year in *Pandora's Box* (1929).

In Dupont's film the race card acts – mixed-metaphor time – as a two-edged sword. The Limehouse sequences with the passion between stricken impresario and sensual Chinese dancer, and between the black and white couple on the local pub dance floor, are defiant gestures which in the sound era of the 1930s would have been wiped out by stricter censorship. Yet the plot's dénouement is itself a compromise, some would say a betrayal. The jealous white lover faints, it later transpires, before she has a chance to shoot her darker rival, who is killed instead by an even more jealous rival her diminutive Chinese associate Jimmy, who may be her lover or brother, or indeed both. This is a timely *deus ex machina* to rescue the white dancer from the crime of murder (one thinks here of Hitchcock's *Murder!* (1930) made a year later where actress Diana Baring, played by Norah Baring, is accused instead of the real murderer, effeminate half-caste Handel Fane). In other words, a cop-out. Bennett and Dupont go so far but no further. They push to a perceived limit and succeed because they don't turn their jealous white woman into a racial killer after all. Yet the plot's crude disclaimer is a flaw in the film's courage, to be repeated in a later age when British cinema had moved out of the age of censorship almost entirely – but of course never quite.

One thinks of that bold transformation of the 1980s where, powered by new television tie-ins with BBC2 and Channel 4, low-to-medium pictures with independent producers started to flourish and deliver feature films that dealt in stark controversies of the new Thatcherite era – social, political, artistic. In

1985, Working Title with Sarah Radclyffe and Tim Bevan produced *My Beautiful Laundrette* for Channel 4, a feature written by novelist Hanif Kureshi and directed by Stephen Frears. A year later Stephen Woolley's Palace Pictures gave us Neil Jordan's racially inflected melodrama *Mona Lisa*, also with some input from Channel 4, and as its swansong in 1992 Woolley's Palace along with Channel 4 films gave us Jordan's transatlantic box-office hit *The Crying Game* which combined strong racial overtones with smart sexual surprises. In one way or another all three are successors to *Piccadilly* in their overt boldness, but also their limitation of vision. The truly strong London social dramas for the end of century have white subjects in their major roles – Alan Clarke's *The Firm* (1989), Mike Leigh's *Naked* (1993), Gary Oldman's *Nil by Mouth* (1997), Gillies MacKinnon's *Pure* (2002) and, most recently, Andrea Arnold's *Fish Tank* (2009) – all this while the racial and cultural complexion of the city is so rapidly changing.

Yet Dupont's interracial love-trope is still echoed in the later films of Jordan and Frears: and as late as 2005 Ken Loach's Scottish film, written by Paul Laverty and shot in Glasgow, *Ae Fond Kiss*, is the first important UK feature to deal with conviction about the cultural pitfalls of white–Pakistani romance. It does so by making its male protagonist Glaswegian and his female lover Irish and Catholic. Though less rated than *Laundrette*, Frears' *Dirty Pretty Things* (2002) works better as interracial drama in its mix of scabrous comedy and serious observation. In Chiwetel Ejiofor's performance as a Nigerian night porter and mini-cab driver protecting Turkish illegal Audrey Tautou, there is something new and powerful to match the film's flair for echoing and uniting modernist style and romantic sensibility. Moreover, Frears and Jordan both remain maestros of the atmospheric London location. Topographical juxtapositions of Piccadilly and Limehouse in Dupont are scenically echoed, for example, in *Mona Lisa*: the five-star hotels and rich clients of an opulent Mayfair where Cathy Tyson as Simone is driven to her assignations and the eerie street life of an expressionistic Kings Cross where her lover-cum-junkie (played by Kate Hardie) dismally plies hers.

In terms of box-office attention the homosexual passion in the films of Frears and Jordan is something of a first for British box-office cinema, though some would argue it is pallid and cosmetic beside the modernist invention of Derek Jarman and Isaac Julien. But to return to homosexuality in 1929 when it is officially forbidden onscreen, I would argue that its oscillating complement, the bisexual triangle, has its original root *as subtext* in *The Manxman*, one of the rare Hitchcock melodramas without a murder. The Hitchcock judgement has to be retrospective, made in light of what happened later in *Rebecca* (1940), *Rope* (1948), *Strangers on a Train* (1951), *I Confess* (1953), in elements of *Marnie* (1964) and *The Birds* (1963) and, more jokily, in *North by Northwest* (1959) (Orr 2005: 179–84). Like Asquith, Hitchcock knows how to play on the triangular poetics of the gaze and in *The Manxman* he makes use of a bold conceit. The innocent gaze of the hard-working fisherman Pete (Carl Brisson) is contrasted with the ambivalent gaze of Philip (Malcolm Keen), the bourgeois lawyer, and the look of innkeeper's daughter Kate (Anny Ondra) shifts from innocence to ambivalence and her allegiance changes as she abandons Pete in favour of Philip. The poetics of the gaze is founded on class difference in Hitchcock's most complex use of visual language in his silent period. These then are the simple formulas that Hitchcock converts into complex cinematic tropes. To be bourgeois is to be knowing, ambivalent. To be proletarian is to be naïve and innocent. To move from innocence to experience is to abandon one class for another.

Written out, the schema seems too simplistic; filmed, it is rich and complex. *How* it is filmed fills out the *what-ness* of its narrative. It is sexual ambiguity that gives class politics its edge: equally, it is class difference that gives ambiguous sexuality its edge. The 'innocent' affection of childhood pals seems in adult life to signify something else, purely through Hitchcock's filming of the gaze or the look, the male arm draped around the male shoulder, and the placement of the camera. Thus when Pete confesses to Phil his love for Kate and his wish to marry her, arm around his shoulder, the answer is 'You and Kate – oh, yes.' Of whom is he jealous? The answer is both of them. Kate threatens his secret affection for Pete; Pete threatens his secret longing for Kate. Hitchcock's tongue-in-cheek mockery of the Romeo-Juliet balcony scene takes it further. We see Pete, Romeo-style, beseeching Kate at her window. The camera tilts to reveal him standing on Phil's shoulders. Pete is literally and metaphorically propped up by Phil who elsewhere also proposes on his behalf – 'You speak for me, Phil' – a classic *mise-en-scène* of mimetic doubling. Hitchcock thickens atmosphere with the flashing beam from the lighthouse and the cinematic framing of separation through door apertures, partitions and divided window-panes. In one brilliant long shot, he films from Phil's POV (point of view) through the divided glass partition of the pub to the parlour where the couple canoodle as Phil jealously watches on. The Hitchcock exteriors are equally powerful, the archway of the rocks on the seashore, the fish gutted at the quayside, the pastoral scenes of the Kate–Philip romance where their affair is consummated after Pete, scorned by Kate's father, has gone away to seek his fortune. At one level, this is romantic melodrama far removed from *Drifters*, but at another it is like a parallel world. Early on the fishermen are on the quayside protesting against steam trawlers encroaching on their fishing grounds, a type of dispute noticeably absent from Grierson's film, but one in which his glorious 'herring fleet' could well be the enemy. The film works because, as Hitchcock said later, all backgrounds must function and this is a grounded film.

In a final take on its transgressing triangle it works subtly through melodrama which seems at first sight to be too obvious. Pete comes back to the island with his fortune, marries Kate who is pregnant with Philip's child, whom she abandons after its birth to her new husband. Carl Brisson, the Danish actor who had played Hitch's tough fairground fighter in a previous film, *The Ring* (1927), is here turned into the house-husband feminised as the surrogate mother of the deserted child that is not his own, a further oblique framing of sexual ambiguity. Hitchcock's studied ambiguities of meaning place this film as part of early modernism. Joseph Losey's cool fabulist *The Servant* (1963) brings the trangressive triangle forward into the neo-modern 1960s and two decades later Jarman's low-budget art-biopic *Caravaggio* (1986) with its tragic and poignant celebration of three-way transgression, heralds a high point in the neo-romantic revival of the 1980s which absorbed modernist style. Both are now classics of UK cinema.

## *BLACKMAIL* AND TRANSITION

Shot at Elstree Studios *Blackmail* existed in two versions, silent and talkie, and Hitchcock has told us how he prepared in the silent version the lineaments of a sound version, already thinking as he shot without sound of how he would shoot *with* sound. As the first UK sound movie, what strikes us now is how the transition to sound can itself be a supreme instance of dramatic suspense. We start with a spinning hubcap which leads into second-unit travelling shots of a Flying Squad lorry speeding through London streets, a radio team in the back coordinating a raid in a working-class neighbourhood. The documentary footage is merged with studio scenography. The Squad raid a first floor-flat surrounded by a hostile crowd outside: Frank, the film's detective lead (John Longdeen), stands with his boss at the threshold of a squalid room where the culprit lies in bed glancing at them in his bedside mirror and glancing at his revolver on a nearby table. Hitchcock plays expertly with the mechanics of suspense. Characters speak silently but their words are given no intertitles. In shot/reverse-shot pattern the police try to stare down the defiant culprit then beat him to his gun when he reaches for it. Dragged out through the hostile crowd and driven away, he is interrogated and picked out in an identity parade by a woman who lays her hand on his arm. Still no sound. He is charged and locked up and only then does the sound start, not to inaugurate the process of arrest but to chart its aftermath. Hitchcock brings it up, almost anti-climactically, in the police station washroom where the triumphant squad chatter amongst themselves. The anti-climax can be read as a different climax altogether, the point at which silence has been superseded in the history of British film by recorded sounds and voices. There is no turning back.

Another brilliant sequence follows. Frank goes with Alice, his fiancée (Anny Ondra), to a Lyons Corner House in the West End (with Hitchcock shooting on location amidst vast crowds). Amusingly, they search and jostle for a free table then argue whether or not to go to a movie afterwards. But Alice has another agenda, a tryst with Crewe, a painter, with perhaps her portraiture in mind. A brief note in her bag, revealed to the audience but not to Frank, shows her intent and as if by magic her painter-prince appears twenty minutes later. She spots him and motions discreetly to the figure of the oblivious Frank: Crewe bides his time. As Frank leaves angrily without her Crewe seizes his chance, but Frank spies her leaving the restaurant with him. Surveillance and betrayal, both hardy Hitchcock motifs, precede and pave the way for the third, larger motif of *Blackmail*, which is of course blackmail. But first we have one of the most powerful Hitchcock murders to grace the British screen.

Crewe (played by song-and-dance artist Cyril Richard) seems to be a clear echo of that famous songster whom Hitchcock had used in *The Lodger*, Ivor Novello, and here the director sends the structure of feeling he elicited in that film into reverse. Novello, the gay matineé idol, is wrongly suspected in the earlier film of being a serial killer but proves himself in the end to be an honourable avenger. In *Blackmail* Crewe, who is very much a Novello clone for the film's purposes, serenades the unsuspecting Alice in his flat not with a view to true romance, but as a prelude to attempted rape. Thus Hitchcock provides us with a sinister lodger in one film we cannot imagine on first sight to be innocent: and here with a Novello *doppelgänger* we could not possibly imagine to be guilty. The switch is fascinating and calculated: it is not motive that counts here, but image. And Hitchcock knows it. After all, Novello was a gay performer masquerading as a heterosexual icon. Here in turn we have a 'sensitive artist' who turns out to be a calculating rapist. And who knows, would he have been a murderer too? But we never do find out because he's the one who is killed. And the mysterious jester in Crewe's painting in the studio, who seems at first to be laughing at Crewe's victim, may well be laughing at him in the end, or rather at his corpse. The jester 'sees' the attempted rape coming, but maybe, much quicker than us, he 'sees' the tables being turned, the assailant assaulted, the victim a killer traumatised. If Frank sees the couple leaving the Corner House and Tracy the blackmailer sees the couple entering the tenement, then the jester-image is a third pair of eyes who 'sees' the unexpected dénouement in that chilling moment as Alice flees – looking on and laughing.

The inanimate male gaze (which is highly animated) thus punctuates the animate male gaze that lurks mutely in the shadows. For after the backtrack down the stairs, Alice's offscreen exit at the darkened doorstep is followed

**Figure 1.1** Offscreen Corpse: Anny Ondra in *Blackmail*

by the onscreen advance of Tracy's elongated shadow caught in the streetlight. Hitchcock at this point is reaching a high burst of creativity in the film. Witness the brilliant offscreen murder sequence: the hand of Alice reaching out from behind the screen to grab the breadknife lying on the table and, moments later, the arm of the dying man flopping vertical from the same aperture. It is a masterly example of closure through repetition and all in the same shot. Then Alice emerges holding the knife as if a trance. Here the director segues quite brilliantly from male to female, from gaze to trauma. For the trance is the beginning of trauma as Alice lurches through late-night London streets far into daybreak in a deserted Trafalgar Square. She is mute, numb, despairing, expressionless. Around Piccadilly at night she sees an animated neon sign for a cocktail glass turn into a knife as she starts to hallucinate. At dawn, as she passes a tramp sleeping in a doorway, she sees in his arm the rigid arm of her victim fallen out from behind the screen. The trauma of the killing repeats itself in the objective images her mind reduces to involuntary memories of the act itself.

Thus Hitchcock sets in motion a trauma sub-genre of horror film and thriller, a brilliant hybrid that permeates British cinema, where the traumatic event defines a life, and the balance between objective and subjective camera is perfectly made. The later landmarks already come into view and we shall look at them in due course – *Gaslight* (1940), *Dead of Night* (1945), *Black Narcissus, The Small Back Room* (1949), *Peeping Tom, The Innocents* (1962), *Repulsion* (1965), *Don't Look Now* . . . Though not endless, the list is long and we can add unlikely titles to the more predictable ones. For Hitchcock this is a first which he repeats rarely and mainly in *Sabotage, Spellbound, The Wrong Man* (1957) and *Vertigo* (1958). Yet it starts here, at the moment of the transition to sound, and having set up near-silent images of trauma in Alice walking the streets of London, he complements it perfectly through the eruption of subjective sound. Back in her father's shop a female customer is gossiping furiously about the murder in the apartment along the street. 'A good whack over the head with a brick,' she proclaims, 'there's something British about that.' 'But murder with a knife?' she asks rhetorically as Alice cuts the bread for breakfast. The word 'knife', sharp, acrid, rasping, rips through Alice's ears and repeats itself inside her head. The breadknife drops dramatically from her hand. Murder with a knife is not the done thing, not 'British'. In her choice of implement, poor Alice may have saved her body, but has put herself beyond the pale. And Hitchcock uses the new invention of recorded sound, including voice distortion, to code the repeating nightmare.

The extended sequence of serenade, attack, offscreen stabbing, image-trauma in the streets and sound-trauma in the shop is one of the strongest in all of Hitchcock's films. Sadly it is undone, at least in part, by the blackmail scene itself. The blackmailer enters the shop, reveals he has Alice's lost glove which can place her at the crime scene and proceeds, with Frank also present, to name his price. Here Hitchcock is at a loss to stage blackmail cinematically. With its fixed frontal shots, stagy dialogue and equally stagy acting, the film becomes too theatrical. The declaiming blackmailer comes straight off the West End stage, the reactions of Frank and Alice straight out of silent cinema. And Hitchcock cannot find the *substance* of the amoral exchange that constitutes blackmail. The blackmailer first demands free cigars and then a free breakfast: the effect is laughable. Only this to cover up a murder? Indeed, the true atonement for the 'failure' of blackmail in *Blackmail*'s primal scene does not come until over twenty years later when Hitchcock makes a British blackmail film-by-proxy in a Hollywood studio. The acknowledged remake of *The Man who Knew Too Much* in 1956 had in fact been preceded the previous year by his unacknowledged 'remake' of *Blackmail.* In a way of course it wasn't, since *Dial M for Murder* was adapted for screen from a stage play by the playwright himself, Frederic Knott. Yet Hitchcock's 'makeover' ensured a key double-blackmail sequence which both echoes and surpasses his first sound picture and it is British. Hitchcock and Knott are English, the actors in the sequence, Ray Milland (Tony) and Anthony Dawson (Swann), Welsh and English respectively. The setting for 'double blackmail' is a ground-floor Maida Vale apartment designed with a naturalistic eye for detail but shaped very much according to Hitchcock's cinematic vision. Briefly we can compare the sequence in the two films.

In *Blackmail* Tracy manipulates Frank and Alice through his possession of the lost glove in the shop and then parlour of Alice's family home with (echoes of *The Lodger*) mum and dad in melodramatic attendance. At first helpless, Frank then counters with the blindingly obvious. Tracy is a shady character with a criminal record, well known to the police, who has been lurking suspiciously near a crime scene, thus putting himself in the frame. It is the word of a policeman against that of a criminal. Of course, Hitchcock plays on the irony that a criminal is prepared to tell the truth while a detective is prepared to lie to protect his fiancée. But all the moves are telegraphed in advance: the framing is clumsy, the action awkward. In the later film Hitchcock duly keeps his audience guessing, mixing shock and suspense. Again, the movement is interior but this time rhythmic and dynamic, a superlative mix of multi-angle montage composition which has the effect of moving the spectator around within the flat's tight interior. The swift cutting using the deep focus of the 3-D format matches the cut-and-thrust of dialogue: this is a polite yet deadly power-play between two dodgy Cambridge alumni who are equally amoral and prepared to commit murder. The 'restaging' of blackmail thus also takes into account the class shift: from lower-middle-class parlour to elegant Maida Vale apartment, from the modestly respectable to the educated but flakily criminal.

We can set out the 'restaging' sequence in the apartment living-room in more detail. With a heavy inflexible 3-D camera, Hitchcock responds to lack of mobility by depth of field and sharp editing, adding narrative momentum through nuanced spatial variation. Here he starts off separating Tony, the husband-plotter, from Swann, the confidence man he blackmails, in reverse-angles then a swish pan (right to left) of the money thrown from husband to thief (as downpayment for murder) unites them in a single shot. Swann's subsequent movement to the desk (left to right) to join Tony completes the symmetry and a series of two shots suggests complicity – no longer antagonists but protagonists side by side in medium shot. Hitch then cuts to an extreme high-angle two-shot, shattering the illusion of the fourth wall unconventionally by 'going through' the living-room ceiling. This is a balcony shot with no balcony, like a technician's POV of the shoot high on a cross-beam in a studio. Tony has second-guessed Swann's feeble attempts to blackmail his faithless wife by betraying her affair, and thrown things back into the blackmailer's court by gaining evidence of the blackmailer's involvement in the mystery death of a wealthy widow. He thus offers Swann the prospect of another murder, his wife played by (Grace Kelly), as a trade-off for concealing the previous one. But Hitchcock is not content with the power of words alone. As Tony shows Swann how to plan his entry into the apartment and kill his wife from behind the curtain to the French windows, he acts, reflexively speaking, as stand-in for the director himself, blocking out for the watching actor-assailant the 'murder sequence' to come. Within the classical canon, Hitchcock fabulates his own thriller, laying bare its devices without ever losing its suspense.

## CONSTRUCTIVE AND DECONSTRUCTIVE: *NUMBER SEVENTEEN*

*Number Seventeen* baffles and infuriates many digital viewers watching it in the new century. It is not a readable thriller in its wilful scrambling of plot and identity, its devil-may-care take on narrative indeed not what they expect at all. For the new sound era this film, though based on a stage play itself based on a novel, runs like a charade created *ex nihilo*. It is exceedingly difficult to work out what is happening, who is who and who has done what to whom. The first part takes place exclusively on the stairwell of a mysterious house; the second revolves around one main prop – a train set complete with miniature stations, signals and boat ferry for the film's disaster finale. Yet this division points forward to a key division in Hitchcock himself – the maestro of the single set in *Lifeboat* (1944), *Rope, Dial M for Murder* and *Rear Window* (1954) and the maestro of the train – or bus – journey in *The 39 Steps*, *Sabotage*, *The Lady Vanishes* (1938), *Spellbound* and *North by Northwest*. Moreover, it is a perfect and perfectly balanced division between stasis and motion. The first part creates six seemingly random characters stuck on a stairwell: the second part, courtesy of a fantasy exit in Number Seventeen's basement which leads to the nearest station platform, creates a train chase that ends in a crash on a dockside boat ferry and a watery nemesis. In other words, the first part is shiftless, the second ceaseless.

It is pure early modernism but also as Barr has pointed out, brilliant hybrid, surreal and constructivist at the same time, creating a dream world and yet laying bare the construction of the film itself with its non-plotting and non-identity – Breton meets Pirandello, oneiric yet with no suspension of disbelief (Barr 1999: 123–6). It also creates, with its calculated stitching of order out of chaos, Hitchcock's first true MacGuffin, the pretext for crime and transgression conjured out of nothing, in this case a jewel necklace discovered, with Hitch's roguish flair for the discreetly obscene, in a toilet cistern. Everybody wants it, everybody chases it and makes it the first point of connection in primal chaos. While the chase and the MacGuffin repeat themselves through Hitch's long career, it is not until the 1950s that his full-on powers of modernist invention return, in a different world and a different life. But here is the primal scene and let us not forget it.

CHAPTER 2

# *The running man: Hitchcock's fugitives and* The Bourne Ultimatum

In the first chapter we looked at the romantic origins of the fugitive film in *A Cottage on Dartmoor*. In this chapter we go further and examine its central figure, the 'running man' in talking pictures. In this let us go back to front. Where today would we find this fugitive figure? The most common answer, in box-office terms, might well be *The Bourne Ultimatum* (2007) – American Matt Damon as Jason Bourne in a film most would think American, but is in part British, made with a partly British crew and a Surrey-born director, Paul Greengrass, who sprang to prominence through his drama-documentaries *Bloody Sunday* and *United 93* (on the 9/11 hijacks). *The Running Man* is also the title of Carol Reed's 1963 feature whose fugitive hero is disappearing conman Laurence Harvey in a film most would rate as one of Reed's weaker films, a pallid echo of *The Third Man* (1948). It is a term Raymond Durgnat appropriated for his study of fugitive films in *A Mirror for England* and one recycled in the next two chapters, where it should be noted that memorable acting in the genre also comes from 'running women' – Madeleine Carroll in *The 39 Steps*, Margaret Lockwood in *The Lady Vanishes*, Alida Valli in *The Third Man*, Claire Bloom in *The Man Between* (1953) and *The Spy Who Came in from the Cold* (1965). In the second of the Bourne trilogy, *The Bourne Supremacy* (2004), we witness the killing of Marie Kreutz, Bourne's girlfriend (played by Franka Potente), another running woman who had established her pedigree for the Bourne films through her cult role in Tom Tywker's *Run Lola, Run!* (1998), where her kinetic tour of a reunified Berlin set the standard for the hyper-modern version of the 'running woman'. Deprived of Marie, Bourne, the loner in the third part of the trilogy, keeps on running – just like those before him. If history moves forward in a straight line, it also goes in cycles too.

## Jason's Waterloo: Hitchcock, Greengrass and deepest fears

What links *The Bourne Ultimatum* way back when to *Number Seventeen*? Both are studies in non-identity with Macguffins to match. In Hitchcock's film the jewel necklace was the Macguffin – his very first – to set in motion the train chase among characters whose identities were confused and confusing until

**Figure 2.1** Fear, Flight, Betrayal: Robert Donat, Peggy Ashcroft and John Laurie in *The 39 Steps*

the very end. In the *Bourne* trilogy the Macguffin is more abstract, a cliché (or tired trope) lifted from American conspiracy movies of the 1970s, the rogue CIA experiment. In fact, Jason Bourne is not really Jason Bourne (real name: David Webb), but a techno-invention of 'bad' chiefs, a Running Man with No Name. But in reducing paranoia to an action trope Greengrass also reprises Hitchcock's double-chase pattern of the fugitive seeking out his villainous tormenters. Born technically speaking out of the kinetic modernism of *The Battle of Algiers* (1965) and *The French Connection* (1971), the Greengrass thriller also has echoes of an even earlier age. It echoes the pattern Hitchcock inaugurated in *The 39 Steps* with Robert Donat as Richard Hannay framed for a murder he did not commit, and escaping his lawful pursuers in attempting to pursue the real culprits – foreign intelligence agents. In the Greengrass scenario 'Bourne' (Born?), the fugitive with a false identity, tries to track down the CIA rogues headed by Noah Vosen (David Strathairn) and sift them out from the 'good chiefs' who are also pursuing him because of disinformation and can thus be 'turned' in his favour. On the face of it this is such a cliché that what matters most is the roller-coaster ride of the double-chase itself, the sheer exhilaration, shock and suspense its fast-cutting provides for the age of PlayStation gaming whose culture of speed, spills and lightning reaction it simulates through filmic means. And yet there is something deeper – a vague disquiet, unease about what is never made explicit. There are close parallels here between Hitchcock's classic thriller and the Greengrass hyper-modern hit with its *cinéma vérité* trimmings, in what *remains unspoken*, in what is hinted at but never really exposed. For 1930s Hitchcock it was the British fear of Germany and a second world war: for Greengrass post-9/11, it is the universal fear of both global terror *and* global surveillance in the twenty-first century. Both films struck a raw nerve in ways, probably, that most of their viewers would not suspect, obliquely tapping into a collective consciousness that did not wish to articulate its deepest fears. Yet in this film Bourne is a post-romantic, a man without a woman, a guy without a girl. Greengrass edits in subliminal flashes of Marie's death-by-drowning which marks *The Bourne Supremacy*, trauma flashes that assail a running man still haunted by his lost love: it makes of the traumatised Bourne a post-romantic loner. Romantic love was only yesterday; but now it is a lost age, a prehistory, an imagistic trace, and all the passion is now in the chase.

The Waterloo Station sequence in the Bourne film, where Greengrass is briefly on home territory, is fast, inspirational and shot on the hoof, the complete opposite of Hitchcock's meticulous story-boarding technique. Yet there are similarities. We may recall that Hitchcock caused a stir among the crowds when he shot location sequences at a West End Lyons Corner House in *Blackmail*. Such is the public ubiquity of screens and film crews today that Greengrass shoots his extended chase sequence – in which Bourne first *escapes* CIA assailants and then *chases* in vain their special assassin who has just killed his journalist contact – *among* the commuting crowds at the station, admittedly out of rush-hour, but still Bourne is chasing and being chased among crowds of ordinary travellers coming up to Town or returning home, or looking for Eurostar. No Central Casting here. Though we don't know what lies on the cutting-room floor, one is struck by the sheer *lack* of curiosity registering on the faces of passers-by as film crews run speedily by in tandem with Damon through the station forecourt. We can also note that in moving from England to Morocco the film reverses the pattern of the remade *Man Who Knew Too Much* but also has similarities with Hitchcock's kidnap thriller. Both did Morocco shoots during the month of Ramadan and both had to overcome the cultural tensions that arose from filmmaking conducted during the fast. Yet fifty years on the Greengrass film both benefits from and demonstrates a more globally connected world. In London, too, differences emerge: Hitchcock shot his film on near-deserted streets where his suspense *mise-en-scéne* with its unnerving chapel and taxidermist sequences bordered on the surreal. By contrast Greengrass gives us constant action immersed in noise, bustle and movement, 'hyper-classical' in style to use Bordwell's *au courant* term for now Hollywood narration (Bordwell 2006: 67–8). It is a virtuoso exercise in speed and fragmentation, outrunning at times our own powers of perception, yet still has a readable narrative and predictable climax. Here Bourne's new lifeline, Simon Ross, a *Guardian* journalist (played by Paddy Considine), who suspects that 'Bourne' may be victim of dirty tricks, is like the Mr. Memory of the Greengrass thriller, but shot not on onstage while reciting spy-facts as in *The 39 Steps* but among the crowds at Waterloo, panic-stricken while trying to gather them (facts), as if in the middle of a terror attack (which he is) and running for his life.

Nothing but not ingenious, Greengrass uses the CCTV cameras at Waterloo Station for his own actuality footage, both for images we see directly and as images we see via his CIA monitor screens in Langley, which in the age of the Iraq war conveys metaphorically, we could guess, the political servitude of Britain to the United States in the nebulous domain of 'security'. Political surveillance thus strikes terror in our hearts, but random terrorist bombings even more so. The film's station forecourt and Underground sequences strike another uncomfortable echo – that of the July 2005 London bombings which took place in underground trains and on buses, especially as CCTV has brought us images of the assailants before the outrage, though replayed after the event. If Greengrass plays on the panoptical vision of such ubiquitous footage, his film also shows its limitation. Bourne moves in and out of shot, a chameleon who cannot be frozen by the grainy video image, the maverick spook who finally gets away. Prior to the electronic age, however, Hitchcock seems just as chillingly contemporary, or perhaps even more so. In *Sabotage* he updated Conrad's version of an anarchist bomb outrage at Greenwich Observatory to a bomb aimed at Piccadilly Circus but unwittingly carried by a schoolboy (the young brother-in-law of Verloc, the terrorist) who is delayed on a London bus and thinks the bomb a spool of film from the owner of the seedy bijou cinema in south-east London. Using cross-cutting montage as the bus makes its way towards Piccadilly Circus Hitch ratchets up unbearable suspense then creates genuine shock in the sudden explosion which kills all the bus's occupants. This West End bomb-on-bus scenario often scorned by critics as 'implausible' no longer is, because seventy years later it happens. And if there are any doubts, we can also say that in the interval between film release and new century atrocity, London bombings had also been the hallmark of the IRA for over twenty-five years.

## The fugitive kind: pre-war, wartime, post-war

Let us go back to the first running man in *A Cottage on Dartmoor.* Is this, the fugitive film that Asquith sets in motion, a British genre? The answer is yes and no. It is *more* pronounced in British film than elsewhere and in the post-war period it runs parallel to American *film noir*, that sub-genre inflected by the American Dream of money, murder and sexual betrayal we can name as 'a criminal conspiracy of passion'. But the British scenario was different. Flight was all and in the pre-war period, as we have seen, Hitch had added the double-chase as a key variation to the fugitive flight pattern. But the scenario is never exclusively British, not would we expect it to be. After all, Hitch took it to America for *Saboteur* and *North by Northwest* and it has been copied many times since. Back at home post-war directors like Reed, Hamer and Cavalcanti had added their own variation, strongly influenced by French poetic realism and its *single-chase* pattern of the 'criminal' fugitive, which pivots around the iconic figure of Jean Gabin in *Pépé le Moko* (1936), *Le Quai des Brumes* (1938) and *Le Jour se lève* (1939). It is Gabin who conveys the stoicism of impossible escape more powerfully than anyone in film history, a stoicism that makes his 'crime', whatever it is, seem secondary. Reed, Hamer and Calvalcanti inject the 'Gabin effect' into their own iconic fugitives – James Mason, Orson Welles, John McCallum and Trevor Howard. Yet there is more to context than this. Throughout the 1940s the UK film industry, exempt from invasion and the censorship of Fascist occupation, and thriving in the absence of European competition, became the new epicentre of flight narratives: indeed, the power of the genre is echoed through to the twenty-first century in *Performance* (1970), *Frenzy, The Crying Game, Naked* and *Dirty Pretty Things.*

The ambient history is well documented. The Second World War was a time of mobilisation, of retreating and advancing armies, of fleeing civilians and refugees. The UK was both a haven for refugees and a sanctuary for its own routed army after Dunkirk: internally, the onset of the Blitz displaced many children and families from its large cities for their safety. Vast, reluctant movement in a country that only just escaped invasion was a cultural fact, a wider sign that flight in wartime could affect anyone. In the post-war period with broken armies and displaced populations on the move around Europe, the UK again became a refugee haven and a place of homecoming for its troops and POWs from Europe and South-East Asia. Post-war scarcity also created a black market in rationed or stolen goods, a secret, fugitive life for opportunistic criminals exploiting shortage and the imbalance of supply and demand, a fugitive *demi-monde* with great film potential. Mobilisation also changed people's lives. It brought young women into the forefront of the economy and into the armed forces where it created the 'mobile woman', stimulated political awareness and created greater sexual and cultural freedoms. This often generated a paradox. Fear and excitement coexisted in equal measure as a response to upheaval and danger: yet the impulse to survive and the daily grind prompted a stoical response to the deprivations of life under duress

It was a fertile atmosphere for fiction and film. In both forms Greene became a dominant figure, writing landmark screenplays for Carol Reed and having his fiction directed onscreen to great effect by Cavalcanti, Fritz Lang and the Boulting brothers. Here Greene rewrote Terence Rattigan's screenplay for the Boultings' *Brighton Rock* (1947), which launched the career of Richard Attenborough as teenage gangster Pinkie Brown. Almost thirty years later in his modernist American fable *Badlands* (1974), Terrence Malick paid homage to the British classic in the voice-o-gram sequence where Kit confesses his thoughts to Holly as he embarks on his fugitive murder spree. In the Greene original the sequence takes place towards the end of the film. On the run from both racketeers and police, Pinkie records his voice in a kiosk on the pier as a wedding present for the gullible Rose (Carol Marsh), but once inside the kiosk, begins to confess to the machine his disgust for his new bride. In the film's last sequence after the hunted Pinkie has drowned under the pier, the deluded Rose plays back the recording, only for the needle to stick on the romantic 'I love you', words uttered before Pinkie's true animus is revealed. That Pinkie and Rose were the inspiration for Kit and Holly can be gleaned perhaps from Malick's desire to produce a remake of the Boulting picture, a wish that nearly bore fruit in this century. At the same time, the bitter ironies of disenchanted love are part of Greene's cinematic legacy. For a reprise of them as ingenious wartime pastiche one should look no further than Neil Jordan's *The End of the Affair* (1999).

Another way that fugitive romance caught the popular imagination was through the POW escape narrative, a key part of the genre which found its culmination in the 1963 cult film *The Great Escape*, shot on location in Bavaria by American John Sturges and made iconic through the 1960s Mod look of Steve McQueen, an example of fugitive cool complete with airborne motorbike which made the British POWs in the film seem stiff and old-fashioned. Much earlier, the Ealing POW drama, Basil Dearden's *The Captive Heart* (1946), had been a post-war bridge between pre-war romance and male escape thrillers like *The Wooden Horse* (1950) and *The Colditz Story* (1955) (Murphy 2000: 212–14). It was also a fable of wartime's adjusted identities, with Michael Redgrave playing a Czech officer in a POW camp who takes on the identity of a missing British officer to avoid death at the hands of the Gestapo. After interrogation and protected by British POWs, he has his right hand smashed by a sledgehammer and writes love letters 'home' to the officer's wife (Rachel Kempson) with his left hand, thus disguising his true identity and paving the way for his eventual 'homecoming' where he must persuade her to accept him as her husband's replacement – which he duly does. Its solemn naturalism seemed appropriate to the mood of the time, its celebration of romance-by-default an antidote to Hitchcock's anxieties of identity and reinvention, a wish-dream for a new generation of war widows. But it also taps into a wider collective desire for post-war unity and for the healing of wounds: Hitchcock, by contrast, rediscovered romance by taking refuge in his adopted country across the Atlantic Ocean.

While romance continues powerfully in American Hitchcock right through to *North by Northwest*, in his 'returning' Brit movies it is upended by the romantic ironies of double-cross in his short Resistance film *Bon Voyage* (1944), by reflexive theatricality in the deceptive *Aventure malgache* (1944), by the sly deconstructions of human frailty in his fugitive *Stage Fright* (1950), and the suffocations of kidnap-trauma in the remade *Man Who Knew too Much* (1955). Finally, it is blown to pieces in the dark disenchantments of *Frenzy* where Hitchcock shifts fluently from black humour to stark horror and back again, without appearing to blink. In Reed there is a parallel shift, though it is not as pronounced. The narrative balance favours the romantic structure of feeling until his partnership with Graham Greene where a more complex post-romantic irony prevails. The dating of the transition in both directors is close, Reed only four years on from Hitchcock. The romance element had been whimsically present in *Night Train to Munich* (1940), Reed's wartime reprise with Launder and Gilliat of the political imbroglio of *The Lady Vanishes*, and was seriously present in his patriotic *The Way Ahead*, which celebrates the army as a source of community where the camaraderie of training and combat overcomes the class obstacles of peacetime. By far the most realised of Reed's romantic films, however, is his version of F. L. Green's Belfast-set 1945 novel *Odd Man Out*, scripted by Green and R. C. Sherriff, perhaps the fugitive film *par excellence* in cinema history. After that the narrative tone has wider registers, becomes more ironic and disenchanted. His four great films here are his collaborations with Greene, is *The Fallen Idol* (1947), *The Third Man* and *Our Man in Havana* (1959) and his underrated Cold War thriller without Greene's direct involvement, *The Man Between.*

A key difference remains between Hitchcock and Reed. Hitchcock thrives on sudden transformation of circumstance and setting that takes people across boundaries and frontiers. He also deals in the imagination of insolent transformations that often defy plausibility and put heroes and heroines on the spot, posing quite casually and comically the deeper question of lost identities (Orr 2005: 35–6). In that respect Iris Henderson, searching for the elusive Miss Froy in *The Lady Vanishes*, is a practical example of a young woman searching for her true self as she pursues just cause but is still unsure about the evidence of her senses. Identity crisis is a constant in Hitchcock, leading to humour, romance and irony but also, in his darker films, to destruction and disaster. Reed's films also question fixed identities but his great strength lies elsewhere – in the single-minded exploration of the city and the concept of ambiguous boundaries within, both physical and moral. The city is a mysterious labyrinth to be explored on location in its own right. In *The Fallen Idol* this works in a minor key but still illustrates the case. The central relationship between deferential butler and lonely diplomat's son reads like a brooding fable of destroyed innocence spurred by misrecognition of the adult world, but it's also a topographical upstairs/downstairs relationship in a vast Francophone embassy in Belgravia. Reed is best here at exploring spatial tensions in the contrast between the tight, enclosed world of the servants' quarters and the vast empty mansion with its magnificent staircase where the child roams in desultory solitude. But the London of this film pales into insignificance compared to Reed's filming of *non-English* cities, of post-war Belfast and Vienna, of 1950s Berlin and Havana. Here he is in his element with his own variation on the fugitive genre: with the twin concepts of subterfuge and internal division feeding off each other, with his camera's sinuous exploration of a city's subterranean life where nothing is quite what it seems.

## British Hitchcock: from romance thriller to post-romantic fable

With his stated contempt in the Truffaut interviews for what he called 'the plausibles', Hitchcock never saw his romance thrillers as a means to enhance our sense of reality (Truffaut 1984: 130–4). Instead he saw sudden, implausible shifts in narrative as a way of guiding his viewer's imagination beyond the constraints of everyday existence, an exemplar of the magic of the moving image in a darkened auditorium. The figure of the fugitive couple engages both the implausible and the magical. Their compulsion to flight leads to the great suspense question: will they or won't they be caught? If so, how and when? Our closeness as viewers to the couple creates some level of empathy, a form of screen propinquity that strengthens our attachment. The couple are in motion – on foot, by car, bus or train – and sitting still in our seats, we 'move' with them and share the romance which is movement and feeling simultaneously. Hence we are prompted to put ourselves in their position, experience their emotions as our own. Kinesis and empathy are interlocked processes: emotion is always a moveable feast. But for that to happen, the *psychology* of the flight process must be plausible even when the event is not. This is precisely where Hitchcock excels.

The narrative options of the fugitive film are two-fold. Either the flight takes priority over the quest or the quest over the flight. The first option is the formula for *Young and Innocent* and *The 39 Steps*, the second the formula for the *The Lady Vanishes*. Here overcoming all obstacles the couple are reluctantly brought together by searching for the 'disappeared', the lady who implausibly vanishes, a formula that Redgrave as Gilbert and Lockwood as Iris act out to near-perfection. Subterfuge is the key semantic figure connecting kidnap and flight, from the Latin *fugire* – to flee. When Redgrave and Lockwood smuggle out Miss Froy under the noses of the kidnappers they are themselves fugitives, recruiting the remaining Brits as their close allies in the train's dash to freedom across the border. We should note that although the film refuses to name names – no dictators, countries, ideologies – the studio miniatures of train stations and Alpine villages seem to oscillate between a Balkan and an Alpine identity and can be read as either. The unnamed country is likely to be an ally of Germany, and it is a masterstroke of Hitchcock to make of this something unspoken in the midst of Europe's gathering storm.

We should also note the unique pattern that shifts the fugitive double-chase into reverse. Lockwood and Gilbert start as pursuers (of the kidnappers of Miss Froy) but later turn into fugitives, intent on fighting off their (fascist?) pursuers and getting the train and Miss Froy, the most implausible British spy ever invented, across the border to safety. The gender relationship is also inverted. In *The 39 Steps* Hannay has first to convince Pamela of his innocence in order to get her to join him. Here the hapless Iris who is a flawed, uncertain witness to the 'lady vanishing' has to convince a sceptical Gilbert that Froy was in fact kidnapped when all around her fabricate a cover-up, including a substitute 'Miss Froy', and claim she has been hallucinating. Hannay enlists Pamela against all odds: Iris similarly recruits Gilbert. Romance thrillers indeed – handsome heroes, beautiful heroines, couples with real chemistry: why then would Hitchcock not repeat the formula on his post-war return? Or indeed, why not return more often to his homeland to repeat it?

The cynical answer would be that he did it better in Hollywood with Cary Grant – Cary and Ingrid, Cary and Grace, Cary and Eva. Yet there is a sea-change in Hitchcock's attitude to his homeland, prompted, I would argue, by the 1944 return in which he witnessed the destruction wreaked by Nazi bombers upon his native city and this percolates through into the work thereafter. It could well have been exacerbated by the documentary footage he compiled and edited from Bergen – Belsen and other concentration camps just after liberation in the following year when he had agreed to make a final war film for Sidney Bernstein (McGilligan 2003: 373–4). After the desolation of a blitzed London followed by the horrors of camp atrocities it could well be that the New World separated off more clearly from the Old in Hitchcock's imagination, though his continued anti-Nazi commitment was obvious in both spheres. Whatever the reason, we find in his short Resistance films and post-war British work an absence of romantic figures, the spectre of a disenchanted director returning to his homeland with a distant, critical gaze. Romance had by now become an 'elsewhere'.

Hitch may well have seen Reed's wartime update of *The Lady Vanishes*, his spy thriller *Night Train to Munich* again scripted by Launder and Gilliat, again starring Lockwood plus the 'two stooges' Caldicott and Charters (Naunton Wayne and Basil Radford) in a suspenseful train journey; but he might also have noted how its joking, jolly tone was incongruous with the Nazi pursuit of total war which had intervened in the meantime to cast its shadow across Europe. In fact, the plot of his first Resistance short, *Bon Voyage*, shares with *Night Train to Munich* its opening gambit. In Reed's film Lockwood plays the daughter of a Czech scientist who has just escaped the German occupation of Prague, but is herself arrested by the Gestapo and sent to a concentration camp – the best sequence in the film – where she meets a fellow-prisoner whom she sees brutally beaten, but who then helps her to escape. Later, she discovers he has been planted to accompany her back to England in order to kidnap her father. She then transfers her allegiance to handsome Rex Harrison, an English spy masquerading as a seaside entertainer (sic). On the eve of the Nazi invasion of Poland, she is abducted back to Germany with her father, and Harrison follows: he disguises himself – implausibly – as a German army officer and tries to rescue both of them. Together, they take the night train to Munich at the outbreak of war and end up in improbable escape at the end of a cable car on the Swiss border. In a time of total war Reed's 'implausibles' are too implausible. He enacts rapid changes of setting and circumstances *à la* Hitch, yet his 'escapes' become whimsical and silly in light of the rapid German invasion of Europe. Three years on, Hitchcock may have taken his lead from this glaring shortfall. If you went overtly political, then plausibility did begin to matter – the realities of wartime treachery and deceit run deep and have sobering consequences.

## The Poetics of Treachery: Dickinson and Cavalcanti

This difference in tone was registered by two other key films before Hitchcock's shorts, popular dramas of internal treachery produced by Ealing Studios with the wartime aid of the Ministry of Information. A key link was Angus MacPhail, whose collaborative script work was a feature of both films before he went on to write *Bon Voyage* for Hitch. The first is Cavalcanti's *Went the Day Well?* (1942), which deals with an unlikely German raid on a southern English village, and Thorold Dickinson's *The Next of Kin* (1942), which explores German espionage in wartime England, treachery that sabotages a British raid on the French coastline. Both films occupied the uneasy period between the Dunkirk evacuation and the Normandy landings and both arise out of the culture of suspicion in a country that had been heavily bombed and feared invasion. 'Careless Talk Costs Lives' was the government poster slogan of the time and Dickinson's film literally brings it to life. But there were other threads too. In occupied Europe, Nazi collaborators – quislings – had already come out of the woodwork, and often out of the ranks of the prosperous and the respectable. These two films test a virtual history with the European example unfolding before their eyes. What would happen here? What of potential traitors who could easily be pillars of the community in peacetime but monsters in war? Should those you feel you can trust most be those you can trust least?

Adapted from a Greene story, Cavalcanti's thriller has much in common with Hitchcock's anti-Nazi cinema. Treachery is to be found in the most unlikely and most respectable of places, not the least respectable and most suspicious. Thus 'the enemy within' at Bramley End, the idyllic village occupied by German parachutists posing as British soldiers, is a treacherous German spy played by Leslie Banks, an actor usually typecast as an upright bourgeois. Once the Germans are exposed by the locals, they become duly nasty and lock the villagers in the parish church: they are only discovered outside the village through the escape of a poacher's boy who manages to raise the alert. In a final shoot-out scenario which borders on the surreal the Germans in British uniform are indistinguishable from the British regiment that destroys them. Both British and German soldiers were in fact played by extras from the ranks of the Gloucestershire regiment stationed near the film location at Turville, Buckinghamshire. Thus the film is gently paranoid but also bizarre. Hidden identity (the enemy within) is a Hitchcockian implausible that clearly taps into a greater wartime fear and parallels Hitchcock's American fable of Nazi subterfuge, *Saboteur*, which was released in the same year. And Hitch would surely have approved of Cavalcanti's revenge moment when the vicar's gentle daughter rumbles Banks as a traitor and guns him down with a service revolver: farewell gentility, but long live community as everyone pulls together and the dead Germans end up in the church graveyard.

Dickinson's *The Next of Kin* is much more challenging and paranoid: all the more so for starting as a War Office film made for military training purposes. But Dickinson had larger ambitions, and at Ealing (where he was not a resident director) Michael Balcon supported transformation to a full feature by doubling the budget. Like Cavalcanti, Dickinson wanted to create a drama of everyday life in wartime but his real interest lay in the contrast between the stoic and casual attitude to life under long-distance siege and the active menace of the enemy close at hand. His film captures the sense of an enemy so near and yet so far, the in-between or liminal state of being that afflicted Britain at war right up to the Normandy landings and beyond. The German spies in his film are as 'ordinary' in some respects as the people they dupe, and thus unlikely suspects: a bookseller, a factory worker, a dentist, people who in a Jennings documentary would be faces of a proud resistant Britain are here figures of treachery. And romance, which traditionally is the core of resistance to treachery in the Hitchcock thriller, here becomes something else – a catalyst for 'loose talk'. A glamorous stage stripper is persuaded by her dresser to get her unwitting date to divulge military secrets. The Nazi bookseller's Dutch assistant unwittingly gives him military information passed on by her soldier boyfriend. One of the London Nazi agents is able to swap briefcases with the military officer collecting aerial reconnaissance photographs when he is distracted at lunch by a pretty girlfriend. At the Westport factory where peripatetic Nazi agent Davis (Mervyn Johns) is temporarily working, he woos an ATS girl at a local dance to gain intelligence on troop movements and departures from the port. Thus every romantic encounter leads down the slippery slope to 'loose talk' and espionage. The film turns the implausible on its head. In pre-war Hitchcock loving couples discovered plots; here they unwittingly aid them with the same poetic licence.

Dickinson may eschew melodrama in his storyline, since no one raises their voice in love or anger. But he also proves himself a master of suspense. Will the spies get caught or won't they? Some do, but some don't. Davis is the supreme survivor, the 'undead' agent who in the film's final scene is seen in a train compartment listening to 'loose talk' from our old friends Radford and Wayne, the witless double act of *The Lady Vanishes* and *Night Train to Munich*. But more chilling and unexpected is Davis's casual murder of bookshop assistant Beppie Leemans (Nova Pilbeam), as accomplished in its staging as any Hitchcock murder of the same period. Realising she has been blackmailed by her boss Barrett into giving away secret information, the innocent Dutch refugee kills him with a knife (echoes of *Sabotage*) and ends her political innocence. A sure connection to Hitch since Pilbeam was the carefree Chief Constable's daughter in *Young and Innocent*, here she is still young but not innocent, no longer a political virgin as Pilbeam delivers a much more telling performance. In her sudden killing, pre-war and wartime are worlds apart. Seeing his contact murdered by Beppie, Davis casually knocks her out and, in a chilling ground-level shot through the legs of a table, turns on the gasfire beside her prone body without igniting it. And of course Davis is never caught. No wonder that to Dickenson's consternation Selnick demanded and got thirty minutes cut from the American version of this dark, pessimistic film.

The diminutive figure of Welsh actor Mervyn Johns also dominates Ealing's *Dead of Night,* which could well be an unofficial sequel. But his disturbing longevity here, as a fugitive figure who perfectly matches flight to subterfuge not as a hero but as a villain, is matched by the dramatic power of the disastrous raid on a Breton port which his intelligence betrays. Though *In Which We Serve* may be the best wartime war film, the coastal raid in *The Next of Kin* is perhaps the best single sequence. Using the Cornwall fishing port of Megavissey and active army units, the fluent location shoot is matched by the live recording of gunfire, artillery and dive-bombers. Dickenson also inserts actual war footage into his staging of the event with equal fluency. The film was prescient because of the forthcoming raid on St Nazaire and soon after, the aborted and disastrous landing at Dieppe (a trial run for the Normandy invasion), which took place just before the film was released. For both reasons Churchill tried at different stages to stop the film, only for the resulting press furore to make him reluctantly consent to its release. He did, however, demand more dead Germans and fewer dead British in the final cut, with the result that Dickenson trimmed twenty feet of film in the interest of 'balance' (Richards 1997: 90–3). In the event, the film's release was something of a minor miracle, a landmark, fusing the format of the Hitchcockian spy thriller with that of the wartime docudrama, powerful in both aspects and excelling in its perfect match of these unlikely opposites.

## THE TRIUMPH OF THE SHORT FILM: *BON VOYAGE* AND *AVENTURE MALGACHE*

In shooting *Bon Voyage* made from the vantage point of 1944 when the tide had turned in the Allies' favour, Hitchcock starts with the same signifier of treachery as that used by Reed in *Night Train to Munich*, a POW escape engineered by a sympathetic friend who then turns out to be a cold-blooded traitor. But while Lockwood's naivety in believing her betrayer is redeemed by her subsequent love of a handsome English spy, Hitchcock's naïve escapee, an RAF sergeant who is similarly used and betrayed in *Bon Voyage*, has no such get-out clause. Instead, his gullibility becomes tragic in its consequences. If *Night Train* unofficially remakes *The Lady Vanishes*, then *Bon Voyage* in turn remakes Reed's tenuous and brittle film via the interventions of Dickinson and Cavalcanti – and thereby opens a can of worms. The key to Hitchcock's twenty-six-minute narration lies in the mix of time compression and flashback. The film starts with a debriefing of an escaped POW, an Air Force gunner, by Free French officers in London: he thinks he has been helped to escape by a sympathetic Pole who stays behind in France. Flashback tells his side of the story but the interrogating officer, with his alternative flashbacks, suggests the Polish POW is in fact a Gestapo agent who has used John Dougall (John Blythe) to trace key members of the Resistance in the locality and also to pass on a coded message to a German agent in England on his return. Hence the French farmer's daughter, a Resistance worker who helps Dougall catch a special plane back to England and with whom he falls briefly in love, is murdered by the Gestapo agent straight after his departure, though eventually the Resistance, in the officer's counter-version, catches up with the agent and his accomplices and metes out its own rough justice. Yet on the Free French counter-version a nightmare scenario is also born. Dougall has unwittingly betrayed the girl who saved him to the Gestapo agent who promptly kills her. The film juxtaposes the flashback accounts of Dougall under interrogation with 'the correcting' flashback version of the French officer. But again given the factional conflicts within the Free French themselves, Dougall may be offered in turn a sanitised version full of wishful thinking about a messy, complicated truth, one that may overturn his obvious naivety but also introduce its own fabrications.

In this vertigo of interpretations, Hitch challenges us – *Rashomon* style – to work out what the truth actually is, or whether in the treacherous world of secret agents there is any single truth to be extracted and set in stone. The airman's story is a heroic-romantic escape yarn, while the officer's counter-story is a fable of deceit, murder and double-bluff: the Hitchcock short is a dark antiphon of enchantment and disenchantment, romance and moral fable. The spectator faced with the time compression of short, taut narration and the greater conviction of the counter-story is left to figure out the perverse computations of a secret, paranoid war. That is to say they have to figure it out, metaphorically, as quickly as Hitchcock edits it. By comparison Dickinson's *The Next of Kin* uses the full-length feature to make its tale of fifth-column betrayal in wartime England lucid and unambiguous. In Dickinson's cautionary fable can be read clearly a conspiratorial sequence of events in which 'loose talk' literally costs lives, but in Hitchcock the plots thickens to a poetic density where meaning is opaque. No wonder the film had a limited release and soon ended up in cold storage: but no wonder that it strikes the viewer today as a minor masterpiece.

Filmed under studio conditions, the *mise-en-scene* is beautifully pitched to capture the reflexive fable, all tight, compressed chiaroscuro interiors to match voice-over, flashback and elliptical dialogue: this is poetic realism by proxy, shot in a studio outside London, instead of one outside Paris, and shot too with subtitles since Hitchcock avoids the future trope of British war movies which have all foreigners speaking in broken English. The French language is a calculated alienation effect for a British audience, though the film, which had a French distributor, was intended for a French one: here, though, it works as an alienation effect too. The divisions and treachery among the French themselves are something in the climate of liberation many French viewers of the time had preferred to forget and did not want to see on cinema screens. It is not until Marcel Ophuls made his extensive retro-documentary *The Sorrow and the Pity* (1968) and Jean-Pierre Melville, an ex-Resistance operative, directed his dreamlike, elliptical *L'Armée des ombres* (1969) at the end of the 1960s that the mood Hitchcock created here is reincarnated at feature length for a French audience in two very original films. But for a post-war British audience seeing a loyal Scottish POW stranded, helpless and stupid in Occupied France would have been no joy either. It was not until 1993 that the Hitchcock Resistance films resurfaced in a video release from the British Film Institute. Yet in the fifteen years since, the diptych has established itself as one of the great buried moments in British and European cinema.

Let us go on to look at the follow-up film *Aventure malgache*, which also sets the cat among the pigeons, but in a different way. It starts too as a flashback story with a French actor belonging to the Molière Players, a Paris theatre company in exile which served as the cast for the film itself, sitting in a dressing room narrating the events surrounding his escape from colonial Madagascar where he had been based at the time of the French surrender and the establishment of the Vichy regime. Is this the real-life memoir of a member of the cast that Hitch is using for the story? Or have Hitchcock and writer Angus MacPhail simply made it up? Are we, moreover, meant to believe his story, or does the film try to show us, tongue-in-cheek, how people in wartime reinvent themselves when they move from one country to another? In any event Clarousse, the narrator, makes himself out to be a Resistance hero who opposes the Vichy collaborators on the island, in particular Jean Michel, the local police chief who tips the balance in favour of Marshal Pétain's regime. The action starts with Clarousse as a star lawyer ostentatiously showing off his theatrical skills in court. From then on it flashes back and forth from the story told in the dressing room and his two fellow actors: it is a loosely constructed narrative of 'resistance'. Clarousse clandestinely organises escapes from the island by Gaullist sympathisers while pretending to be a hard-line Vichyite. In a typical Hitchcock touch, a Resistance escapee mentions his name to his fiancée before departing, and the girl betrays him. A romantic farewell turns into act of treachery. Imprisoned and awaiting court-martial Clarousse must then avoid the traps of his 'defence lawyer', who is also trying to incriminate him. Pétain commutes his death sentence to five years imprisonment due to his First World War service. On the point of being transferred to a penal colony on the mainland, the British Navy boards his boat and he becomes a Resistance radio operator broadcasting propaganda messages to the island. In some inserted documentary footage we see the British occupy the naval base at Diego Suarez in 1942. Michel now knows the game is up, so takes down the portrait of Pétain on his office wall and replaces it with one of Queen Victoria. In this Chinese-box theatricality, Clarousse has told the story to fire up his fellow actors in their stage roles as Gestapo officer and a Vichy policeman while he is dressed in peasant clothes as (we presume) a member of the Resistance. They joke that they have finished their rehearsal in the dressing room as they are called to make their stage entrance.

## POST-ROMANTIC FUGITIVES: *STAGE FRIGHT* AND *FRENZY*

In both short films there are key narrative devices that Hitchcock will take further in *Stage Fright* – from *Bon Voyage* the unreliable flashback and from *Aventure malgache* the ambiguities of theatrical role-playing. At feature length he intensifies both. The London thriller starts with a couple on the run, or rather fleeing the city in a sports car through the bombsites surrounding St. Paul's Cathedral. The so-called 'lying flashback' in which Jonathan Cooper (Richard Todd) tells to Eve (Jane Wyman) his version of the murder of Charlotte Inwood's husband (for which he stands accused) lasts a full thirteen minutes: meanwhile Charlotte (Marlene Dietrich) is a celebrity actress and Eve an aspiring one at RADA, so theatricality is both metaphoric in the film's endless round of impersonation and role-playing and metonymic in terms of what the two women officially 'do'. The flashback to the crime scene is realised with such panache, with such Humean force and vivacity in Hitchcock's cinematic staging, that it becomes the most compelling section of the whole film. Yet in retrospect we come to realise it is false, and that the director has pulled the rug from under our feet. And he has done so, as Chabrol and Rohmer note, in a specific way. The images are true: it is Cooper's voice-over commentary that is false (Rohmer and Chabrol 1992: 105). The 'truth' of the images would mean Cooper is wrongly accused, a good-looking, innocent man. The falseness of the commentary means that he turns out, much to Eve's consternation, to be a psychopath and a charmless one to boot.

Hitchcock also deconstructs the convention of female beauty he has so often employed in his Hollywood films. The bespectacled Jane Wyman is naively enthusiastic, plain, ungainly; Dietrich is as charismatic and glamorous as ever, playing a role that is clearly moulded on her own persona. But she is also a middle-aged *femme fatale*. Eve's alternative to Todd's charmless killer is the quietly manipulative policemen played by Michael Wilding who is not exactly a brilliant detective. Hitchcock thus severs all the usual points of identification that can draw an audience into a film. At the same time Eve is a straight continuation of Iris from *The Lady Vanishes* – an uncertain young woman searching for a new identity who tries to find it through an addictive quest, in this case not by rescuing a vanishing spy but by planting the murder rap on her glamorous rival. Cooper starts out as a wrong-man update of Richard Hannay and Robert Tisdall from *Young and Innocent* but ends up as 'the right man' after all. In this way just as Hitchcock reprises the innovation of his wartime shorts, he echoes and inverts themes from his pre-war thrillers. And he maintains as well the scene-changing intensity.

Hitchcock's substitutions for passionate romance here are theatricality, the knowing stress on storytelling and fabrications of plot; the generous use of irony and of dark humour. Of course, romance never vanishes, as Hitchcock reprises the old standby of *Blackmail* and *Sabotage,* the slow but sly copper who 'rescues the heroine' for his own purposes. More importantly, the severing of star identification from the spectator's gaze coupled with the duplicity of the flashback is extreme. Critics dismissed it at the time as a cheap trick played on an audience attuned to the conventions of classic narration. With *Frenzy* (1972) times had changed. The veteran Hitchcock is now the acclaimed director of *Psycho* (1960) and *Frenzy*, as a Hitchcock serial killer film for Universal Pictures, can be hyped and read in that idiom. At the same time other London developments had caught the director's eye. In 1966 he had admired the expatriate gaze that Antonioni had cast on the city in *Blow-Up*, a mystery film that lacks any central romance at its core and plays instead on the unnerving disconnections of the modern city. Yet English Hitchcock is never a true modernist and *Frenzy* remains a hybrid of the inventive and the old-fashioned, a film that seems both very contemporary and very nostalgic (adapted in fact from Arthur La Bern's post-war thriller *Goodbye Piccadilly, Hello Leicester Square*). From *Stage Fright* he takes to extremes the conceit of the male fugitive as good-looking but petulant and egocentric. In the earlier film this anti-romantic trope had slotted into the eventual revelation of guilt. But here the ex-RAF officer down on his luck, Richard Blaney (Jon Finch), is innocent, yet just as charmless as Jonathan Cooper. Thus Hitchcock eventually drains identification and romance out of the fugitive film and takes the genre to the point of no return. But 1972 audiences now liked the point of no return and, contrary to *Stage Fright*, he had the satisfaction of a massive box-office hit.

At the same time the subject matter is truly dark and disturbing, not least because Hitchcock's sharp humour and flair for understatement seem to increase with the enormity of the crime. In addition, the Covent Garden market sequences are very much the stylised recreation of a famous city venue as a glorified stage setting, a theatrical scene that is in no sense an attempt to portray the 'real' London. If we analyse *mise-en-scène* in the two central murders to break down Hitchcock's neoclassical style, how fluidly he operated in his stylistic understatement, we can also see how he crosses the line into modernist montage and filmic tropes of absent presence. But for Hitchcock this was also a return to origin, down and dirtier than any previous British film and taking the fugitive film to the edge of the abyss.

## EPILOGUE: THE *FRENZY* MURDERS

The *Frenzy* murders are two discrete instances of modernist intervention in neoclassical narrative. Here our chapter epilogue zooms in on the running man's double, the standing, strolling man who in *Frenzy* is the unlikely murderer. Rusk, the wholesaler, is forever around the market, lounging, chatting, checking delivery lists, always ready for a laugh. While the farouche Blaney is constantly ducking and diving, Rusk (Barry Foster) does his cockney salt-of-the-earth routine, showing off his mum up from Kent, reassuring the ladies, joking with the lads. Yet by halfway through the film we know he is the necktie strangler. So Hitchcock simultaneously poses two questions: how does he get away with it, and for how long will he continue to get away with it? The answer to the first is that he takes people into his confidence: the answer to the second is right until the very end. Hitch and screenwriter Anthony Shaffer check in with a comic copper subplot where languid Inspector Alec McCowen is a less of a detective than his batty wife (Vivien Merchant), who prides herself on her Michelin star cuisine but has no culinary skills at all. Hilariously, the anxiety of gastronomy takes over from the solving of crimes. So we have time to see Rusk acting normally for most of the film except when he commits murder or, in the case of Blaney's lover, Babs, has to fight with her corpse for rigor mortis possession of his tiepin in the back of a potato lorry. It is important therefore how Hitchcock films the two onscreen murders because they represent the eruption of the unnatural into the natural order and demand in their staging something special since *mise-en-scène* in the film is largely functional and conservative throughout its duration.

Working closely with Shaffer he does it through contrast, antithesis. The first murder is brutally explicit, the second unseen and, with the first murder already implanted in the spectator's mind, everything is left to the imagination. The onscreen/offscreen opposition quickly becomes a question of staging and style. In the Brenda Blaney marriage bureau Rusk has slipped in at lunchtime after the secretary has left. Blaney's estranged spouse (Barbara Leigh-Hunt) is alone. As Rusk's murderous intent unfolds, slowly at first, Hitchcock starts with reverse angles and then cuts from medium shot to close-up to increase the sense of entrapment. This is broadly within the format of classical style. The first physical contact is over the disputed phone call for help. As Rusk takes preventative action, his hand enters the same frame as her hand for the first time. Next Hitch moves fully into two-shot; he then pans to capture the two bodies pressed tightly against the office wall as Brenda tries in vain to escape. This tight sequence of close shots signifies a bodily aesthetic that moves into modernist design. Entrapment then morphs into a brutal rape-murder montage as bold, if not bolder, than the shower scene in *Psycho*. It is technically complex and emotionally harrowing, an example of time-image delay where though the cutting is fast, the sequence seems to take an eternity. According to Krohn, Hitchcock shot the scene in one day from fourteen angles, keeping his camera on the victim for most of the rape sequence and on the killer for most of the murder sequence, though the four close shots of the dying Brenda from Rusk's POV are the most memorable and haunting images of desperation in the whole sequence (Krohn 2000: 272–3).

For Rusk's murder of Babs (played by Anna Massey, who had escaped the clutches of Carl Boehm in *Peeping Tom* but has no such luck here), the staging could not be more different. The money-shot in the first sequence may well have been the extreme telephoto lens that captures the spittle from Brenda's lolling tongue as the killing is completed. Here the money-shot is more subtle and comes right at the start. As Babs the bar-girl walking out on her job encounters Rusk outside the pub, Hitch swiftly fades out the sound to match a silent zoom-in on her face as she senses someone behind her. We then see Rusk at her shoulder, just behind her in two-shot. But this is casual Rusk not demented Rusk, so the disturbance is in the *camera alone* not in the actor's demeanour. It is a brilliant modernist conceit. There follows a long backtrack of the two in cheerful conversation walking through the covered Covent Garden market, brightly-lit, transparent, there for all to see, and completely anti-noir with no shadowy menace as Rusk offers Babs accommodation for a few days at his flat while she sorts herself out. As they reach the building, the camera precedes them, allows them to overtake it, then follows as Rusk closes the door uttering the fatal words he has used to Brenda in her bureau: 'You're my kind of woman'. Thereafter the camera's descending back-track is eerily silent until Hitchcock fades up source sound, traffic noises, bird song, and then with a cut disguised by a passing porter's truck, opens up the full market bustle of the street outside, oblivious as in *Rope* to interior killing. Babs had spent the previous night with Blaney the fugitive, an enjoyable one-night stand by her account: but here she spends her last moments with the running man's cheery double, the standing, strolling man who does not need to run because his 'normality' fools the world. A traumatic encounter – or it would have been if she lived long enough to be traumatised.

# CHAPTER 3

# *Running man 2: Carol Reed and his contemporaries*

Carol Reed makes the same shift as Hitchcock from romance to disenchantment but takes a very different route. He works closely within a mimetic idiom: his films rival those of the Italian neo-realists in the immediate post-war years. Here he is part of a wider movement in which fugitive film is just one dimension, the historic moment of *romantic realism* in British film, which is over, we could argue, almost as soon as it has begun. Romantic realism has three main components, all variations on the new mimesis. The first is the wartime documentary series of Humphrey Jennings, in particular *Listen to Britain* (1942) *Fires Were Started* and *A Diary for Timothy* (1946). The second is the combat drama-documentaries of Reed, Lean and others. The third, the wider remit of the fugitive genre which includes at a tangent two of Lean's most popular films, *Brief Encounter* and *Great Expectations* (1946). Of these the Jennings trilogy is arguably the most startling, the most innovative and the most compelling. In the fugitive genre the most important feature is Reed's Belfast tragedy, *Odd Man Out*, closely followed by Robert Hamer's East End drama for Ealing, *It Always Rains on Sunday*.

To speak of 'romantic realism' is to stress a British form that combines the poetic realism of the pre-war French with the neo-realism of the post-war Italians. In wartime it transforms the moving image by capturing the everyday dramas of ordinary people and does so because they are seen as part of a wider community, a broader fabric of social being. The war itself is vital: the drama-documentary exalts the war effort and does so by showing the courage and resilience of ordinary men and women, civilian and military alike. One feature common to the patriotic and highly naturalistic war dramas and the poetic short films of Jennings dealing with the Home Front is the capture of a particular mood: the willingness of the disparate, varied by class and culture, to stand firm in the face of the enemy, to endure and prevail. Thus the stress on flight and subterfuge in the post-war fugitive film is the *absolute antithesis* of its patriotic predecessors, but there is continuity of form. The romantic patriot of wartime inhabits a collective subjectivity; he or she is part of a social whole and has special privileges: the romantic outlaw, or post-war fugitive, is singular and isolated, and the film obliquely laments the wider fabric of community that has been rent asunder, but necessarily so as war gives way to peace and different dramas take centre stage. Jennings' role is vital. While most patriotic fiction narratives tried to render communal lives through professionals with familiar faces, Jennings directly recorded the voices and faces of ordinary people at war. His images have an unequalled freshness, immediacy and vitality. While his cross-cutting and his surreal power of juxtaposition are breathtaking, at the same time he makes them integral to poetic composition. His films remain narrative but they are not fictions loosely based on real-life incidents. There are for the most part the incidents themselves.

It was the high point of a particular kind of romantic sensibility, never to be matched again until the memory films of Terence Davies where it is substantially modified by modernist style. In general, romantic realism was the beneficiary of many things: the new detail in location shooting, both day and night, the use of precise, naturalistic studio interiors to match location footage, the use of greater camera mobility and deep-focus lenses. It was also enhanced by more complex forms of lighting and framing that come from a new generation of cinematographers, in particular from Robert Krasker, Guy Green, Otto Heller and Douglas Slocombe. It had a broader cinematic vision that differs markedly from the vivid fantasy worlds of Powell and Pressburger, which embodied anti-naturalistic romance at the time, especially in *Black Narcissus* and *The Red Shoes* (1948). Equally, its power transcends the parochial concerns and moralistic tone of its near-neighbour, the social problem films of the post-war years. Romantic realism represented a stylistically heightened exploration of the life-world: its pivot was the romance of changed fortune that offered redemption from dire circumstance. Yet for the doomed fugitives of *Odd Man Out* and *It Always Rains on Sunday* the change in fortune never materialises. It founders on the tension between the ideal and the actual that drives fugitive narration and it is the drawn-out suffering of the transgressor in flight that attracts us to him as a sinner searching for grace before his fate is sealed. Thus it is with Tommy Swann and Johnny McQueen. They have transgressed under law and yet neither we feel deserves the fate that awaits them. To identify with them is an audience romance – a shared transcendence of the post-war gloom of the material world in the flickering darkness of the cinema.

The transformation of romance into realism is, in literary terms, a descent from high to low. In Northrop Frye's literary formulation romance is based on the quest, often mythic, and the heroic adventure: it has a noble pedigree in the myth of medieval chivalry and the figure of the knight. It is, we could say, the exalted search by different means for the Holy Grail (Frye 1976: 35–8). In the relationship of film and modernity fugitive narration performs a special kind of volte-face. Not only is it in class terms a descent from high to low, from aristocratic to proletarian, from the lives of the privileged to those of ordinary working people or from the lawful to the transgressor; it is often *a reversal of pattern from noble pursuit to criminal flight.* The noble hero quests and pursues: the transgressing fugitive hides and flees. The opening of *Great Expectations*, the chance meeting of Pip and Magwitch in the churchyard on the Romney Marshes, is in many ways a meeting of complete opposites who become kindred spirits, the confused young orphan who is spiritually lost with the confused convict who is physically lost in his desperate effort to escape the law. The Dickens romance will later reunite them after chance has favoured both of them and their lives are changed. But the post-war fugitive in film is a different kind of figure altogether, a loner who is usually doomed or else survives as a damaged figure.

We can link Reed with the near-documentary melodramas of *Waterloo Road* (1945), *Brighton Rock, The Blue Lamp* (1949) and *Night and the City* (1950). Yet two other features stand much closer to his work – *It Always Rains on Sunday* and *They Made Me a Fugitive.* Here *Odd Man Out* has a closer affinity to *Sunday* than to his later film, *The Third Man*, which in turn is more aligned to Cavalcanti's dark masterpiece. Often critics have wrongly reduced fugitive film to a special kind of social comment, to a form of 'spiv' movie highlighting the flash black market criminals of the post-war underworld, risk-taking villains without a conscience in a ration-book world governed by scarcity. But all four films go way beyond this. In Cavalcanti's film Narcy, his philosopher-black marketeer played by Griffith Jones, is both worldly and unnervingly articulate, a Mephistopheles for his age, almost allegorical. At the same time his bold artifice is expressed precisely through the excess of body language and clothes in a time of material lack, an iconic play on surfaces and on extravagance, which conceals a deeper malaise. While Narcy is a deeply comic Nietzschean super-spiv whose portrait goes beyond naturalism and spiv culture, in *The Third Man* it is Harry Lime's *proximity* to espionage, not spying itself, that helps nail his elusive character. Narcy and Lime both defy obvious labels as spies or spivs, and for different reasons Hitchcock's fugitives are neither spies nor spivs either; never the former since they start as innocent bystanders, and never the latter because even when criminal, their demeanour is too stylish and bourgeois. Paradoxically, the villains of his American films such as *Shadow of a Doubt* and *Strangers on a Train* share the Nietzschean amorality of Narcy and of Harry Lime, and are equally fascinating.

The young, impulsive gangster, sadistic, frightened, manipulative and spiteful is another matter. This explains why Pinkie Brown in *Brighton Rock* and Tom Riley in *The Blue Lamp* prompt our deep ambivalence: they are repellent, but also lure our feelings in the final act of retreat. They are cool sadists when on the offensive but on the run we feel the trap closing in them, sense the senselessness of wasted youth, and endow them at the end with a secret sympathy they do not deserve, especially when they are boxed in by both police and rival criminals. Yet we do so also because, as bold young actors, Dirk Bogarde as Riley and Richard Attenborough as Pinkie have the temerity to upstage their boring police pursuers (and unconvincing fellow-actors). While many critics have seen *The Blue Lamp* and *Brighton Rock* as the main films in the so-called 'spiv' series, made to extol the values of police work and camaraderie in the face of tough young hoodlums, Kynaston claims there was little contemporary evidence that Bogarde had really scandalised his audiences in his role as a police killer. He was soon to reprise it on radio, and become, briefly, a cult figure (Kynaston 2008: 72–3). It seems more likely that audiences wanted to have their cake and eat it, to be reassured by moralistic closure and the wide sense of community inherited from wartime but also enjoy the audacity of the teenage killer-on-the-run and his perverse individuality in a grey and uniform post-war culture. What adds to the appeal in both films is the contemporary, documentary look, a recognisable post-war Brighton with locations at the racecourse, the station and Queen's Road, posing as Greene's pre-war city in *Brighton Rock*, or the extensive car-chase locations around Paddington, the Edgware Road and the White City dog-track which were handy for the Ealing mob in *The Blue Lamp*. Here the candid camera sequences at the dog-track stadium of Bogarde fleeing through rough and hostile crowds unaware they were being filmed has the authentic candour of *cinéma vérité* and is a bravura sequence to atone for all the earlier tedious scenes at Paddington Green police station.

The fugitive films of Reed and Hamer are richer and more intricate: neither is mired in the popular legend of cops and robbers, which they easily transcend. Two key factors unite them and make them stand out. Both work through bold use of time compression, of a lifespan lived in twenty-four hours. The action of *Odd Man Out* proceeds from late afternoon to just past midnight. Hamer's film is nearer twenty-four hours, starting very early on a Sunday morning (2–3 am) and ending very late on Sunday night. And, both dramatise the special *active passivity* of their fugitive hero, though by different means. Both are fugitives: but only for a brief time are they running men. Johnny McQueen (James Mason) is badly wounded in the botched factory raid that makes him a killer, no longer a gunman on the run but a delirious victim who can barely walk. Tommy Swann (John McCallum) spends most of his fateful Sunday in hiding at the Sandigate house: his active flight from the law simply bookends the film. Yet the repose/movement rhythms are crucial to the momentum of both films. McQueen starts as an escaped prisoner on the run holed up in his girlfriend's family home, but then assumes his role as local IRA leader to oversee one last raid. Thereafter he has no true resting-place in the city. Swann heads off to the East End home of Rose Sandigate (Googie Withers) after his breakout from Dartmoor and recruits the aid of his ex-lover, now a married woman. While he is in hiding, the fractious world of the Sandigate family carries on around him and without him. There is a contrast too in focus. The hunted, ever-haunted McQueen is always at the centre of Reed's narrative. However, *It Always Rains on Sunday* focuses on the domestic life of Rose, and Swann is now an outsider to the multi-layered world of the East End community he once inhabited. Similarities of pattern thus top and tail films that otherwise deviate sharply from each other at the narrative core. At the end, both men make a final, doomed bid for freedom late at night, where the atmospheric deep-focus photography of Krasker for Reed and Slocombe for Hamer enhances the atmospheric locations that offer their fugitives the fleeting hope of freedom – the Belfast docks for McQueen, the East End shunting yards for Swann. Of course, neither gets away. In line with the censorship code, onscreen justice is meted out in accordance with the gravity of the crime. McQueen is gunned down, like the cashier who had been his unintended victim: Swann, an armed robber but no killer, is finally captured as he throws himself on the rails in front of an approaching train.

Hamer, perhaps, gives us the lesser film. It centres on a working family in a cramped terraced house with no bathroom – the appellation 'two up, two down' seems almost a euphemism. But the location shoots in Bethnal Green and Whitechapel, the shabby houses and bomb sites, the ration books and passing figures still in uniform, the studio evocation of a teeming Petticoat Lane market and the backstory of simmering tensions between Jewish and Gentile locals all lend an authenticity that makes it seem now a film document as much as a dramatic fiction of the post-war years. If *Brief Encounter* two years earlier gave us the tortuous near-affair of a gentle middle-class couple, this film shows us a more abrasive 'brief encounter' in which passion is earthier and more powerful, and finally a one-way love. Both women fashion their own kind of subterfuge. While Laura travels furtively to her secret assignations with Alec Harvey, Rose is trapped in her own house by Swann's return, a house now converted by his presence into a prison she never leaves the whole day. Here she bends the usual domestic strategies of manipulation into something different – a cover-up for the convict she still loves. Judicious cutting gives us a choice in deciding whether or not her passionate embrace of Swann in the marital bedroom (one of the great screen kisses of British cinema), leads on to raunchier things. We suspect that it does, but of course this is 1947 and if it does it cannot be shown. What can be shown is the pressing weight of fate – almost unbearable, a pressure felt in nearly every frame. At the start Hamer uses oneiric flashback in a brilliant double-mirror shot not only to register Rose's earlier life with Swann but also to lift that pressure of entrapment, to shoot Withers briefly as a lustrous blonde in soft lighting, to include a summer picnic scene with the lovers dressed in white and an engagement ring passed between them. The idyll is everything the rest of the film is not, the romantic promise of something that is never fulfilled and never will be, since Swann is a natural chancer who will move from woman to woman wherever opportunity knocks.

For Hamer as a constrained bisexual director, you sense that Rose could well have been a projection of his own tortured persona. Nonetheless, the film takes on a momentum of its own. Rose's attraction to the dark unshaven fugitive out of her past, mute, expressionless but ever ruthless, has its own sexual dangers. Two-way desire: one-way love, and in her own words 'ten years too late'. First hiding out in the backyard Anderson shelter, a poignant reminder of the war just past, then smuggled by Rose up to the main bedroom after the rest of the family go out before lunch, Swann is the metaphorical skeleton in her cupboard who turns into the escaped convict in her marital bed. He is what-might-have-been but never was, and Rose like many others in the war has to reinvent herself to move on. She is thus married to a man old enough to be her father and must deal with stepdaughters precocious enough to be her rivals, or indeed her 'younger sisters'. The family side of the multiple plot-line, defiant teenage daughters cavorting with older men and giving their step-mum lip, fits in with the wider ambience of the time – wideboys fencing stolen goods and general petty crime – that would become the stuff of British television soap. But television can be dull and prosaic whereas this film is tight and poetic: it makes nothing reassuringly familiar and leaves its audience at times feeling claustrophobic. And its sense of time and place is vital. You feel the East End is a place that has taken a battering from a distant enemy, as the Blitz and the war remain something unspoken and working people try to pick up the pieces and get on with their lives.

The muted but palpable romantic feeling in Hamer's classic thus pivots on the figure of Withers, who creates a feisty local housewife with the same power and conviction she had shown in playing the middle-class newly-wed of Hamer's 'Haunted Mirror' episode for *Dead of Night*. In the short film, Hamer brilliantly balanced romance and fable but here a different contrast is suggested – between *Sunday*'s romantic realism and his exquisite fable made two years later, *Kind Hearts and Coronets*. In the latter Dennis Price plays an upstart from a noble family, the D'Ascoynes, but has fallen on hard times. He plots revenge by murdering the remaining lineage, while planning to marry the beautiful widow (played by Valerie Hobson) of his second victim and thereby inheriting the family fortune. It is an amusing tall tale, narrated as such by Price from his diary in his prison cell as he awaits execution and made even taller by the casting of Alec Guinness in the multiple roles – one female – of all his noble victims. Where Hamer had used romantic realism as a quasi-tragic form to explore the fraught lives of an East End family, here he uses dark satire to mock England's fading aristocracy, thus inverting the traditional formula of European literature – the high form as tragedy and the low form as comedy. At the same time this is post-war England: his 'comedy' is too dark to be comic and his 'tragedy' too stoic to be tragic. The result, modification of the romance balanced against modification of the fable, suited the Ealing format of popular cinema perfectly. Yet both films were much more and Hamer's failure to find a true niche in Ealing or elsewhere has been one of the great losses to British film.

*Odd Man Out* is a cinematic masterpiece, and *is* tragic in its sensibility, far transcending the politics in which it is rooted but which at the same time are indispensable to its dramatic impact. To call it 'British' would do damage to its nature. It is strictly Anglo-Irish in its inception and corresponds to that great contemporary film that combines Irish film talent with an English director, Steve McQueen's *Hunger* (2008). The main difference between the two films is also crucial: *Hunger* is a prison film of turbulent stasis; *Odd Man Out* a poetic film of wounded flight. Here Reed manages to create a remarkable fusion, a filmic homology to the Stations of the Cross with the time–space unities of classical tragedy. The film takes place in just over eight hours within the boundaries of a single city: the large clocktower near the docks is ever-present in many of the film's wide-shot exteriors to remind us of time passing. And as time passes, the hero's slowed and suffering movement – the bullet wound in the shoulder – signifies the weight of an invisible burden. This is a modern version of the Passion and simultaneously a vision of tragic fate. To merge the two – a risk-taking venture at the best of times – *is* a romantic conception but one that Reed achieves through a tightness of genre matched against a breadth of vision.

Reed's film shares many things with Hamer's fugitive romance but works itself out on a larger scale in its vision of the human condition. Whereas Swann's escape is secondary in the lives of Hamer's East End characters, apart from Rose, McQueen's fugitive status affects everyone in Reed's film. It is a legend in the making. For the East Enders life goes on; for the Belfast locals who encounter the wounded man life is altered. The motif of the gunman on the run is not new to Irish writing. Sean O'Casey had cast a wry look over the new mythologies surrounding the 1917 Easter Uprising in his great 1924 stage play *Shadow of a Gunman*, where the hapless Donal Davoran tries to weave a false myth around his inflated persona. It is a self-aggrandising strategy that has both farcical and tragic results. Yet Reed's film pushes farce back into the secondary realms of action. For sure, the wounded McQueen is a shadow of his former self and hence one update of O'Casey's 'shadow of a gunman'. But he is more. All mythology is external to him, the work of others who encounter him, who transform his suffering figure into a legend – hence the perfect match of his active passivity with the reactive interventions of others. Wounded and delirious, haunted by guilt and governed by the primal instinct to flee, he understands little of what others are making of him. The absence of tactical thinking in his damaged psyche thus acts as the springboard to a rebirth of innocence and tips the balance between right and wrong, good and evil. The armed robbery gone wrong that ends in the cashier's accidental killing is the sign of ruthlessness and a compromised morality: the *via dolorosa* through the bleak post-war city in winter that ends with a snow storm is a sign of expiation, the transformation of anti-hero back into hero, the potential Antichrist transformed into a modern Christ. Out of such things are myths forged and this film can be read in this double form, as a flight from the law but also the poetic forging of myth in its purest cinematic form.

Here Reed's poetic form gets its main charge from the haunted figure. While fugitive films often increase the degree of disorientation as flight progresses and as the city becomes more and more of a menacing labyrinth, Reed's strategy is much bolder. Disorientation starts with the first exterior sequence. For the back parlour plotting of the robbery in the home of McQueen's girlfriend, the staging is objective and naturalistic. But with the car drive to the linen mill that follows, things change. This, we understand, is McQueen's first venture into city daylight since his prison break into the hills six months earlier. Krasker's camera is mobile and subjective; Reed's cutting is swift and sharp. Subjective camera, speeding car shots, swerving tram lines and tilted angles make up a montage of jagged forward movement to indicate a leader who has lost his bearings and is out of touch with the world around him. After the hold-up and the flight to the waiting car when the alarm is sounded, there is further disorientation. Blinded by the sunlight on the steps outside the mill, McQueen fatally hesitates. The cashier catches up with him and pulls a gun. In the struggle McQueen is wounded and the cashier killed.

Perceptual confusion thus pre-dates the wounding that aggravates it and creates hallucinations on the verge of consciousness. There are three main sequences. After McQueen falls from the getaway car and has to make his escape solo, he finds the sanctuary of an air-raid shelter near a bombsite. A prison warder enters the shelter, caught in a single shaft of light, to recover a kid's football that has just bounced inside. McQueen talks to him as if he is back in jail, the place of refuge now a prison cell. Reed fades out the image of the jailer into that of girl on a single roller-skate holding the ball. Later in the pub where he has been shut in an alcove for his own protection, he sees the faces of familiar characters appearing in the bubbles of the beer he has spilt on the table. Finally, as his end approaches, he is brought into Lukey's bizarre art studio where the paintings on the wall fly away at strange angles around the room: then he begins to hallucinate the figure of Father Tom, the priest who wants to save his soul, preaching to McQueen as he prepares to make his final dash for freedom. It is a spasmodic lapsing in and out of delirium, set against the objective world of his pursuers, helpers and betrayers. Yet as a whole, it is their objective world that prevails. McQueen is *object*, viewed by a composite collective gaze – ours as spectators and those (as characters in the film) who encounter him.

Here Reed makes some unusual moves in the chronology of flight: the black marketeer played by Maureen Delaney should be a good ally but turns out to be an informer interested only in police rewards. Conversely, two Englishwomen skilled in first aid through their wartime air raid work take him in and tend him: one takes his incriminating gun and drops it down a drain then sends him back out in the driving rain with a flat cap as a disguise. The young girl with one roller-skate who sees him in the air raid shelter senses an instant affinity with him, a lost waif who seems instinctively to identify with the lost-ness of the wounded man she has discovered. Belfast street urchins express in guttural terms the ambivalence suppressed by the adults he encounters. They rib the police by making Johnny their hero, but in the same breath demand their share of the reward money for sighting him. In the pub run by Fencie (William Hartnell) the wounded fugitive is locked into an empty cubicle to avoid embarrassment to all: he is neither protected nor betrayed by people who are not fully on his side but still secretly moved by his plight. On the one hand, the film is a neat moral fable that puts us in the position of those who encounter him. What would we do? On the other, it softens the dilemma by romanticising its fugitive. To see him suffer so passively, to see him without malice or anger, to see him lurch in pain towards death moves us all. And the love of a good woman who radiates innocence and devotion as Kathleen Ryan does so winningly throughout, in what some might see as an update of the Mary Magdalene figure, is the icing on the cake. Romantic fate on the broadest scale is primed by couple-romance on the gentlest of registers.

This would not be the culmination of romantic realism that it is without the serendipity of nature itself. It had begun snowing, quite heavily at times, during Reed's Belfast shoot in the winter of 1946–47, one of the coldest on record, and he absorbed this harsh magic of the seasons directly into the look and mood of the film. As McQueen staggers through a purgatory of alleys and backstreets shot in wide angle, the snow caught in the street-lamps lightens the darkness of the oncoming night: thick flakes soften the contrast of harsh lighting and black shadow. This gives to his martyrdom, that culture of creating legend out of disaster, a magical aura that Krasker's

**Figure 3.1** Painter Meets Gunman: James Mason and Robert Newton in *Odd Man Out*

black and white cinema seems to extract from the very depths of nature itself. We associate the Passion with a burning sun and a desert landscape, but Reed's Passion is Nordic and snow seems like a cushioning of death. Yet he is careful enough not to overbalance. When Lukey the painter-obsessive (Robert Newton) wishes to capture the face and figure of the dying fugitive he remarks: 'All the others I painted were living . . . but he's near death. You can see it in his eyes.' But we see in the canvases strewn around Lukey's baroque shambles of a studio other portraits of staring eyes, which merely mirror the demented eyes of the painter himself. Do we thus mould, asks this muted version of Protestant doubt, the sacred image of Jesus into a profane likeness of our own ego? Thus we suspect that McQueen will be given the same eyes as the painter himself, as Lukey tries to endow his putative Christ with the look of a desperate fanatic. Of course we never see the painting because Lukey throws it away in disgust after the wounded gunman has grabbed at the easel to keep his balance and brought it crashing to the ground: the attempt at consecration ends in bathos. But the point is taken. Each of McQueen's Others wants to see him in their own way, to construct their own variation on the growing legend, including the director himself, who repeatedly moulds his iconography as a latter-day Jesus in a northern city in winter.

## Fable versus romance: *The Third Man* and *They Made Me a Fugitive*

The fable is often the instrument of romantic disenchantment used by the disillusioned romantic. Hence that disenchantment is itself romantic, as these two films demonstrate. At the same time they are acerbically comic, and necessarily so, in their observations about the lack of fit in human affairs between appearance and reality. The best disenchantment is comic before it is tragic: post-romantic because romance is its absent presence and still lingers. Since Europe was now in ruins, destroyed by total war, that comic scepticism seemed justified. Any new concept of enlightenment had to be built out of the ashes, and with the coming of the Cold War two very different re-versions emerged from West and East respectively, neither of them at all convincing. *The Third Man* is at the very core of this disenchanted Europe in a black market Vienna still occupied by the Allies. Cavalcanti's film too seems to have a disenchanted Europe somewhere in its lineage. It has a London setting with like-minded racketeers to Reed's who use a funeral parlour as a front for their black market operations. But Drazin has suggested that its origins lay in Cavalcanti's disenchanted return to Paris in the immediate post-war to supervise location shooting for *The Captive Heart.* Here he saw friends who had become crooks and collaborators living sumptuously, while those who had led decent lives starved (Drazin 2007: 131–3). Reed too was quick to absorb local mood and detail. The racketeering in penicillin, which was in short supply for a destitute civilian population, was a contemporary evil that Greene picked up from his visit to Vienna to fine-tune the film's screenplay. So close parallels: both films are British artworks using a popular genre to gloss a widespread European malaise. And it is not just scepticism about human motive that drives both films, it is also the imagination of evil and here the respective villains are as intelligent, articulate and laconically amoral as British cinema has ever produced.

Of course, the portraits are very unalike for they encapsulate two different sides to evil in modernity. Griffith Jones is a flash sadistic narcissist who openly flaunts his treachery, thus justifying his name 'Narcy', which can be read as either 'Nazi' mispronounced or as shorthand for manufactured self-love or narcotics. His 'Valhalla' funeral parlour which fronts his black-market operations and the coffins that carry his secret contraband, including narcotics ('white powder'), were a morbid joke too dark for many critics and audiences of the time. But the ambience also has beyond its gallows humour the aura of a Nazi death cult gone wrong, as if the institution were a hangover from the nightmare just past. If the Valhalla parlour suggests the twin spectres of the death cult and the undead as two sides of the same coin, then the figure of Orson Welles as Harry Lime might equally be seen as a chilling version of the 'undead', the malevolent residue of a war just past. He is also a one-man disappearing act, an enigmatic fugitive intent on constantly reinventing himself in an expatriate world of floating identities. Narcy takes a visceral delight in the manipulation and torture of others. Lime seems by contrast to be energised by the impersonal nature of the process where people are treated no better than what they seem to him from the top of a fairground big wheel – ants, insects waiting to be crushed. One villain seems, more predictably, to embody the face-to-face dimension of terror and extermination just past; the other more boldly signifies the impersonal nature of destructiveness-from-distance where the guilty are inured from the death of the innocent, just as Lime never witnesses the children suffering from tainted doses of his diluted penicillin. As this is a moral fable for the age of classical cinema, justice will be done and seen to be done: Cotten and Howard, fall-guys cheated by the evil of their erstwhile friends, will take part in the process of vengeance. But their romantic life is in pieces.

Howard as Clem Morgan escapes from Dartmoor to settle it in a Soho shoot-out as a personal score before the police move in: Cotten as Holly Martins is given his part in the official chase through Vienna's sewers of his old high-school buddy who is now Vienna's Most Wanted. Yet justice is never fully done. In both films it is partial, incomplete and found wanting, and romance cannot really triumph. The flow of black marketeers will not cease: the plight of refugees like Anna who are cruelly sent back to countries under dictatorship will not go away. Cotten will never win Anna, (Alida Valli) who walks straight past him after Lime's funeral and remains Harry's girl: Narcy's dying words do not confess his obvious guilt but again falsely implicate the hapless Clem, already framed by the woman in the Dartmoor cottage who kills her drunken husband with the gun that has Clem's fingerprints all over it. And is the mistreated Sally, Narcy's girlfriend who has switched allegiance to get her revenge, likely to remain loyal to him? There is no knowing, no guarantee. There is no guarantee, in fact, that Clem's nightmare will not start all over again.

As fables we can read both films as satirical disenchantments of civilisation, offering little hope that in a post-Nazi world morality will thrive in the midst of ruin and scarcity. Even if the ruins are rebuilt and scarcity gives way to prosperity there are no guarantee that spiritual values will follow. For what are they? Romance is dead, religion is dead, idealism is dead. Meanwhile the Cold War is born. Irony thrives . . . and how. In Vienna Anna Schmidt is beautiful but still in love with a dead man when he is in fact alive and even more afterwards when he really is dead. Love of death, rejection of life. Love of sewers and subterfuge, rejection of the light of day. American accents,

Russian voices, Austrian city but drinking buddies by night and actors by day, Trevor Howard and Bernard Lee in khaki reassure us of the 'Englishness' of what is after all the British sector in the city in a picture still acclaimed the greatest British film of all time.

The elusive Harry seems to know every sewer escape route into the Russian sector where he is a protected species. But why is he protected? He may be American but the plot evokes a very local backstory as Drazin and Wollen have both shown in some detail (Drazin 1999: 144–54; Wollen 2002: 138–42). In the film a bystander at the car 'accident' that kills Harry Lime mentions the presence of a 'third man' who turns out to be Lime himself, who has in fact faked his death and put one of his dead rivals in his coffin. In the early 1950s when the film's popularity was at its height there was metaphorical talk of a 'third man' in British intelligence who had aided the Moscow defection of notorious MI5 agents Guy Burgess and Donald Maclean. Many years later this 'third man' defected to Moscow before he was arrested and his name proved to be Kim Philby, who himself had been in Vienna as a communist partisan during the defeated socialist uprising of 1932. Then recruited by the Soviets as a double agent, he disguised his allegiance by espousing *right-wing* causes like Franco's Civil War. Thus, it can be surmised, Philby *was also* the real 'third man' of Reed's picture, a wartime colleague of Greene in MI6 and the main model for the character of Harry Lime. How much did Greene know of Philby's treachery before anyone else did? Nothing for certain, but he may well have guessed, especially as he remained an occasional intelligence operative *after* the war (but part-time and covert) *on the other side* to Philby, openly espousing Leftist causes but reporting back on his many travels to Central Europe, South-East Asia and Central America to his Whitehall handlers. While Philby had 'played' Right but was covertly Left, post-war Greene played 'Left' but for a while at least was covertly Right, or more accurately was both at the same time, believing in Leftist causes but disliking the baleful influence of the Soviets around the world.

Lime embodies this maze-like duplicity, the new espionage world of smoke and mirrors. Plot-wise he is a cold and cruel racketeer pretending to run a children's charity, but something more is being concealed. Since Harry Lime is also shorthand for Graham Henry Greene, he embodies something of his screenwriter's professional duplicity while Lime's anxious friend and double Holly Martins, a drunken scribbler of pulp fiction Westerns, embodies that other aspect of Greene, the novelist who self-consciously wrote 'entertainments' for a mass audience. In both the telling of the tale and the substance of the tale, Reed and Greene are as thick as thieves. There is something more to Harry even when he has been exposed and we never know what it is – racketeering seems just the tip of iceberg. The film's rich indexicality

**Figure 3.2** Lime's Last Stand: Orson Welles in *The Third Man*

here makes its construction a politico-philosophical maze, a genealogy of Cold War knowledge before the 'war' had really started, with a dense, alluring quality that Reed feeds into the very texture of his Dutch tilts and his inspired images – the streets, buildings, shadows and squares of post-war Vienna. This is a film that turns itself inside out just as it turns our view of the world upside down. It became the template for the Cold War thriller of years to come, as well as a radio franchise for the opportunistic Welles who brought back Lime once more from the dead and found another source of money to help finance his risk-taking films. Unnoticed by critics, the substance and style of Reed's film also feeds into Welles' later European ventures, into *Mr Arkadin* and *The Trial,* so ultimately Welles made use of Reed as much as Reed, in debt like many to *Citizen Kane*, made use of Welles. There are also fascinating links between Reed's two later films, *The Man Between* and *Our Man in Havana*, and the picture some regard as Welles' masterpiece, *Touch of Evil.*

## REED AND SUBTERFUGE: *THE MAN BETWEEN* AND *OUR MAN IN HAVANA*

Reed's espionage pictures not only provide the connection to the new Cold War thrillers of the 1960s, they also feed into the flamboyant fantasy world of James Bond. After all, one of the early directors in the Bond series – signing in with *Goldfinger* (1964), *Diamonds are Forever* (1971) and *Live and Let Die* (1971) – was Guy Hamilton, assistant director to Reed on *The Third Man* and in a padded overcoat its original running man as body double for Welles during the famous flight along Schulhof, his moving shadow thrown high onto the wall, the clatter of his feet echoing on the cobblestones. Here then is a Jekyll-and-Hyde effect. The heritage of Buchan and Greene goes in two different directions – on the one hand, the exotic, globe-trotting novels of Ian Fleming and, on the other, the tight, harsher Cold War fiction of John le Carré and Len Deighton centred on the Iron Curtain. With its grim ironies and complex double-cross *The Man Between* seems the key link between Green and Le Carré, while the light, tongue-in-cheek humour of *Our Man in Havana* provides a perfect lift for the Bond series. At the very end of all this, in the twenty-first century we have the amusing sight of Le Carré's literary pastiche of *Our Man in Havana, The Tailor of Panama* (2001) being adapted for the screen by John Boorman (with Le Carré and Andrew Davies) so that he can cast Pierce Brosnan, at that time a Bond on the wane, as a seedier but realistic version of his fantasy 007 persona. If *Our Man in Havana* was a source of tongue-in-cheek action for the Bond franchise, then Boorman's film symbolically buries the myth of Bond in a post-Cold War world by encouraging Brosnan to mock his reason for being famous – which he does with relish.

It was not Hamilton as *auteur*, however, that kick-started the Bond series: it was the working-class milkman Sean Connery cast for the film out of nowhere, or more precisely the wrong side of Edinburgh. Dalry is a far cry from Fettes, the exclusive public school for the Anglo-Scot that Fleming had in mind for his hero's pedigree that leads on to exotic adventures, fast cars, the latest gadgetry and one-night stands with beautiful women who may or may not be Cold War updates of Mata Hari. But Connery, who can transform a scene simply by entering it, made all the difference to the franchise. For the Le Carré Cold War film, the acting was different, better suited to James Mason, Claire Bloom, Richard Burton, Simone Signoret and Michael Caine, all of whom carried it with equal aplomb. If *The Third Man* is latent Cold War, then *The Man Between* is the explicit version only five years on. It leads on to Sidney Lumet's *The Deadly Affair* (1966), Hamilton's *Funeral in Berlin* (1966), Ritt's *The Spy who came in from the Cold* and Sidney J. Furie's *The Ipcress File* (1965) – and many more. With the Fleming, Le Carré and Deighton franchises in full flow, British film, following British fiction, has a near-monopoly of the spy thriller for the whole of the Cold War period, even though it is sustained in part by North American directors and occasionally by Hollywood studios. Without the fugitive film of the 1940s this would have been impossible and, significantly, *The Man Between* is loosely adapted from a German and not a British source. For Reed there was no obvious successor to Greene.

Reed carries over his concern with divided cities from Vienna, then soon to be reunified, and Belfast (still partly divided) to Berlin, soon to be physically segregated for nearly forty years by its infamous Wall. Soviet dislike of *The Third Man* (and the hint that it tolerated black marketeers like Lime) meant that Reed was refused permission to film in the East German sector. However, he filmed as close to it as possible in venues like Moritzplatz where the war ruins of the Eastern sector acted as an atmospheric backdrop (Snow 2007: 72). He also filmed the Funk Sports arena, then one of the city's eighty-five camps for refugees and placed forbidding portraits of Stalin (who died in March in the middle of location work) at strategic points around his street locations. As in Vienna he mixed daytime and night-time shooting using two DOPs (directors of photography), Hans Schneeberger by day and Desmond Dickinson (who photographed *Hamlet* for Laurence Olivier) by night, directing hands on in a day-and-night double shift: if anything he did more daring night-time work here than in his earlier film with Krasker. In the drama that runs in part-parallel to *The Third Man* Claire Bloom as Susanne Mallison replaces Joseph Cotten as the naïve innocent abroad and James Mason as Ivo Kern succeeds Orson Welles as the enigmatic male Other who is topographically on the other side, but this time as a redeemable bad guy whose heart may be well be on the right side. Mason in fact lives up to the film's title as 'the man between', shuttling back and forth across the city's control points, a man with a foot in both camps and, like Lime, carrying a compromised and criminal past that is never made explicit.

The familiar espionage motif of blackmail looms large because of situation: desperate people in a new world need to reinvent themselves and are vulnerable. Reed constructs a chain of vulnerabilities and, as in 1948 Vienna, he uses a current scandal, the spate of car kidnappings done by both sides to recruit or 'return' people they deem necessary to their own sector of the city. He also adopts a device copied by Hitchcock at the start of *North by Northwest* – the mistaken kidnapping. The naïve, inquisitive Susanne is kidnapped in mistake for her German sister-in-law, Bettina (Hildegaard Knef), targeted by the communists because of her refusal to collaborate in the abduction of Kastner, who is running refugees out of East Berlin to the West. Susanne turns from amateur sleuth into a bewildered prisoner at risk and then a fugitive whom Ivo frees and hides before returning to the Western sector, except that his duplicity is by now well known and he is shot at the border crossing where Susanne escapes to freedom – the film's one true moment of soft romance in which Reed finally drops his guard.

This late lapse in tone and the muddled plot structure bequeathed to Reed by writer Harry Kurnitz threaten the quality of the film, but the saving grace is twofold: the superlative acting of Bloom and Knef, who out-perform their male counterparts, and the way Reed can fuse the mystery and uncertainty of the city itself with the oblique and shady motivation of its political players. He uses night-time shoots to create the effect of the divided metropolis as a labyrinth without seeming exit, and daytime shoots on open, desolate, bombed-out streets to evoke the arbitrary nature of all borders and division. Visually speaking, it is as effective as anything he ever did. The child witnesses of adult folly in *Odd Man Out* and *The Third Man* are replicated here by an even more haunting figure, Ivo's young lookout Dieter, wearing a baseball cap and endlessly circling desolate city streets on his modest bicycle. He is Ivo's 'eyes and ears' but you wonder about the loss of innocence displayed in his perpetual stalking. It is a brilliant, near-wordless image, the potential of goodness – he helps in the final escape – set against the lure of corruption that is everywhere.

Reed's film is also prophetic of the firming up of political division by the East Germans and their ruthless prevention of mass flight – the Wall that was constructed several years later to divide the city and provoke an international crisis. The seeds of that crisis are all here and in that respect Reed's film shares the power of uncanny prophecy with Wim Wenders' *Wings of Desire* (1987) made thirty-five years later, a magical and romantic fable which in its own way is prophetic of the Wall's impending demolition. Both Reed and Wenders filmed locations very close to or against the border within the divided city: just as Reed constructed imaginary checkpoints for his shoot just inside the Western sector, so Wenders replicated sections of the Wall for his own shoot very near to the Wall itself. The spy thrillers that followed often seemed sedentary by comparison with Reed's kinetic locations, but by then the Wall would have forced film directors to replicate East Berlin in other European cities. Reed had seized the moment, and for this reason alone his film endures.

His reunion with Greene came from the writer's willingness to sell him the film rights to *Our Man in Havana* at a knockdown price after refusing the higher price of his great artistic rival, Hitchcock. Here, finally, Reed moves sideways from fugitive to subterfuge mode. Though Noël Coward strides briskly and ostentatiously through Havana arcades as an MI6 operative of the old school, there are no running men. Yet there are key continuities for Reed amidst the switch. He again got an extended location shoot in a city in crisis and transition, and this time his new DOP, Oswald Morris, is able to use black and white to explore the look of the Hispanic city in the newer format of wide-angle Cinemascope. The book is set just before Castro's revolution, the film made soon after with approval of the new authorities when Reed convinced them he would paint their deposed Batista enemies in the worst possible light. Hence the 'Havana' of Reed's film is reflexively divided between old regime and new, a metaphorically divided city. Where Belfast, Vienna and Berlin had been spatially divided, Havana is time-split: but that time-split is rendered spatial by foregrounds of the 'old' and backgrounds of the 'new'. Reed and Greene told the new Ministry of Interior that Captain Segura, played by American comedian Ernie Kovacs, who was loosely based on Major Esteben Ventura, a notorious Batista torturer, would be the villain of the piece. The revolutionaries duly obliged by facilitating location shoots and providing crowds who spat at other extras dressed in the blue uniforms of Batista's police (Wapshott 1990: 299–301). Castro and Hemingway both visited the film set and Reed was allowed to restore the 'decadent' Tropicana nightclub and its pre-revolution strippers for one of his key sequences. The location shooting thus captures the city at a momentous point of transition in the country's history and Reed's film again has a hard documentary gloss that does not fade, and makes it fascinating to watch again and again.

During the war Greene has been intrigued by the technique of lazy operatives in the field of reporting nonexistent conspiracies or networks in order to satisfy their handlers in Whitehall. He thus suggested to Cavalcanti, who turned him down, the idea of such fictitious revelation as the core for a comedy thriller set in Estonia at the start of the war. In his new novel Havana became the centre of this invention. Yet despite his superb comic plot-device of salesman Jim Wormold (Alec Guinness) recycling diagrams of his latest vacuum cleaner as photographed blueprints of a new atomic weapon, there remains something uncanny – Greene's knack of creating comedy where potential tragedy is, historically, soon to be unfolded. The earlier scenario for Calvacanti used Estonia in early wartime, bridging the moment of its forced absorption into the Soviet Union and later conquest by the Nazis. Cuba in 1960 had also seen regime change and is just a year or so away from the Cuban Missile Crisis, sparked by American spy photography of sites in the country's interior being constructed for Soviet nuclear missiles. Thus Wormold's packaging of the design for his Atomic Pile cleaner is both hilarious and no laughing matter. It is about ridiculous invention, a true Hitchcockian implausible – MI6 believing that Batista had created his own atomić weapons in the mountains of the interior! But it was also eerily prescient of the actual espionage that followed on almost immediately from the release of the film, when the United States put Castro's Cuba under close surveillance – as well as invading it without success in the abortive 'Bay of Pigs'.

Tongue-in-cheek, the true 'romance' of the film lies in the brief encounter between Hawthorne and Wormold as Coward tries to inveigle Guinness into entering the new world of espionage. The venue is the men's toilets in a country club, with the result that spy subterfuge crosses over with a version of 'Carry on Cottaging' and Guinness and Coward play it up for all it is worth.

As for the straight romances, the police chief's interest in Wormold's teenage daughter is strictly off limits while Wormold's 'romance' with Beatrice, his new Whitehall secretary, is as pallid as any relationship in a Reed movie. As satire on a sclerotic Establishment culture the film hits the jackpot, but for audiences looking for new forms of heroism as wartime exploits faded into the collective memory, something else was needed and this rejuvenation was provided by a young, wisecracking, arrogant Bond. Connery, the working-class Scot soon to become an ardent nationalist, ironically injects through his defining 007 a new mythical life into 'Britishness' as it enters its uncertain post-colonial epoch. It was a way forward in the midst of worldwide ideological fermentation and Cold War crisis that audiences craved to take with a pinch of salt. Taking on the dangerous second world of the Soviets, the third world is Bond's oyster, a set of exotic locations into which he jets for exotic intrigue and gorgeous girls. For this, of course, socialist Havana was out of bounds, but the Caribbean, Latin-America, the Near East, South-East Asia, all would figure as the franchise stretched itself out until the end of the Cold War and the end of the century. Hitchcock had provided the Bond prototype with 'the double-chase' spy thriller which the Bond narrative slavishly follows as Connery becomes the first of the bold pursuers on a mission, and Greene here provided the tongue-in-cheek comedy that Bond's screenwriters put into the wise-cracks of their macho hero. It was a formula that could not fail, but its enormous success was not guessed at by critics at the time.

## REED'S SUCCESSORS

The 1960s alternative to Bond came, as we have noted, in the screen versions of Le Carré, in particular *The Spy Who Came in from the Cold* and *The Deadly Affair*. If Bond onscreen deals in hi-tech, exotica and spectacular success, the Le Carré films deal in desolation, betrayal and failure. The Bond fantasy is a celebratory form of autistic romance. Bond is in love with himself bedding nubile woman, a sucker for serial seduction. Le Carré's burnt-out operatives are compromised and betrayed: there is no couple-romance as fallback in a lonely world, for none can flourish. Both the Ritt and Lumet adaptations also contain key elements of the expatriate gaze, an outsider's vision of London embedded in the look of the film. Extensive location shooting and the desire for an authentic look echo the fugitive films of the 1940s: but these are Cold War narratives and both Ritt and Lumet see London in a different light. This is not the 'swinging' London of the 1960s. It is drab, austere and wintry, a place and culture of scarcity rather than plenty. Lumet encouraged photographer Freddie Young to develop a method of pre-flashing the negative to wash out the colour on the film and get the look of London in winter. Oswald Morris's black and white photography for Ritt looks cold, harsh and hygienic, with none of the softness or subtle shading he rendered in his Havana shoot for Reed. James Mason appears worn and distraught as a middle-aged cuckold used and betrayed by a close wartime comrade: Richard Burton gives his whisky-drinking fake defector, Alec Leamas, an air of still and chilling desperation that channels itself through the hypnotic power of the eyes. His encounter with fellow librarian Claire Bloom is a true cinema of loneliness where even sex with a young, attractive idealist fails to thaw emotions that are in deep-freeze. As in Reed's film, Bloom is the political ingénue in great danger, but this time she is not saved. While the Bond saga reduces romance to hedonistic fancy, the Le Carré films literally paralyse the moral power of the fable, for at the height of the Cold War morality has ceased to exist.

Here we must jump ahead and finish where we began, with the present. *The Bourne Ultimatum* now seems a suitable new century epilogue to British Hitchcock: ditto *The Tailor of Panama* for the Reed–Greene legacy. Bourne is the prototype hyper-modern fugitive: Brosnan as the seedy MI6 agent in the Boorman/Le Carré picture is Bond's post-modern *alter ego*. With John Boorman, one of the great neo-romantics of British cinema who had made *Point Blank*, *Deliverance* (1972) *Excalibur* (1981) and *The Emerald Forest* (1985), this switch with its perfect Panama locations seems almost like a repetition of the path that Reed had earlier trod from romance to comic disenchantment. Equally, Greengrass seems to be offering us pure hyper-modern Hitchcock. Both features are disenchanted fables of the corruption of global power but work, therefore, in different ways. Greengrass buries the stench of corruption in screen pyrotechnics and commodified paranoia: Boorman flaunts it as a running gag without end but not without genuine pathos. You pays your money you takes your choice.

CHAPTER 4

# *David Lean: the troubled romantic and the end of empire*

We have already looked at Lean as a contemporary of Hitchcock and Reed, but of course he was more. It is usual for admirers to make a critical leap from the post-war success of *Brief Encounter* and the Dickens' diptych (*Great Expectations* and *Oliver Twist* (1948)) to the big-budget location shoots produced by Sam Spiegel, *The Bridge on the River Kwai* (1957) and *Lawrence of Arabia*, both of which set up Lean as a global figure in the film industry. Within that period, however, and bridging the gap, are three neglected films in which the English stage and film actress Ann Todd, who became Lean's third wife, is the central female protagonist, if not the focal point of each narrative. *The Passionate Friends* (1948) and *Madeleine* (1949) were box-office flops; *The Sound Barrier* (1952) successful in the main as a novel action picture about the jet technologies of post-war aviation. Yet Todd's films with Lean in which her thin lips, fair hair, pinched cheeks and cool demeanour had earned her the unlikely tag of the 'English Garbo' have an unsettling aura in those five brief years before she dropped out of sight after her marriage to the director folded. Before we tackle his two great epics that book-end the start of the 1960s, Cinemascope followed by 70 mm Panavision, let us consider what preceded them and why. Let us look for the signs of a troubled romantic, that is, before he engaged with the end of Empire.

## Forgotten Lean: the Ann Todd trilogy

The Todd trilogy is an intriguing one, unjustly forgotten, not just for her acting but for her role as muse, an inspiration in Lean's pushing of classical film form and the stylised oscillation of romance and restraint that shapes so much of his work. The partnership pre-dates other pairings that spring to mind: Godard and Karina, Antonioni and Vitti, Bergman and Andersson, and, significantly, Hitchcock and Hedren. These were all seminal, if not sensational, in the careers of both actor and director and helped forge new and exciting forms of 1960s modernism. But Lean's trilogy, which is a lost preface, has really gone nowhere. What it does suggest when we look at an Englishman who admired the classical poise of Hollywood directors like

William Wyler is the paradox that lay within Lean himself – an *auteur* who was always old-fashioned yet very often before his time, a conservative revolutionary in British cinema.

Theme-wise the trilogy is a continuation of Lean's earlier concerns. *The Passionate Friends* and *The Sound Barrier* gloss the relationship of romance and restraint in post-war Britain echoing *Brief Encounter*, while *Madeleine* is a further examination, after Dickens, of the nineteenth-century heritage, this time in bourgeois Victorian Glasgow, to offset perhaps the novelist's teeming, proletarian London. All three films are complex studies of the relationship between dependence and autonomy (female) under the watchful eye of the patriarch (husband or father, or both). It also echoes the theme of Compton Bennett's *The Seventh Veil* (1945) in which Todd had excelled as a gifted young pianist torn between artistic suitors and her dominating guardian (played by James Mason). All three Lean films have very different outcomes and all three have Todd in different guises. In *The Passionate Friends* she is a prosperous, unfaithful wife taking up once more with a former lover and, unlike Laura in *Brief Encounter*, carnally so. In *Madeleine* she is the transgressing daughter of a respectable Glaswegian lawyer, and in *The Sound Barrier* the demobbed wife/daughter back to things domestic after the war yet locked into aeronautic obsession through her pilot husband and ruthless magnate father. The image of the cool English rose is often undermined by the lingering severity of Todd's gaze, by a facility for changing look and expression from one shot to the next. The cliché is further undermined by the very Scottish *Madeleine,* modelled on the true story of Glaswegian Madeleine Hamilton Smith tried for murder in Edinburgh as an arsenic poisoner, a role that Todd had previously played onstage in 1944. (The play was Harold Purcell's *The Rest is Silence.*) But then the 'rose' cliché does not fit any one of the trilogy. For something far more unsettling is in place.

What exactly is this? It is a triad of enigma variations in which Todd is neither defiant victim in the style of Hitchcock's 1940s heroines nor dark *femme fatale* in the style of American *film noir.* Unlike Celia Johnson's rendering of the near-faithless Laura in *Brief Encounter*, which delivers a febrile guilt-transparency where what you see is what you get, with Todd something more subtle and complex takes place. The gaze, the voice, the gesture are all shrouded in tight ambiguity. The poise and politeness of her middle-class pedigree enable her to go through the line or undercut the action with sustained double meaning. She is articulate, confident, confessional: yet often we don't know quite how to read her. In *The Passionate Friends* Lean's stylistics add to the iconic appeal. At times he photographs Todd as Mary Justin in the style that Lee Garmes adopted for Dietrich in Von Sternberg's 1930s melodramas, soft and lustrous, with the shimmer of backlighting. Yet there is no shallowness in the staging. For Lean expertly blends soft-focus with deep-focus photography, as Welles later did with Dietrich in *Touch of Evil* (1958), so that his long shots retain the consistent detail of high contrast and the grain of the object. Moreover his travelling shots, though sparse, have an elegant fluency that reminds us of the film that Garmes shot for Hitchcock two years earlier – *The Paradine Case* (1947), where he introduced the crab dolly to inject fluid circling movement into Hitch's long takes, which Selznick then butchered in editing. Featuring in that film as defence lawyer Gregory Peck's jealous wife was, of course, Ann Todd.

The look of Lean's picture also shows the versatility of cinematographer Guy Green, who was able to shift effectively from the high-contrast look of the Dickens epics to the mellower rendering of contemporary English life. Robert Krasker is well remembered and revered for his work on *Brief Encounter* and *The Third Man*. Green should be revered not only for the Dickens' diptych but equally for the luminous subtlety of the first two trilogy films. This blends well with Lean's own subtlety in the very first – a contemporary setting that is also a meditation on time. Crucial to Lean's narration in *The Passionate Friends* is the complex flashback in which Todd's voice unfolds her past attachment to Steven Stratton (Trevor Howard) through a multilayered time-frame. The film starts in the present (1948) with Mary's first trip abroad to Chamonix in the Swiss Alps for a holiday with her rich banker-husband Howard (Claude Rains), where she finds herself, by chance, in a room adjoining her former lover. She then thinks back, not to her very first meeting with Stratton, but to her first *reunion* with him nine years previously, at a New Year's Eve ball to usher in 1939. Now married to Rains, she re-encounters Howard *after* her *previous* mid-1930s romance with him but *before* her marriage to another man. Not only is this a before-and-after film in which the war itself is an absent presence. The flashback template sets the lyrical tone for the film: she remembers in sheets of time unfurling backward. One memory leads to another, one flashback to another, and the world of desire is trapped in perpetual fantasies and actualities of reunion. If this isn't a version of Deleuze's time-image *avant la lettre* I don't know what is. And even within the structure of the present she daydreams of her love for the ex-lover who is beside her. So that although narration is predicated on flashback – the remembrance of a love past – the accidental encounter in Chamonix which starts the picture also suggests something else: Chamonix could almost be structured as a flash-forward, a wish-dream of love's reunion in future time with a departed lover who will happen 'by chance' to be booked (by fate?) into an adjacent hotel room, when her husband is away on business and yet to join her.

No wonder critics and audiences were baffled in 1949. While Lean clearly borrows from *Citizen Kane* (1941) (deep focus and multiple flashback) which earlier confused audiences, his own double usage is much more. It becomes a technical foundation for romantic delirium. Although we are flashing back and forth through layers of time, from 1948 to New Year 1939, then to the mid-1930s then forward to the year 1939 which prefaced the Coming Storm and then finally back – or forward – to 1948, we feel somehow the remembrance of love past is so vivid that every sequence is in a perpetual present in which time itself is a labyrinth. Thus the scene after the New Year's Eve ball where Mary and Stratton take up their old (or young) intimacy again, feels and looks like a *post-war* sequence where Lean makes no obvious concessions to the previous decade in terms of fashion or production design. Where he does differentiate the look is in the first romance flashback of the young lovers, shot in soft focus with shallow backgrounds and pastoral settings signifying the look of innocent passion. Yet even here the pattern is set. Mary will reject Stratton's passion as too imprisoning and desire to escape: Lean ends the flashback with a beautiful low-angle shot of Todd all in white, her dress fluttering as she descends the steps outside the house in parting, effectively in flight. Here Lean slows down the image gracefully as she moves closer to the camera with the descent, almost to freeze-frame before the point of cutting. As *mise-en-scène* it is a truly stunning farewell that predicates, of course, a future return of the same.

The reversion to 1939 in the months after the ball is shot in deep-focus high-contrast, especially in Justin's large, empty London townhouse which has the monumental look of a Selznick studio set, with its vast circular staircase a true signifier of full-blown melodrama. At the same time, Lean continues the softness of the earlier look through the overhead lighting on Todd, the sheen creating highlights on her fair hair as a recurrent visual trope that endures until the last frame. Yet this is a triangular picture and the other two figures in the triangle have a filmic pre-history that Lean subtly teases out. Trevor Howard continues the role of the handsome lover (this time for real) he began for Lean as Alec Harvey in *Brief Encounter*, while Claude Rains as Justin continues the role of suspicious cuckold which Hitchcock gave him in *Notorious*. As an actor, Howard at times seems shell-shocked by repetition – yet more brief encounters, lots of them, and staggers into trysts renewed like a punch-drunk boxer as if he had seen it all before. Rains, however, grasps the chance to become a truly wounded human being and not just the expatriate Nazi he was in *Notorious* (the film has a pre-war scene where he decries the fascist hysteria of the mob). Here he is a jealous man in a pragmatic marriage who will finally fall in love with Todd *as a result* of her infidelity, and still knowing full well that she will never reciprocate. Rains hones to perfection the poetics of suspicion that started with Hitchcock, becoming its maestro and taking a leaf out of Cary Grant's book by conveying through the slightest flicker of the eyes the alert gaze that renders the full impact of suppressed emotion, in this case marital jealousy which kindles unlikely desire.

We can see this early at the New Year's Eve sequence – Rains watching Todd in their reserved box on the balcony, looking down at Stratton dancing in celebration with his new girlfriend Pat (Isobel Dean), who later becomes his wife. Lean cross-cuts sequences to inject tension, as Stratton mentions to Pat his chance meeting with Mary and her nervous gaze mirrors the suspicious eyes of Justin in the box as he watches Mary watching the distant figure he recognises as his rival from the past. And Mary too is looking down at Stratton and his partner with a slight hint of desperation, a mix of regret, jealousy and desire. Thus visually Lean captures with a few succinct camera movements the intertextuality of jealous lovers and spouses, a perfect four-way split. In doing so he simultaneously doubles the gaze of desire and the gaze of suspicion, the loving gaze and the jealous gaze. All are inseparable, interpenetrating. And later he repeats other Hitchcock motifs too. The binoculars with which Rains had spied on Grant and Bergman at the Rio racecourse in *Notorious* are used here by Rains to spy on Todd and Howard in the speedboat on the lake by the hotel. Suspicion sustained through a lens darkly. His brief glimpse of their distant parting kiss echoes the famous (notorious?) wine cellar embrace of Grant and Bergman in Hitchcock's spy thriller. But here there is no espionage, no political aftermath of war to give passion its political edge. Lean must mould tension out of peacetime banality, and does.

As in *Notorious* love is predicated on mimetic rivalry. For Justin to see his beloved with his rival is often to incite passion and hatred in equal measure to which Stratton duly reciprocates: yet Mary's passion is predicted on difference. The handsome science professor-lover is so unlike the diminutive banker-husband that Todd forges a rapture of oscillation – moving between polar opposites, unable to choose or reject one in favour of the other. In one instant her instinct is to throw herself into the arms of her resurrected lover: in another it is to nestle in the bosom of her reassuring patriarch. The faithlessness with its in-built love of love is undoubtedly a form of Bovaryism, and when Lean later became self-conscious about the literary model, as in his moulding with Robert Bolt of the storyline for *Ryan's Daughter* (1970), the results are disastrous. But here he is offering something much sharper, more visceral. Instead of Flaubert's unsurpassable parody of provincial life, he has upped the romantic stakes by going cosmopolitan: his cuckold-banker is no fool but sharp, measured and ruthless, a winner in a harsh, material world. And the faithless wife is not pursuing, like Emma, the amorphous love of love, but constantly resurrecting her passion for the *single lover* she has left in the past and will leave again in the future. Todd acts out with great conviction the role of a troubled romantic who is also a strategist playing a dangerous game. The turn-on is not difference and exploration – playing the field – but repetition and reincarnation – the return of the same. The 'passionate friends' are protagonists in the passionate revolution of the same and yet each return is also entropic. In the hotel scenes Howard is no longer shot in soft focus. His face is lined and pitted – Todd tells him he looks like a 'ghost'. The fixation on the return of the same can only come, in this instance, from the fixity of marriage as level continuum. Passion is predicated not on freedom and autonomy but on the structure of faithlessness.

Lean's other great visual concern in cinema is the intersection of culture and nature, where a story's momentous events are not only framed against landscape settings but also integrated into the very texture of the image that his camera produces. Hence the celebrated meeting of Pip and Magwitch in *Great Expectations* where the atmospheric skyline of the Medway estuary standing in for the Romney Marches, one Kent location for another, seems to enfold the characters in three-dimensional space. Lean's pantheistic tendency (Silver and Ursini 1992: 5–7) finds its outlet here in the Swiss Alpine setting of Chamonix, a welcome journey for Todd out of post-war austerity where she marvels during the plane journey at white bread, butter, copious fruit and real cream. After seeing Stratton by chance on the hotel terrace the next morning they plan a day out before he must leave and before Justin arrives: it is their speedboat journey across the lake followed by the cable-car ascent through the clouds that gives the fleeting renewal of the intimacy its genuine enchantment. Lean could easily have given us kitsch, syrupy imitations of landscape photography, but his staging and cutting blend so fluently that his evocation of the romantic sublime is linked, inextricably, to his *découpage* and sense of place. The image has its own power of conviction. This, of course, is merely a foretaste for more extensive visions – the jungle in *River Kwai* and the desert in *Lawrence of Arabia.* The romantic sublime here is an obvious move in an obvious melodrama, but it translates later into something less obvious and more disturbing – the fanatical sublime of his great epics where the cruel grandeur of landscape matches the perverse fanaticism of his English protagonists.

The film also points forward to the modernist deconstruction of romance in *Vertigo* and *Last Year at Marienbad* (1961), the former with its disturbing undercurrent of the compulsion to repeat and its fixation on a second chance, the latter with its formalisation of time as a perpetual present in which the cut is always a play on sameness and difference. Different palaces, hotels, corridors, gardens, statues and costumes, but also for Resnais the same three players, jealous husband, torn and divided heroine, seductive lover who always uses mention of a past encounter as the first move in his erotic game.

Lean, of course, never approaches the darkness at the centre of either film. In Hitchcock there is a formalisation of the compulsion to repeat as male neurotic obsession whereas Lean's film would have been consciously made as 'a woman's picture'. While Lean makes it clear that Mary always makes the first move in the consummation of reunion and brings Stratton with her, for Hitchcock it is the obsessed Scottie Ferguson who calls the shots and lures Judy Barton into repeating her impersonation as Madeleine. As cinema moves on, Resnais's abstract meditation on memory and Hitchcock's carnal metaphysics of renewal thus shift the Lean template, which is at heart naturalistic, into new time–space continua. Yet Lean's film feeds obviously into both of them. It has made love enigmatic and time problematic. Forced to choose between husband and lover, Todd chooses the triangle in which love is more past and future than present, a pure reincarnation of that which is already memory. In her end is her beginning. She chooses death in order to await rebirth.

This is of course upper-middle-class England, an ordered world, and Mary Justin is neither Emma Bovary nor Anna Karenina. As if to make the point, Rains rescues Todd in the last sequence from her intended leap onto the rails of the London Underground, her false solution to love's impasse where for the first time reincarnation seems no longer possible. But the rescue is also another kind of triumph, internal to the film itself. The rescue is justified dramatically by the sense that Rains had acted out his part more convincingly than Howard, a dramaturgic victory for the husband over the lover which makes for perverse, if not subversive, melodrama. The triumph is reflexive. In terms of sheer presence, Rains moves winningly forward from *Notorious*: Howard goes mechanically backwards from *Brief Encounter*. The subtle powers of surveillance that Rains incorporates into every gesture, glance and movement show Lean at his most conservative and, it has to be said, most effortless. The tone of authorial condescension that had lingered over the skittish suburban Laura in *Brief Encounter* – an inheritance from Coward – is conspicuously absent here. Lean has escaped Coward's clutches by going upmarket for wealth, glitter and power, his conservative instincts exonerated in one sense, but laid bare and indefensible in another. The triumph of the patriarch here is as bold as it is reactionary.

## *MADELEINE*: THE PERVERSE UNVEILED

The germ of the perverse that incubates in *The Passionate Friends* spreads rapidly to *Madeleine* where Todd's persona is recast in a more explosive role, and Lean swaps the surety of a literary source (a 1923 novel by H. G. Wells) for an original screenplay from Stanley Haynes and Nicholas Phipps, based on a nineteenth-century *cause célèbre*, the 1857 murder trial of Madeleine Hamilton Smith. It is in effect an attempt at provocative biopic which anticipates *Lawrence* and sketches out the fanatical resolve that will later mark his charismatic anti-hero of the Arabian Desert. There is of course another Hitch reference to dispatch first. We noted that Todd appeared in *The Paradine Case* as the spouse of lawyer Gregory Peck watching from the balcony in the Old Bailey as Magdalena Paradine is tried for the murder of her blind husband by poisoning. Three years later, Todd gets her chance centre stage. Now *she* in the dock also charged with poisoning. Instead of Hitchcock's fluid crab-dolly sequences and an open Old Bailey, Lean's Edinburgh High Court has an enclosed horizontal look which he films largely in static-shot/reverse-shot sequences. It is a method and style closer to the gangster court sequence that ends Fritz Lang's *M* (1931). And here the flattened horizontal is spatio-visual continuation of the crime scene itself which doubles as the scene of passion, the basement of the family home where Madeleine secretly meets her French lover Emile (Ivan Desny) and is alleged to have served him cups of poisoned cocoa. And let's just end with the forking of the plot-lines. Hitch's Magdalena pleads not guilty then confesses everything: Lean's Madeleine pleads not guilty and confesses nothing.

At the start Lean takes the bold step of a sweeping pan across the rooftops of contemporary Glasgow followed by an impersonal voice-over also set in the present, finally alighting on Blythswood Square as it is in 1949 with modern pedestrians and cars, the shot coming to rest outside the basement railings of the large Georgian house at number 7, before flashing back a hundred years to 1857. A studio set replicates exactly the basement yard at the bottom the steps and the pavement above. Lean then shows us the inside the property as Madeleine and her family visit with a view to purchase. Interior shots of the vacant rooms are unsettling and the primal emptiness is uncanny, as if the house has an identity of its own as a place of fate that precedes the family's moving into it. Madeleine herself is attracted to the empty basement whose barred windows look out onto the street at foot level. In this empty room Lean both tracks and dissolves to future time as we see passing feet through the barred window at night. A letter is dropped down through an opening in the window. 'What was that?' Madeleine younger sister demands as she is listening to a bedtime story. Lean has cut to the room's bedroom's interior, now furnished, ornate and cluttered in true Victorian style, and framed the sisters in long shot on the bed they share. Todd had visited the actual house before the shooting began to get a flavour of her part. 'I attract spirits,' she said, 'and in that house Madeleine Smith came and visited me . . . I felt most of the time we were making it [that] she was there' (Brownlow 1996: 69).

There are good filmic precedents for the uncanny abode of the previous century, classic instances of Victorian Gothic. One is by Lean himself, his richly textured version of Satis House, Miss Havisham's cobwebbed mansion in *Great Expectations*, and prior to that we can think of the aunt's adjacent house in *Gaslight*. The Gothic convention usually stresses the deep recess, the attic, the secret room. But here it is the opening onto the street and the basement that are vital to Madeleine's strategy of arranging secret assignations with her French lover. He drops letters into her bedroom. He has a key to the basement door. She arranges to meet him in the maid's room across the corridor when her family is in bed upstairs and the maid discreetly relocated to the kitchen. At one level this is the upstairs/downstairs divide of the respectable Victorian abode. Yet the troubled Madeleine adds something else to the equation. Hers is the transgression of the free spirit, the prodigal daughter who refuses to play along with the conventions of the virgin bride and the arranged marriage. Her attraction to the dandyish Emile also reminds us of the paradoxical romantic strain in Lean himself as Madeleine struggles to free herself through passion and Emile veers in the opposite direction, towards bourgeois convention through the prospect of a prosperous match. Madeleine wants Emile to spirit her away from her family: Frenchman Emile wants Madeleine to introduce him to her family. For both figures are constrained – Madeleine by her class and sex, Emile by his nationality and meagre income. Their paths cross, as it were, because they are heading in opposite directions.

Thus both figures reflexively gloss aspects of Lean's biography. The narcissistic Emile has the deceptive look and bearing of the bohemian romantic, while the plain-looking Madeleine embodies the spirit and energy of a bridled romanticism. We should also remember that Lean reacted against his strict religious upbringing in a very special way: he chose to make a career in that very medium denied him as a young boy because it was considered unworthy and unchristian – cinema. The patriarchal structure of the Smith family, with Leslie Banks as the severe, domineering James Smith, surely possesses an echo of the tight constraints of Lean's early upbringing. In fact, we might want to see in Lean's attraction to his subject matter a deep homology between the English Quakerism of his childhood and the Scottish Presbyterianism of the previous century, an ambivalent attraction that lured him north of the border for the first and only time. Of course, it is not the Christian faith *per se* but its cultural impact that concerns him. For the most part Madeleine plays out the role of a dutiful daughter in her daily life, but when the cards are down she defies the rules of the game. She draws her father's ire by refusing suitable suitors in preference to her secret lover, who in turn is found wanting. Likewise, Lean breaks the rules of romantic melodrama, for in the end there is no thwarted passion that provides the key to Madeleine's happiness once its barriers are broken down. For everything stays problematic, devoid of solution. It is Madeleine's divided soul that creates the divisions in her attraction to men, and these endure.

The model of intimacy is thus a different from Lean's previous picture. The eternal triangle of *The Passionate Friends* is replaced by the formula of the doomed quartet – heroine, father, suitor, lover. The formulation in the subtext is extreme. Only the radical solution of unbridled romance can break the oedipal tie to the Victorian patriarch, a fateful either/or as William Minnock (Norman Wooland) the worthy but ineffectual suitor, caring, kindly and a model of respectability, is largely ignored. Minnock is courteous and handsome with no clear defect that would provide the get-out clause of most melodrama. In fact, he is the only model of virtue in the doomed quartet, a fact that gets him nowhere, or rather stranded in no man's land between the polar opposites that entice Madeleine, the extremes of transgressing romance and unreasoning patriarchy.

In Madeleine's infatuation with Emile there is an echo of the measured attraction that dour, canny Lowlander David Balfour feels for the cavalier Highlander Alan Breck in Robert Louis Stevenson's *Kidnapped*. But Emile L'Angelier is no flamboyant adventurer, just a would-be man-about-town with a great line in cravats. Emile fails abjectly to live up to the romantic archetype Madeleine has conjured out of her fervent imagination; he is certainly no Edmund Dantes, not a patch on Julien Sorel. The clandestine meeting they have near the family summer house in Rowaleyn proves the point, and becomes the point of no return. In a clearing in the woods away from the house they hear the sounds of a ceilidh coming from the village below. Leans cuts to the villagers in full flow, dancing a Highland reel then back to the nocturnal couple where Madeleine too starts to dance and solicits Emile to follow her. The parallel cutting here between the uncertain couple and the raucous dance hall not only stresses class difference but also the limits of Emile's romantic progeny. He tries to dance while, dandyish to the last, still holding his cane: when he drops it the attempt at an improvised reel ends in farce. Madeline runs off and falls on a grassy knoll, an act of exasperation and despair. Below Lean's Highland reel in the packed hall is by contrast in full swing, the most full-blooded and sensual couple in the foreground of his shot. As the dance reaches its climax, accelerating all the time, so does their sensual attraction, and as the music ends they rush off to continue their intimacy at closer quarters. The contrast here is of the many doubling motifs of the film: the raw, desiring village couple in perfect harmony set against the isolated, awkward couple on the hillside above. Class difference is a difference in sensibility, the self-consciousness of the bourgeois romantic model that

Emile betrays, with the unselfconscious energy of villagers and crofters who do not use words to convey the attraction of the dance.

The doubling of the dance itself follows on from the doubling of the couple. We later see the decorous version of the Caledonian reel during a ball in Glasgow in which Minnoch proposes to Madeleine, and Emile, a cloaked and jealous outsider, watches on, a great high-angle long shot by Lean, furtively from the balcony. Minnoch's awkward proposal is drowned out by the music but he is the one that dances with Madeleine, decorously, properly, as befits a Scottish gentleman of his time. Madeleine, however, has earlier waltzed with her father and *this* is the dance in which she is most elegant, most fluent and self-assured. The ritual 'passing over' of the daughter from father to suitor follows the time-honoured convention of family approval, but you feel that, disenchanted with Emile, Madeleine changes tack to please her father more than to accept her suitor. Later, when the angry Emile threatens to blackmail her by exposing her letters to him, it is more the fear of what 'papa' will think than what her future husband will. Her solution is to take Emile back as her basement lover and thus set the cycle in motion all over again. Or is it? Is the buying of arsenic, ostensibly to wash and treat her skin, simply a pretext for the premeditated act of poisoning?

The whole point of the film, and one that Lean's audience would have found exasperating at the time, was that we shall never know in cinema any more than in history. The prolonged sequence of the trial fills us in with the circumstantial detail but brings us no closer to the truth, just as it brought the jury of the time no closer to the truth. L'Angelier, a laudanum addict, might even have died of a combination of the drug that he sporadically took with the poison that Madeleine administered, if at all, in the cocoa. Lean certainly doubles the visual motif of powder placed in liquid. Christina, the maid, stirs the cocoa into a saucepan of milk in the kitchen before Madeleine serves it to herself and Emile. Earlier in his lodgings Emile openly stirs laudanum into a glass of water in the presence of his landlady, who suggests a drop of whisky would be better for him. The doubling motif of the film, by implication, runs to the very end: class duality, love duality, romance and restraint, powder and liquid, suicide *and* murder, overdose *and* poisoning. Emile could have killed himself by intent or by recklessness. Madeleine could have killed him solely by arsenic poisoning. They could *both* have killed him in a cocktail in which neither knew the ingredients of the other. Such ambiguity in a veiled, implicit and open ending goes way beyond the classical code of melodrama (or even its contemporary hyper-classical version) where a murder trial is supposed to establish guilt or innocence one way or the other of *somebody*. In that sense Lean's trial is the serious version of melodrama rule violation that Welles did comically with the trial scene in *The Lady from Shanghai* (1948). The

**Figure 4.1** Opium or Arsenic? Ann Todd and Ivan Desny in *Madeleine*

intermediary status of not knowing – or of not proving beyond a reasonable doubt – is the unique Scottish verdict of 'not proven', a juristic agnosticism where the defendant is suspended in limbo between guilt and innocence.

In the literature of mimetic rivalry the rejected lover is usually jealous of the successful suitor. But the jilted Emile does not try to compete with the courteous and caring Minnoch; rather, he tries to usurp the power of the father. In the first instance of usurpation he appears uninvited at the front door when the rest of the family are away, treats the maid with contempt and demands to be shown to the drawing room. It is symbolic appropriation of territory, of the drawing room as the father's abode to which all other family members and guests are summoned. He is served cocoa and demands that Madeleine play for him on the pianoforte, thus replicating an earlier scene where she has played for her family, accompanying the French love songs she sings out of tune. Now Emile is sitting in her father's chair. In further pursuit of visual doubling Lean doubles the abject posture of female submission – the kneeling that is humiliation as Madeleine genuflects to influence events that have spiralled out of control. First she appears to seek mercy when Emile threatens to blackmail her with her love letters. As Emile throws her to the floor, her body face down in the same prone posture as her fall following the dance on the hillside, her sustained crying is that mixture of intention and emotion that defines her elusiveness – a combination of despair and tactical tears. The posture of submission turns quickly to seduction as Emile's body bends over her and his cane crashes on the hard, glittering surface of the kitchen floor.

Later on during the visit of Thuau (Eugene Deckers), fellow Frenchman and friend of Emile who reports his death to James Smith, as well as the existence of Madeleine's letters – the visual gesture is repeated before her unforgiving father. Since this is melodrama Lean adds to the romantic irony with Madeleine, unaware in the bedroom, trying on her bridal gown before being summoned to the drawing-room dressed all in white where she denies knowledge of L'Angelier without realising what Thuau already knows. As her mendacity is exposed, the damage done and Thuau departs, Lean assembles a remarkable double shot, two deep-focus set-ups to create a visual symmetry of reversed protagonists, an original variation on the staging dynamics that so enthused Bazin about Welles and Wyler. As Madeleine stands at the door through which Thuau has departed, Lean shoots on the acute angle slightly above Smith's inflated profile in left foreground toward Madeleine's figure in long shot by the door. The axis is one of descent, a perspectival illusion that deep focus can happily produce and Bazin conveniently ignore. Madeleine returns pleading in vain for her father's forgiveness, still denying what was lefty to deny. Lean's camera then cuts to a low angle from the same position, a floor shot as Madeleine drops to her knees before her father. 'We are naked,' James Smith declares, meaning of course the family is exposed to a sexual scandal that it cannot reverse and which now makes Madeleine unmarriageable. Yet the Oedipal subtext lingers. Madeleine wears the bridal gown that is meant not to please the suitor who is now the betrothed, but the father who will deliver her to her future life. As she beseeches him he casts her aside and walks to the door in a couple of steps. He leaves it open and the railing on the hall stair can be seen in clear detail behind him. It is a perfect depth-of-field moment that again combines the close-up with the long shot. The angle of descent from the father's profile in left foreground to the daughter at the door has been transformed and inverted like a mirror image. It is matched by the angle of ascent from the prone daughter profile in right foreground to the receding figure of the father as he walks out. The patriarch is rigid and upright, the daughter bending and abject, the dress signifying the patriarch's symbolic rejection of the bride. The orchestral strings on the soundtrack strike a sudden crescendo, for this shot is the defining emotional moment of the film.

After her arrest for murder, the religiosity of the film erupts suddenly in Lean's perverse inversion of the Passion in the gospels. Madeleine's abject entry into Edinburgh to stand trial is prefaced by mob orator John Laurie's

Calvinist haranguing, denouncing her as a 'murderess' and a 'daughter of Satan' as the mob howl for a hanging and angrily rock her prison coach as it makes its way along Princes Street. This plays out like an inversion of the triumphal entry of Jesus into Jerusalem where he is showered with palms by adoring crowds. Deep under the High Court itself another deep-focus shot from Madeleine's POV shows the sharp ascent up stone steps into the courtroom with the crowd peering over the balcony above: the camera dollies after her, signifying perhaps her uphill road to Calvary. Yet after her release the gospels story goes into reverse. On her exit from the High Court she is greeted by the cheering crowd as a heroine: her triumphal exit is her resurrection. But it is a dubious resurrection based on the verdict of 'not proven'. At the end Lean breaks with the classical frame of invisible narration which has sustained his melodrama. His impersonal voice-over which began the film now returns to ask her in its local accent 'Well Madeleine Smith, are ye guilty or not guilty?' Todd looks long and pointedly at the camera but does not reply. Her face remains a pure enigma, betraying no trace of guilt or innocence. The voice-over address and the look to the camera come three years before the famous turning of the head by Harriet Andersson halfway through Bergman's *Summer with Monika* (1952) towards her audience and fixing it with her alluring stare. Monika is playing with us in open flirtation. Madeleine is drawing a veil over the high-octane performance we have witnessed for the previous 100 minutes, freezing her face into the enigmatic stare of a Mona Lisa and just, but only just, playing with a smile.

## *THE SOUND BARRIER*: THE FALTERING SUBLIME AND THE END OF EMPIRE

In the third of the trilogy there is, looking back, a sense of anti-climax. Todd's role is much reduced, the emotional tenor of the film is low-key, the male acting indifferent and the action is one in which machines dominate the mortals who are trying to control them. Lean's fascination with jet planes was part of his fascination with nature and the human conquest of it. In a way the film takes up where the cable car journey through the clouds in *The Passionate Friends* had left off: this time the ascent is wireless, the new jet fighter prototype of the post-war era zooming up to 40,000 feet to launch its attack on the speed of sound. Lean, to his credit, creates a visual balance between man and machine and dramatises the human struggle that surrounds the speed of sound. But Todd as the wife/daughter of the jet fanatics who dominate her life plays second fiddle for the most part to the arena of the action, mediating our own anxieties by voicing her concerns about a dangerous obsession. Meanwhile the Promethean symbolism of Lean's film is a little laboured and in places more than a bit functional. Yet while many British films of the

1950s like *The Dam Busters* (1954) and *Reach for the Sky* (1956) would feed their audiences stirring wartime sagas of winner's history, Lean was fascinated by the new technology of the sky that would come to define the rest of the century. There is continuity too with *Madeleine*. He likewise invokes as a central axis for his docudrama the vexed relationship of defiant daughter and ruthless patriarch, the plane manufacturer John Ridgefield, played by Ralph Richardson and partly based on the de Havilland dynasty which dominated the air industry in post-war Britain.

Though Lean uses state-of-the art prototypes from Vickers and De Havilland in the making of the film and bold second-unit filming for impressive aerial photography, he is also myth-making for post-war Britain. Tony and Susan take a day trip by jet to Cairo looking down at Paris, the Alps and the Parthenon on the way in an aerial Cook's tour of Europe for British audiences still stuck on their side of the Channel. At Cairo airport they stroll out onto the tarmac as if it were a simple extension of British airspace and British territory, a unique pre-Suez moment. Back at base Ridgefield claims the British aerospace industry is two years ahead of the Americans, a claim accepted as documentary truth by gullible audiences who were not to know that the Americans had gone beyond Mach 1 several years earlier, but at the start of the new Cold War were keeping the information classified. Still an Empire, still ahead of the global field – the twin illusion that the nuclear arms race and the débâcle of the aborted Suez invasion of 1956 were about to shatter. And which shows in Lean's further meditations on Englishness which soon followed, the two post-Suez epics that made his name in the new age of Cinemascope and Panavision. Here he forges a new strain of fanaticism in his English protagonists and places them on overseas terrain – Lawrence operating on Arabian territory just beyond Suez with a tribal guerrilla army, Nicholson in *River Kwai* defying and then capitulating to the Japanese occupiers of colonial territory (Burma), which at the time of filming was no longer a colony at all.

The fanatical sublime generated by these two pictures comes from two sources: first, Lean's boldness in leaving a hothouse, enclosed Britain that now constrained him for foreign locations which inspired him (he was never, location-wise, to come back); and second, the revival of a strain of religiosity that gravitated to the sublime landscape – the jungle or the desert. Metaphorically, cinematic colonisation replaces political colonisation, but only through an oblique register of the latter's nemesis. The two films are corrosive on the limits of empire but also bittersweet laments for its demise. In this there is little room for Todd or anyone like her that Lean might look to. Yet Todd it was whose bold performance of the perverse in *Madeleine* leads to the fanatical strain that Lean takes further with Guinness in the figure of

Nicholson and with O'Toole in his myth-making reinvention of Lawrence. Lean also built on the previous performance of Todd in which she had displayed her talent – not only *The Seventh Veil* but also the costume thriller from Lewis Allen, *So Evil My Love* (1948) in which she sparks remarkable onscreen chemistry with Ray Milland and again plays a poisoner. The subsequent shift to *Lawrence* could not be greater, from films about women to a film with no women at all.

## Enthusiast or fanatic? The paradox of Lean's 'Lawrence'

Lean's transition from *River Kwai* to *Lawrence of Arabia* reverses the pattern of disenchantment to be found in post-war Hitchcock, Reed and Powell. He continued to work within the frame of classical narration until 1960 but while *River Kwai* is a disenchanted romance and a parody of British military stupidity – though lumbered, courtesy of producer Sam Spiegel, with a typical Hollywood love encounter for screen idol William Holden – *Lawrence of Arabia* is the very opposite: an inspired act of re-enchantment, a transcendental vision. Nothing could place it further from *The Third Man*, *Peeping Tom* or *Frenzy*, all films that Lean could never have made. The paradox is this: though its hero eventually becomes disenchanted with the imperial politics that constrain his love of Arab culture, the Arabian Desert and his desire for a new Arab nation, the force of that love and the force of that desire are the motor-forces of the film itself. The film is a full-blooded romantic dance with the image of its troubled desert hero. Yet because Lean at heart is a conservative revolutionary, the film is reflexive: *his* Lawrence is forced to regulate his enthusiasm through obligation to the British military just as Lean, as director, is constrained to temper his romantic vision through the structuring of the well-made film. For Lawrence, the conflict is a heartfelt dilemma that finally shatters him, but for Lean one suspects the paradox is latent, not manifest. This after all is a film made by one of the great film editors working within the orbit of classical narration and it seems to come naturally. But it also breaks with traditional filmmaking in its scope and ambition. Its hero remains a supreme enigma and Lean films his epic in four countries on three continents. He made his commitment to the 'impossible' location – the desert – an absolute one in which his Panavision camera becomes the tool that intensifies mimesis of the image to a point unparalleled in all previous filmmaking. For that alone he touches base with the fanaticism of his flawed and troubled hero whose commitment to Arabia was equally absolute.

We can look at Lean's predicament another way, by placing *Lawrence* at a midway point between two 'landscapes' films which defined their respective decades – John Ford's *The Searchers* (1956) and Michelangelo Antonioni's

*The Red Desert* (1964). One works as a Western epic within the framework of classical narration but maybe foretells its coming crisis; the other fractures narration and alters our concept of vision as a modernist artwork. Both have been praised as great landscape cinema, as of course has *Lawrence*. What Lean shares with Ford is a monumental theme, one man's fanatical quest as a lone figure confronting sublime landscapes, and here the awesome Wadi Rumm north-east of Aqaba is Lean's equivalent of Ford's Monument Valley. Likewise, John Wayne's Ethan Edwards is an edgy, neurotic obsessive figure who is clearly not the jocular Wayne of *Stagecoach* or *Rio Bravo* (1959). Edward's ruthless revenge scalping at the film's climax shows a darker side of the brutal settler struggle against Native Americans that Ford's previous films had not. Similarly Lawrence's thirst for revenge against the Turks that sparks the Tafas massacre in Part 2 of Lean's film abruptly shatters any lingering illusions naïve spectators might have had about the blue-eyed Peter O'Toole as an uplifting war hero. O'Toole's Lawrence is even edgier and more neurotic then Wayne's Edwards: and by the end, shattered by the complexities of the betrayed ideal of Arab liberation, deranged, fanatical and empty, a casualty of conflicting worlds.

If we fast forward a few years to *The Red Desert* we encounter a different film formula that Pier Paolo Pasolini had teased out of his discussion of modernism in his famous essay on 'The Cinema of Poetry'. Pasolini contended that the new, free, indirect discourse in film language allows a modernist *auteur* to set up his neurotic bourgeois subject (in this case Monica Vitti's Giuliana) as a filter for his own film form, a delirium of style rendering the dystopian realities of Italy's industrial 'red desert' as a terrible beauty that fascinates and repels in equal measure (Pasolini 2005: 178–81). This double register of disturbed protagonist and visionary *auteur* is one in which Vitti is central to Antonioni's portrayal of man-made landscape through her constant and disturbing presence. In the same way O'Toole's commanding blue-eyed figure had been at the centre of Lean's narrative for most of its 216 minutes, a constant presence through which personal and political fate unfolds and through which Lean mediates his own vision. The key difference between the two films lies in narrative dynamics. As Lawrence changes, the desert changes and so does fate. By contrast, Antonioni's vision of bourgeois malaise as a permanent crippling condition sets up a challenge of narrative entropy for director and spectator alike. For Lean this would be one challenge too far and inimical to his vision which is linear and dynamic, and romantic. Lawrence *has to change* – from visionary to fanatic, from man of justice to bloody avenger, from desert prophet to betrayer of his own vision, from a man of two personas, British military and Arab guerrilla, to a man of none.

In cinema's mythic reworking of history, famous figures are often a compromise between the source material and the ambition of the director who seeks, perhaps subconsciously, to recast the protagonist in his or her own image. There is an element of this here. The diminutive Lawrence of history is replaced by the tall, rangy O'Toole, who in stature looks like a younger version of Lean himself. Moreover his height helps to dominate the image, and the crisp Panavision lenses capture his intense rapture in both middle distance and close-up against the horizontal grain of the desert. O'Toole's blue eyes can be limpid and lucid, or fiery and fanatical. Lean's *mise-en-scène* is crucial as he transforms his charismatic leader's expression from one to the other. In Part 1 he is a genuine visionary with a mission: in Part 2 a deranged fanatic who finally comes to realise that his mission has failed. Yet the cause and the campaign have not significantly changed and are in fact achieved: to defeat the Turks and drive them out of Arabia. But Lean's Lawrence, with the aid of writer Robert Bolt and the source memoir *The Pillars of Wisdom*, is a changed man, a prophet of freedom who has turned into an avenging angel. And of course that is only one side of him; the other is the awkward British officer in Cairo, a reluctant cog in a military machine used by strategists to expand British and French interests in the Middle East once the Turks had departed.

Thus Lean's Lawrence has two uniforms, British military and tribal Arab, but a triple identity and, if we add his troubled homosexuality, a fourth: officer, prophet, avenger, repressed homosexual. This dazzling multiplicity stretches any idea of heroism to breaking point but offers up great cinematic possibilities. As the outsider prophet who has the daring to instigate the taking of Aqaba through the desert to the north, his dazzling white robes make him a metaphorical figure of desire. He is Lean's John the Baptist, a prophet in the wilderness, but also the director's version of an Egyptian sun-god (the origin of Judaic monotheism). In the age of modern Empire he is for the Arabs 'El Aurens' with hundreds of tribal admirers who follow deliriously in his wake. (In *The Pillars of Wisdom*, though not the film, they also expect him to convert to Islam.) Though Bolt saw Lawrence's self-betrayal in modern terms, as a sign of 'romantic fascism', Lean makes that betrayal biblical in scope, almost immune to secular analysis. The religiosity is everywhere. No wonder that Roy Stevens, his assistant director, said: 'There was a feeling of going to church when you went onto his sets' (Brownlow 1996: 461). In Part 1 Lawrence reinvents the figure of the desert prophet for the twentieth century: in Part 2 he takes on the role of the ravaged disciple, the mimetic double and shadow of the pure prophet whose bloodlust now betrays his former self. It is the road to Aqaba (Part 1) that evokes revelation, or rather is conjured up by it in the 'miracle sequence' where Lawrence contemplates alone in the desert night, and the road to Damascus (Part 2) where murder, mayhem and massacre snatch revelation away again. The function of Lawrence's relation

**Figure 4.2** Prophet or Avenger? Peter O' Toole in *Lawrence of Arabia*

to Sherif Ali (Omar Sharif, the film's true acting discovery) also changes: in Part 1 they become covert and constrained romantic lovers, black-robed Arab alongside white-robed Englishman, but in Part 2 Sherif Ali becomes more directly the speaking voice of Lawrence's lost conscience, cajoling and reminding him in vain of his pure mission. Their pure love remains (inevitably) unconsummated and Ali is left helpless to witness Lawrence captured by Turks in Deraa where he is beaten, tortured (and almost certainly raped): but not without a tortuous and masochistic pleasure that is later balanced by his sadistic rapture at the Jafas massacre. Thus the question can never be fully answered. Is Lawrence seeking political revenge for Turkish outrages against oppressed Arabs or personal revenge for sexual humiliation? Or do the two forms of revenge fuse in the maelstrom of war?

There are two key hesitations in the film, which Lean admitted to, which show the conflict between his cinematic daring and his tendency to restraint, between enthusiasm and regulation. One is this, the Daraa capture, the other is much earlier, the celebrated entry of Omar Sharif riding a camel out of the distant horizon like a shimmering figure in a desert mirage. The mirage sequence of course has been hailed as a triumph. Cinematographer Freddie Young had brought special long lenses over from Hollywood to capture the black speck of the tribesman on the horizon of the salt flats at Al Jafr in Jordan. But the sequence, breathtaking in its technical virtuosity, does not have the boldness of the long-take sequence that ends *The Third Man.* Its climax with a sudden shoot-out between the two rivals of different tribes suggests a Western mythos not an Eastern one, tribesmen with rifles aping the mannerism of gunslingers with six-shooters.

Lean had hesitated to make Sharif's long ride out of nothingness a continuous take and admitted afterwards he was wrong not to (Brownlow 1996: 437). He was not bold enough to consider that he could sustain the dramatic tension for his audience without cutting: in retrospect it now seems he puts in too many reaction shots. This is not to denigrate the shot itself, expertly made over by the painting of a wide white line in the desert from the well to vanishing point and discreetly fringed by pebbles on either side to bring it up in the spectator's eye. It still remains one of the great single shots of British cinema. But Lean's editing errs on the side of caution with cutaways to shorten the time of the rider's advance (originally around ten minutes) and Bolt's shoot-out scenario between the tribesman who have never met, lacks plausibility and conviction unless it is read as a plot-device to generate volte-face. (Sherif Ali starts out as a vengeful, tribal murderer but acts latterly as Lawrence's moral conscience when the Englishman is vengeful in the interests of his adopted 'nation'.)

The second crucial hesitation takes us to the edge of censorship, and it should not be forgotten that if classical narration is constrained by rules of filmmaking it was also constrained by censorship. How explicit could a big-budget film released through Columbia Pictures in 1962 actually be about homosexuality in its very masculine hero? Lean's solution was to partly feminise O'Toole's Lawrence without making his desire explicit, but that in turn meant toning down the punishment sequence during his capture at Deraa. One has to infer rape from the prelude to the beating, Lawrence defiantly spitting in the face of the Bey when the Turkish ruler makes his advances. Lean's solution is far better than, for example, the histrionic melodrama of Alan Parker's *Midnight Express* (1978) made less than twenty years later (which proves that rolling back censorship is only part of the solution). A contemporary audience with greater awareness – partly through cinema – of such sexual matters would easily read the scene's inference. But Lean also realised that an audience of his own time was less likely to, and it was to them his film was addressed. Yet on the scale of things these are not shortcomings but minor blemishes, apt reminders that there is no such thing as cinematic perfection.

If we compare Lean's two war epics we see they provide a vital contrast in the portrait of their officer subjects. The ideological divide between the two colonels, Lawrence, promoted officer and hero of Aqaba who returns to the desert in the First World War, and Nicholson, captive officer in the Burmese jungle of the Second World War, is at times a chasm. Lawrence is the daring maverick who breaks the rules, Nicholson the fanatical conformist who upholds them to the letter. Once he gets his way over the Geneva Convention, the latter delivers his POWs entirely to the building of the railway bridge for his Japanese captors. More dangerous than the officer class of Powell's *The Life and Death of Colonel Blimp* (1943) he becomes a *de facto* collaborator, forging an exemplary work ethic in the service of the enemy. Lawrence goes from enthusiasm to fanaticism, but still in the right cause. Nicholson heads in the opposite direction, from fanaticism in suffering pain on behalf of his men to perverse enthusiasm in collaborating with the enemy, which is of course totally the wrong cause. Lawrence's grandiose actions attempt to rival the forbidding grandeur of the desert landscapes that frame his courage and daring: Nicholson does the opposite. His perverse rule-abiding amidst the natural beauty of the jungle are demeaning and result in bathos. Lawrence is at the heart of pantheistic ambition and human longing, Nicholson an acerbic update on the mad dogs of Englishmen who go out in the midday sun.

Lean's experience in both pictures meant that he had lived twice over the journey of war-cinema *auteur* that Coppola pinpointed in his making of *Apocalypse Now* (1979) and where the Philippines stands in for Vietnam. In filming the theatre of war retrospectively in extreme climate and terrain, the filmmaker relives through the difficulty of the shoot the original experience of the nightmare logistics of combat on foreign terrain. For Lean this was slightly different. One film is about POWs, the other about the forging of a guerrilla army. But the adversity of filming conditions suggests that Lean had already been through the Coppola 'experience' a generation earlier, in *River Kwai* where Sri Lanka stands in for Burma and in *Lawrence* where the Jordanian desert replicates with far greater accuracy of terrain the guerrilla campaign in Arabia since its territory was part of it, though only one territory among three. The storming of Aqaba was actually filmed in Spain, on the coast of the semi-desert province of Almeria (Lean got there before Sergio Leone) and the Tafas massacre in southern Morocco. And Lean's shoots had their own casualties through illness and injury in climatic extremes, where cast and crew alike found conditions punishing, and cooks, grips, carpenters, focus pullers, drivers, extras and PAs were all part of an army of grunts in the grand design. But commanders also suffer. After the various desert shoots of *Lawrence* Lean needed eye surgery in London for sand trapped behind the eyelid. In this film of four quarters spread over twenty months, Jordan, Spain, Morocco, England and post-production, there is a clear analogy between Lawrence's arduous desert campaign plus his post-campaign writing of *The Seven Pillars of Wisdom* and Lean's multi-continental shoot followed by four months' intensive editing fifteen hours a day.

History repeats itself, we might say, as art imitates life twice over, but it does so only as the Lawrence myth was dying, as the revered and enigmatic hero, about whom so much had been talked and written, faded away as a historical person in the wake of the Suez débâcle and was reinvented magnificently as screen persona in the Lean epic. This is after all myth-making and speculation on a grand scale and O'Toole will forever mediate our image of a distant figure who was barely three-quarters his size and tried to end his life a recluse. If Lean's epic grandeur is connected after 1956 to the end of empire, his troubled romanticism is marooned period-wise after *Lawrence*, *in* the age of empire. His cinema abandons the present and his subsequent epics go back to the past with a hollow grandeur where the director is a shadow of his former shelf. But for all that, O'Toole and Sharif at Al Jafr and Wadi Rumm remain unforgettable images in world cinema. The imprint of Panavision brands them into the brain and helps create a monumental artwork whose scale and complexity would be impossible in the twenty-first century. In fifteen years, Lean had come a long way from Laura Jesson in a state of confusion, pottering around Beaconsfield.

CHAPTER 5

# *The trauma film from romantic to modern:* A Matter of Life and Death *to* Don't Look Now

What is trauma if not, as in the Greek, a kind of wound? Here it is something more – a wound that seldom heals, a wounding of body and soul from which, often, the subject does not recover. Hence the critical formula for the outcome of the trauma picture: at the least, significant damage; at the most, violent death. If film horror often sources the supernatural, film trauma focuses on the fears of the human and natural world. What is out there as waking nightmare in a dangerous world is often a mirror of what is hidden in here, in the human heart. The monsters that horror films project onto the screen are often the monsters of our dream worlds. The wounding events of the trauma film are by contrast a fusion of life and dream. In film there is no absolute borderline between these opposites – human trauma/supernatural horror but the question of emphasis, one way or the other, is crucial. The threat of aliens, mutants, werewolves, monsters, robots, slasher killers, vampires *et alia*: or the threat of evil that is here and now, that is contingent and recurrent in the life-world, yet also seems onscreen to inhabit the world of dream. Horror is thus the popular genre of superhuman evil, trauma its human and dreamlike subset. (Another subset is the serial killer film, which crosses boundaries and, in Hollywood at least, reinvents the superhuman monster in human form – the homicidal freak possessed of rational cunning.)

Let us look at other differences. Freud suggested that fear has a distinct object, whereas fright is nonspecific. Horror often plays on the eventual appearance of the object of fear after filmic premonitions eliciting fright – spidery shadows, slamming doors, creaking floor boards, heavy breathing, howling wind, stalker phone calls and trails of blood. Something at first nonspecific, it then becomes the opposite when the spectre of monstrosity appears – and strikes. Trauma often works the other way round, as a specific event, a fearful, unexpected happening, then the fear spreads outward and forward in time to attach itself to random events where normal patterns of logic in the life-world are effaced. Thus the wound does not heal. Film trauma also trades on what most neuroscientists have remarked on – the close relationship of emotion and perception where to feel is to perceive and to perceive is to feel. Trauma is not just visceral then, signifying aversion to the threat of the monstrous Other or the devastating Event, it also incorporates the anxiety of incomprehension – the encounter with the Other or Event that *defies understanding* – and the emotional breakdown it induces. The otherness of the Other, the facticity of the Event – these are diffused in the psyche precisely because they defy true knowledge and cannot be absorbed into the fragile self. Sometimes we cannot work out what exactly it is that troubles us, or if by an effort of will a partial understanding is achieved, we then run into a further obstacle. We cannot then figure out *why* 'evil' is what it is. Trauma-fright relates not just to the palpable presence, or imminence of threat, but to the *incomprehension of its true nature*. We demand to know but cannot know. There is no true angle, no hook, no formula that puts it to rest. And – cruel irony – what may be considered a threat may be no threat at all. To be is to be perceived – as evil. But how and why? And is the fear of diffuse evil a spur to desperate retaliation that may well be evil itself? Think here of *The Innocents*, of *Angel* (1982) or of *Repulsion*. Or is such a desperate remedy simply a function of besieged victims losing their mind?

Let us then be perverse by starting at the end of our period with a film that is Irish first and British second, and where the trauma is as much political as it is personal – Neil Jordan's *Angel*. Funded by Channel 4, the new source of finance and exposure for low-budget cinema in the 1980s, *Angel* was produced by Englishman John Boorman and there are similarities in pattern with his path-breaking Californian thriller *Point Blank*, of a man traumatised (betrayal and wounding simultaneously) by a sudden Event he least expects and for which he seeks deadly revenge. Jordan's Danny (Stephen Rea) is close in this respect to Boorman's Walker (Lee Marvin). While playing the saxophone in a showband in a small town nightclub called Dreamland near the Irish border, he sees the deaf-mute girl with whom he has just made love on wasteland outside, gunned down at random by masked paramilitaries harassing the club owner. This is the trauma-event that Danny witnesses and is like any shooting witnessed by any civilian at that period in Northern Ireland where the hapless victim is up close and personal. Just as Boorman had encouraged Marvin to draw on his wartime Marine experience in acting out the role of traumatised vengeance, so Jordan encourages Rea to morph from showband sax player dressed in garish purple to pale-faced, robotic avenger in a shapeless overcoat with an automatic weapon – an updated 'shadow of a gunman' but also a fugitive echoing the flawed heroes of Reed and Cavalcanti.

Let us now formalise things by looking at the enigmatic remarks on trauma in Freud's 'Beyond the Pleasure Principle' and later, near the end of his life, his brief return to the topic in *Moses and Monotheism*. Freud, writing in 1920, was taking on board the traumatic effect of combat experience on front-line soldiers in the Great War, often lumped under the label 'shell-shock'. He contends that trauma occurs with the *unexpected* event that penetrates our protective carapace against external stimuli, a breach which can later haunt us in dreams and nightmares, flashbacks and hallucinations (Freud 1984: 299–305). It is not caused at source through excess anxiety but by an *absence of anxiety* that allows us to be caught off guard first time around. Often our obsession with the event is to ensure its non-repetition, but that in turn can induce the compulsion to repeat the original circumstance where this time we will have the anxiety we need to ensure that we are *not caught off guard a second time around.* In cinema the plight of Scottie Ferguson in *Vertigo* is the prime and pure case. The 'pleasure principle' is put on hold to try to ensure the non-recurrence of pain. Yet the compulsion to repeat may well have the opposite effect to that intended: the neurotic effect of the original trauma is intensified, not diminished, and with it is intensified the feeling of pain. The nightmare of the compulsion to repeat is a vicious circle which has no resolution.

In the fleeting trauma-discourse of *Moses and Monotheism* Freud hints at the loss of that fabric of meaning which Moses had given his exiled people through his ethical God and which was to be rediscovered by the Jewish people only centuries later. He thus makes a key analogy between disassociation prompted by the traumatic Event (modern) and the loss of the ethical God (ancient). Just as trauma hides in latency and returns in altered form, so did Judaic monotheism where the ethical God of Moses is collectively forgotten only to surfaces centuries later, collectively remembered. But should we see this observation of the exiled Freud in London nearing the end of his life as a simple analogy or as a key secular substitution for the loss of the sacred? Is the double substitution of the Freudian project roughly like this: *ab initio* psychoanalysis for theology and, at his life's end, the reverse – theology for psychoanalysis? Moreover, is the delayed pain of the event made worse by the carapace of cognition which monotheism provides? In any event, we can see in cinema a secular parallel to this in trauma-narrative: the horror of cognition-loss matching the terror of original wounding. Know thine enemy and know thy God, the ethical injunction goes. But what happens if you end up in the full sense of the word 'knowing' neither?

## Prelude: Thorold Dickinson and Anton Walbrook

Having started *after Don't Look Now* with *Angel* we can now continue *before A Matter of Life and Death* with Thorold Dickinson's wartime *Gaslight*, the original screen version of Patrick Hamilton's Victorian drama *Angel Street*. Anton Walbrook plays Paul Mallen, a 'respectable' sociopath trying a variety of tactics to drive his wealthy spouse Bella insane. The authority of the Victorian patriarch is used for purposes of secret torment: only this patriarch is an imposter with a secret, murderous past and a deadly agenda. Knowing nothing of this, the innocent (and flaky) Bella (Diana Wynyard) cannot predict when, where or how he will strike, or why he treats her, a loyal, devoted wife, so badly. Yet she knows the resurgence of his venom will come and this fills her with dread and *déjà vu* as if her life is locked into a cycle of repetition over which she has no control. At one point when she is desperate to escape the house in which she has seemingly been imprisoned, he appears to relent and takes her to an exclusive music recital, only to drag her out and humiliate her in front of all the guests. So far, so Gothic. He will hide objects and accuse her of stealing them, flirt with female servants in her presence, tell their friends she is seriously ill. Secretly prowling the adjoining house for some rubies he has failed to find after murdering Bella's aunt some years before, his use of the shared gaslight suddenly lowers the flame in Bella's room and deepens her fears of hallucination. Knowing on his return the accusations will come thick and fast, Bella tries to inure her fragile self: but the cunning of the sociopath lies in the timing. She is never to know when, how or where her married life is locked in a trauma of repetition. As this is melodrama, good finally triumphs, Paul is conveniently unmasked as an impostor and murderer, a bigamist called Louis Bawer, by an ex-Scotland Yard detective: so just in the nick of time justice is done.

In the subsequent history of British film, trauma subjects are usually not that lucky. Including Walbrook once more. Dickinson cast him opposite Yvonne Mitchell in his 1949 version of Pushkin's *The Queen of Spades*, shot seductively in high-contrast black and white by Otto Heller. Walbrook, in this film a Russian captain, is a scheming seducer, but this time the old woman who dies is different, not his wife's aunt but a wealthy countess superbly played by Edith Evans, who turns the tables by opening her eyes on the scheming captain in her coffin, having earlier given Walbrook a false formula for success at cards – a Queen of Spades who grins back at the obsessive gambler as he finally loses a fortune. The old lady thus gets her revenge – perhaps too for the old lady Walbrook has murdered in the earlier melodrama. Taken as a Dickinson double bill, the traumatiser is truly traumatised.

## Juxtaposition: *A Matter of Life and Death* and *Dead of Night*

Two films at the war's end, but like day and night: one is in breathtaking Technicolor and deals in metaphysical healing, while the other is in black and white and deals in perpetual nightmare. One is the Archers' partnership of Powell and Pressburger at their best: the other is an Ealing Studios composite, three writers and four directors. Of course, *A Matter of Life and Death* (*AMOLAD*) does have a monochrome afterlife but visually the romantic rapture of a multi-coloured English countryside, the here-and-now triumphantly prevails. *Dead of Night*, by contrast, has its sinister country house located in Turville, Buckinghamshire, the site of local treason in the wartime *Went the Day Well?* Cavalcanti directed both features and no rural idyll is forthcoming in either. And what of box-office success? The uplifting *AMOLAD* with a special royal première was a magnet for post-war audiences, the dark, unrelenting *Dead of Night* a film they avoided *en masse*. When your country has been battered by a monstrous war, you want to savour victory and then move on. That is what *AMOLAD* explicitly allows, and what *Dead of Night* implicitly denies. Yet I would argue, against the critical grain, that the Ealing composite is just as enduring. For sure *AMOLAD* certainly has some of the boldest sequences in British cinema with back-to-back scenes in the bomber's doomed cockpit and in pilot David Niven's unsteady walk out of the sea to the broad sand-dunes of the Devon shore, one of the most imaginative openings of its epoch. But the film is also poised precariously between direct material trauma and dense metaphysical fable. In a way it was Powell's drive to ground Emeric Pressburger's lofty fable in the material world of war and traumatic breakdown (by consulting medical case-files) that saves it. The lesion in the brain caused by the force of the airman's fall is what gives rise to the spatial hallucinations of a dying consciousness, in Powell's framing, so that we have on view the direct psychic consequences of severe physical trauma refined into a cinematic imaginary. In other words, poet Peter Carter (Niven) is placed poetically on the margin between life and death as if his flair for language had been translated under duress into a flair for extraordinary images (Horne 2005: 125–7).

At the same time, the logic of the afterlife trial which at one level may indicate survivor's guilt on Carter's part also has a momentum of its own as metaphysical fable. It works as part of the film's remit – to celebrate the Anglo-American special relationship as victory against Germany is finally achieved. And here, arguably, classical narration and its hard-edged concern with outcome clash with the overripe romantic imagination and its concern with spectacle as they often do in Powell's films. The banality of dialogue and acting mannerisms often undermine the transcendental staging. This prompts consideration of Durgnat's notorious Powell put-down: 'His central problem as an artist, is another permutation of Lean's, his tendency to escape from realism, yet only play with romanticism . . . Powell lived in a class and a country, and generation which suspects, fears and undermines emotion. Thus his diversity of qualities rarely find their holding centre' (Durgnat 1971: 210, 215). Durgnat is perceptive but nonetheless disrespects the romanticism in both directors: they do not play with it. *They are romantics*. But he does probe the contradiction he detects in Powell between 'the Tory and the pagan', which is an endless source of fascination. At his best, Powell transcends this contradiction: but often it can undermine his vision as he oscillates from one to the other, from the archaic stiffness of rural bourgeois tradition (very southern English) to the imaginative uncovering of a deeper mythic world. And the former, as Durgnat rightly says, *does* hold back the latter so many times . . .

Yet *AMOLAD* sets the baseline of Powellian trauma in its hero's clinical condition and deepens it in his subsequent films with David Farrar and Kathleen Byron, *The Small Back Room* and *Black Narcissus*, before the unnerving thriller made without Pressburger, which obliquely refracts war-trauma some fifteen years later, *Peeping Tom*. With Alfred Junge's grand monumental design and the film's concern to transcend death, *AMOLAD* recalled nearly all of Weimar Lang from *Der müde Tod* (1921) through to *Metropolis* (1926). In its staging of the afterlife, no other British film had ever looked like this or would ever do so again. If *AMOLAD* absorbs and remakes the transcendental sublime at the gates of death, *Dead of Night* does something a little more familiar. It invokes the demonic figure in Weimar film of the destructive 'scientist', ironised here in the character of the hapless psychiatrist Dr Van Straaten, but with clear echoes of those two archetypal doctors of death from Weimar, Mabuse and Caligari. In the Ealing film, of course, with its English country house, the demonic *Doktor* is transformed into something more banal – a crass, insensitive shrink. The film sets him up to become an unexpected victim of his most troubled fellow guest, architect Walter Craig (Mervyn Johns). But in the end the question hovers in tantalising ways. Has his crassness set up the context for his sudden and shocking strangulation? Has his 'rational' talk in fact been a catalyst to madness rather than its cure? Has the story-telling game among the assembled guests, intended to exorcise fright and fear of the inexplicable, only added to its ineffable power?

There is none of *AMOLAD*'s grand staging here, simply the village (somewhere in the Kentish countryside) and country house exteriors plus the cosy studio house interiors and spaces and places where five separate stories; unfold. It is quintessential Ealing. The second and fourth are lightweight ghost stories; the former a children's tale and the latter a pretext for bringing on the comic double-act of Ealing regulars Radford and Wayne. But all five tales are still linked via the framing device of Craig's 'first' visit to the house in which he claims a strong case of *déjà vu* and correctly predicts a number of incidents that duly happen in the course of the film. The girl's tale thus brings up the atmosphere slowly and the golfing tale is a comic interlude before the climactic, most harrowing tale of all – Van Straaten's account of the descent of ventriloquist Maxwell Frere (Michael Redgrave) into homicidal madness. Van Straaten, who has a smug commentating role on all the previous tales, is thrust to the fore for the film's finale as the key tale-teller, with shocking consequences. The build-up is crucial, the spacing of narrative suspense vital. Three trauma-stories with damaged bourgeois protagonists, all male, told to an architect who is also middle-class and equally damaged, and even more damaged after he has heard the damage-tales: narration intensifies suspense by the chain-effect of upping insanity in spaced instalments.

The build-up is crucial. The first tale is told by the subject himself, the second by the subject's young wife and the third by the subject's post-arrest psychiatrist. The staged distancing from male madness here offsets its growing intensity with each story, metaphorically speaking, like a backtrack compensating for a forward zoom. (Let us not forget the actual use of this as a trauma-shot in Hitchcock's *Vertigo* as James Stewart unsteadily ascends the Mission tower.) Yet as the teller shifts further from the subject with each tale (self to spouse to shrink) so the impact of the tale moves in each case closer to the heart and mind of its main listener, the traumatised Craig, the ultimate case study of the traumatised subject further traumatised by increasingly harrowing tales of trauma. As the tellers shift mode from subjective (personal confession of the crashed racing-driver) to intimate (a frank admission by the young bride of her spouse's growing paranoia and uncanny hallucinations in the 'haunted mirror') to objective (the doctor's diagnosis of mad ventriloquist Maxwell possessed by Hugo, his dummy), Craig shifts from distant sceptic to deranged participant until he identifies completely with the jailed ventriloquist and promptly strangles the shrink who has failed to cure either the ventriloquist or his new double, the visiting architect who is now Maxwell Frere's *frère,* his brother-in-madness.

The staging and the enquiry, through a series of related tales, seems at times a pastiche of the country house mystery – Agatha Christie style – where the investigator examines each of the guests in turn before resolving the puzzle of the whodunit. Here, however, there is no whodunit, only a Chinese box formula of trauma-tales in infinite regress doomed to repeat themselves to infinity, a steady-state universe with no end or beginning. The social import of the film should not be missed. Each of the young males starts out as assured, polite, self-confident, but each in turn is damaged by the dangerous Event. Two step back from the brink. The third is not so lucky. Granger, the crashed racing driver, steps back from the town bus which will then crash because the conductor ('Room for one more inside') has the same face as the hearse driver who earlier invited him in a nightmare to his own funeral. Peter, the jealous husband obsessed by Robert Hamer's 'haunted mirror' that shows him a room from its previous owner's past, will be hauled back from the brink when spouse Joan manages to smash the mirror's glass as he tries to strangle her. Maxwell Frere is not so lucky. In Cavalcanti's eternal triangle with queer sub-text, Frere becomes insanely jealous at the attention bestowed on dummy Hugo by rival ventriloquist, Sylvester Kee. He shoots his rival and later, in his prison cell, when Van Straaten tries to reunite him with Hugo, crushes his beloved dummy into powdered pieces. This double crime of passion duly takes its toll. When Kee, now recovered, visits Frere in the asylum, the inmate speaks with the voice of the destroyed Hugo. Identity is no more, and the scene is now set for Craig's own madness in which he strangles Van Straaten and hallucinates condensed Freudian variations on all the tales that he has been told – before waking up in his own bed in his London flat, and then being invited to the country so that the process can start all over again.

The war, only just finished, is never mentioned, so the tales of the three men really function as allegories of lasting damage, juxtaposed against a rural world in which the war might just as well have not happened. The film adaptations of Nigel Balchin's novels *Mine Own Executioner* (1947) and *The Small Back Room* (1948) will subsequently give a literal reading of war-trauma in their damaged male subjects, as does John Maybury's recent Dylan Thomas biopic, *The Edge of Love* (2007). Maybury's retro-pastiche with surreal flourishes offers a portrait of army captain William Killick (Cillian Murphy) as an upper-class, self-confident officer who woos Vera (Keira Knightly) during the Blitz amidst the nightly bombing, but ends up a traumatised veteran after guerrilla combat in Greece, gun-toting, alcoholic and insanely jealous of Matthew Rhys's slimy poet. (Fascinating too, we could add, that Killick was a colleague at the special Operations Executive (SOE) Baker Street office of the young Leo Marks, who later wrote *Peeping Tom*.) Maybury's recent biopic is obviously more upfront about war-trauma than most post-war cinema of the time, as it is about sex. But if we return to the post-war period itself we can see how Powell after *AMOLAD* gives us three intriguing variations on the trauma picture, in which intertwined are the central landmarks of British life after 1945, the end of war, the end of Empire and the birth of a new consumer age.

If Ealing produced a keynote trauma-film for future generations it also produced a triple antithesis in the post-war years – *anti-trauma comedy* in the form of Hamer's *Kind Hearts and Coronets* (1949) and Alexander Mackendrick's scintillating double-act, *Whisky Galore* (1949) and *The Ladykillers* (1955). Indeed, the best of Ealing comedy is premised very precisely on this inversion, where *what might well be traumatic* turns out to be the exact opposite. Hamer's film is biting social satire, in which serial killer Dennis Price, as the outcast of the family and excluded by the vacuous rich, is more sympathetic than any of his eccentric aristo victims (all played by Alec Guinness). As they fall like ninepins one after the other, we can all have a good laugh and applaud Price's elegant cunning. A perfect picture, you could argue, for a new social democracy. The wartime *Whisky Galore* set on the remote island of Todday (toddy?) also plays on inversion, this time on the fear of occupation – an anti-*Next of Kin* or *Went the Day Well?* In Mackendrick's film the fear of invasion is now past but the Scottish island is in fact 'occupied' by an English Home Army captain, Waggett, who has marshalled customs officials to try to prevent the looting of a wrecked cargo ship carrying whisky. A comic version of Anglo-Scots antagonism with its famous montage sequence of looted whisky being hidden by the islanders in rain butts, water tanks, hot-water bottles and under a baby's cot before bemused officials arrive to discover absolutely nothing. The gradual exclusion of Waggett from the island has an edge and a cruel streak that prevents any lapse into sentimentality.

Sentimentality is equally absent from *The Ladykillers* where Mackendrick completely inverts the trauma-effects of Gothic expressionism. A motley gang of train robbers posing as a musical ensemble take lodgings near Kings Cross station to prepare for their heist. At the landlady's door the figure of Alec Guinness casts a dark shadow – shades of the opening to *The Lodger* – but thereafter the threat becomes internal as the eccentric old landlady (played by Katie Johnson) in her parody of a haunted house has the gang tearing out their hair in annoyance and frustration at her blithe eccentricities. In Gothic melodrama we expect villains to terrify, but here they are traumatised to the extent that, when found out, they are prepared to kill off each other rather than kill the 'harmless' old landlady. She who should be terrified is oblivious to the threat; those who should terrify show a collective failure of nerve and eliminate each other. Gothic melodrama morphs into dark comedy, and Ealing comedy runs happily on in a parallel world to Lean and Powell.

## POWELLIAN TRAUMA: *BLACK NARCISSUS*, *THE SMALL BACK ROOM*, *PEEPING TOM*

*Black Narcissus* does not have the post-Suez vantage point of *Bridge on the River Kwai* or *Lawrence of Arabia* but in a way it does not need to. It immediately precedes the end of the British Raj and has about it a deep twilight feel. When the convent Order terminates the experiment in the old palace at Mopu, it is as if the fragility of its enterprise is a register of much wider things British as empires crumble. Sister Clodagh as the Sister Superior of the new 'convent' in the remote foothills of the Himalayas is the idealist with a doomed project among a remote people for a school, a hospital and, as side-effect, Christianity in a Hindu culture. The film begins with their arrival and the renovation of the old palace with its faded, sensual wall-paintings: it ends with the nuns' departure as the rains fall. The plight of the Order at the end of Empire is just

**Figure 5.1** Through the Looking Glass: Kathleen Byron and Deborah Kerr in *Black Narcissus*

as transitory as the elaborate studio set used at Shepperton studios. Powell does of course supplement the studio shoot with exteriors in the lush forest of Leonardslee Gardens (near Horsham, Surrey). But none of the film gets anywhere near India. Instead, what we get is cinematic simulation, a virtual world that gives a new meaning to the word 'Orientalism' – discovering the exotic East without moving out of southeast England.

The film's trauma-tale is inseparable from the doomed project: it is predicated on the vertiginous nature of culture shock. The lofty palace-convent perched on the edge of a mountain precipice (Junge's landscape design makes it look like the Grand Canyon relocated to the Canadian Rockies) seems a visual metonym. Sister Clodagh (Deborah Kerr) may want to heal and enlighten 'a primitive people' but when she looks up and then down from the bell tower, she is completely lost. Powell has transposed the 'edge of the world' from Foula, at the tip of the Shetlands in his 1937 Scottish picture, to India's border with the high Himalayas: from the edge of the Roman Empire to the edge of the British Empire. The former of course was long gone: the latter was about to expire. The end of Empire is literally vertiginous, its trauma doubly embedded, or embodied, in the figures of Clodagh and sickly Sister Ruth (Kathleen Byron). Ruth cannot cope with the chasm of culture that confronts her and wants out: Clodagh, disillusioned after a romance in Ireland has ended when her boyfriend leaves for America without her, seeks solace in the Order. Flashback shows us the rural idyll of Irish sweethearts fishing and riding amidst fields and hills of emerald Technicolor, the flame-haired Kerr slim, free-spirited and ravishing, like a figure from a Pre-Raphaelite painting. Her long auburn hair now concealed under the all-embracing convent habit is never to reappear. As the fragile Order starts to crumble after the unfortunate death of a local child, the febrile Sister Ruth sheds her habit to reappear in scarlet lipstick and a lush crimson dress; for the shocked Clodagh a nightmare return of the repressed – the erotic red of the painted lips matched by the sensual velvet that highlights the shape of the female figure rather than burying it under a swathes of white cloth.

Thus Ruth and Clodagh are established as mimetic rivals, doubles who equally desire two male opposites in their remote life, the young Indian prince in full regalia, 'Black Narcissus' (Sabu), and Dean (David Farrar), the local English agent in short shorts and hair-shirt, a muscular icon who is distinctly kitsch. The doubled object of desire, the first impossible, the other too cynical, may well be Powell's attempt to reverse the conventions of the male gaze by drawing us erotically to the male and not the female body. But this trope is inseparable from Powell's insatiable appetite for spectacularity and romantic melodrama premised without reservation on the art of excess. The figure of Dean might also embody for the two adoring nuns the love for a distant England, the reassurance of the phlegmatic colonial male and the hegemony of public school 'common sense'. Powell's Tory values intrude conspicuously at this point, as Farrar's gruff performance of male imperial 'awkwardness' is produced like a rabbit out of a hat. It can certainly be regaled as an anti-naturalistic device: but emotionally it rings hollow. What really works is the ferment between the female rivals, in which the film risks many of the clichés of female madness, then in a fit of visual inspiration surpasses them. There is too a fragile fanaticism in the acting of Kerr and Byron that is perfectly sustained. It puts them, metaphorically speaking, on the precipice – and also on the cliff precipice where the final showdown actually takes place. It is one of the memorable images in the Powell canon of the doomed sublime – the belltower facing down the sheer cliff to the void; and of course Hitchcock adapts it to the end of *Vertigo* with the intruding nun at the top of the Mission tower who watches the doomed fall of female beauty in the form of a reinvented 'Madeleine'.

In Powell, both Clodagh and Ruth are traumatised but by opposite choices: one takes her vows to escape the disappointments of love, which is no solution, while the other abandons the Order, only to encounter the disappointments of love, which is no solution either. Yet Clodagh's survival after Ruth's death has a cleansing effect: the trauma is partly exorcised with the sacrifice of Ruth, and life precariously goes on with the convent exodus. But you feel too that the Order will never recover. It is a dignified retreat, of course, unlike the British exit from the subcontinent where the post-imperial footprint became indelible with the realities of civil war and partition. Yet Powell and Pressburger are not given to anything as complex as the haunted meditation on Empire that is embedded in *River Kwai* and in *Lawrence* at the start of the 1960s. All the same Powell and Lean reach the pinnacle of their careers as great film artists at roughly the same time – Powell with *Peeping Tom* in 1960 and Lean with *Lawrence* two years later. The irony of vicissitude in fortune is not lost in the comparison. *Lawrence* was a box-office hit and hailed as a masterpiece; *Peeping Tom* was vilified by critics, poorly distributed and ignored by audiences. Powell's UK career was effectively over while Lean overindulged in grandiose epics for global audiences that cost millions and, artistically speaking, went nowhere. This was the swansong of UK romanticism in its purest cinematic form: it was reinvented thereafter in radically different ways, refracted through the prism of modernist narration by Roeg, Boorman, Russell, Jarman and Davies, all neo-romantics with diverse styles and obsessions. But in *Peeping Tom*, it could be argued, Powell was already making the transition from the romantic to the neo-modern and reaching a point from which there was no turning back.

The break with Pressburger, after a string of commercial failures, allowed Powell to consider a partnership with Leo Marks, who had worked in wartime military intelligence as cryptographer and code-master and who, having known the fine line between life and death in his work with field agents, became a strong fan of Powell's *AMOLAD*. Marks pitched Powell a Freudian tale of voyeurism and 'scoptophilia', which had origins in Marks' wartime experience but was set mainly in Soho and the film industry of the present day. If *Peeping Tom* indirectly sourced wartime trauma, then its Powellian prelude was the naturalistic *Small Back Room* about a different kind of expert, bomb disposal man Sammy Rice (David Farrar), now an alcoholic and sporting an artificial leg. The trauma is physical since Rice is still in pain and the absent limb is never explained. Is he atoning for an earlier explosion that has blown it to pieces by now dismantling on Chesil beach a new kind of German bomb with a delay mechanism designed to maim and kill civilians? The answer is never made clear. But the endless self-pity his wound generates is clearly psychic. His lover (played by Kathleen Byron) who lives in the flat opposite (since censorship forbade them living together), aids his recovery. Time-wise the Balchin adaptation, book to film, is almost immediate. Powell makes it a naturalistic fable of redemption, a triumph of grim ambition over physical pain, of sobriety over an expressionistic delirium tremens (reminiscent of Wilder's *The Lost Weekend* (1945)), a gritty tale of enduring love superbly acted by Farrar and Byron – and like *AMOLAD* a trauma exorcised. *Peeping Tom*, however, is a different matter. It ends with trauma's dark, destructive triumph and leaves a bundle of innocent corpses in its wake.

The Freudian wager of Marks and Powell in their creation of focus-puller Mark Lewis (Carl Boehm) lies in their bold evocation of infantile trauma, both neo-Freudian and reflexive. In flashback the father (played by Powell) 'abuses' the young son (played by Powell's own son, Columba) by filming and recording his pseudo-scientific experiments in eliciting the child's fear. In this fusion of science and sadism, the son is treated like a laboratory animal in a behavioural experiment, subject to round-the-clock surveillance, a form of audio-visual rape, a violation of fragile selfhood. Is audio-visual attack a displacement of sexual violation, a metonym of bodily intrusion? Or does it supplement it? The question is left tantalisingly open. In the event, like father like son Mark also becomes a visual rapist, but of a different kind: a killer of young woman, he is too traumatised and impotent to love. Here the scoptophiliac perversion has a concrete outcome. The death-image is matched to the death-instrument – the terrified faces of victims caught on the camera lens to the bayonet concealed in the leg of the camera's tripod extended horizontally toward them. Powell here tries, riskily, to make the victim's look of fear the source of orgasmic delight for his wannabe artist, and hesitates on the brink of cliché. He may identify with his deranged 'artist', but his 'artist' has become a psychopath, and unfortunately for him – and for Martin Scorsese who buys into the conceit too easily – a psychopath is a psychopath is a psychopath.

Hitchcock, of course, evoked the traumas of childhood of his subjects in *Spellbound* and *Marnie* and again in *Psycho*. But he always leaves a gap between actuality and cognition which Powell here tries to elide. The effort of closure, as explanation, through the words (and the recordings) of Lewis himself just before his death at first seems forced, a closure of classical melodrama. At the ending of *Psycho*, Hitchcock by contrast took the plunge into modernist ambiguity by juxtaposing the psychiatrist's simpleminded account in court of Bates' schizophrenia with the prison cell superimposition of the Mother's grinning skull on Norman's docile face. Powell and Marks, on the other hand, cannot convincingly close off the enigma of their killer through the predicate of infantile trauma. But if we take the secondary post-trauma of the 'adult' world as an alternative starting-point for reading the narrative, then the film, fascinatingly, opens up again.

Here the trauma-delay is not only the recurrence of childhood fear in adult life but a supplement of something else, the reflexive transposition of wartime history onto peacetime pathology. The child's history, if you like, has its homology in British wartime: the Soho present is a different kind of disturbance, an adult disturbance in the culture of a peacetime age. Here the other side of film and photography is pornography. Like *Dead of Night*, *Peeping Tom* has a double-imprint of allegory and representation. This is London narrative on location at the start of the 1960s just as *Dead of Night* is country house narrative in 1945. Yet both are trauma-allegories, *Dead of Night* of the *immediate* past, *Peeping Tom* of the *delayed* past. In Powell's film, and in Marks' screenplay, this is conveyed by the Freudian trauma-delay of Mark's childhood repeated (and reversed) in adult life, young boy to young man. It is, one could argue, that compressed space of a generation between wartime London and 1960. Marks' idea of *Peeping Tom* was born of his wartime experiences of inventing codes for SOE agents, an operation surrounded by extreme secrecy. In Powell's film he has translated the linguistic connection between the secret agent's code and the masked reality it conveys (code–signifier–signified) into the relationship between the camera-image and its victim-object. Mark, the focus-puller, who secretly moonlights in magazine porn-photography and the amateur voyeurism of his 16 mm camera, usually conceals the latter in his jacket, a stalker's visual turn-on, Powell's hand-held camerawork every bit as inventive as that on view in the *nouvelle vague*.

There is, here, a key connection to *AMOLAD*. Just as the earlier film sought to spatialise traumatic wounding through visual images, *Peeping Tom* seeks in Marks' screenplay a visual homology for his wartime experience of secret language, the code by which agents in Europe transmitted their messages back to London HQ. This works as an *oblique transfer from text from image* as is made clear in Marks' own statements on the film (Marks 1998: xii–xvii) and indirectly in his 2001 memoir *Of Silk and Cyanide*. Marks was obsessed by finding a code that could not be extracted from his agents, especially female agents, by torture and instigated the use of silk ribbon strips in coat linings that could be torn out, used once only, then burnt. The code could not be memorised and thus revealed to the Gestapo under duress. The key transfer from text to image is highlighted by the role of Helen's blind mother, Mrs Stephens (Maxine Audley), Mark's uncanny lodger who in a brilliant rendition of 'sightless seeing', knows Mark's demented mind without ever seeing the bayonet on his tripod or the camera lens in front of her eyes. Subsequently Helen (Anna Massey) fails to register the look of fear that would seal her fate, as it has of all his other victims. Mulvey deems this a crucial moment in the film, an instance of 'the light that fails' in Mark's fetish-obsession with the image of fear that drives him to kill. Helen, whose eyes are wide open, shows no trace of the fatal emotion (Mulvey 2005: 153). Likewise *absence of code-knowledge* in Marks' obsession with captured female agents, *as immunity to torture*, is transposed here through his anagrammed anti-hero (Mark Lewis = Leo Marks) into the *absence of the image as the sign of immunity* (symbolised by the figure of the blind mother). The young Marks was trying to do his patriotic duty: the middle-aged Marks with more than a touch of survivor's guilt was turning himself into one of his imaginary enemies, a torturer who in wartime would have been a Gestapo officer and in peacetime, fifteen years later, a psychotic porn-photographer.

How else can we explain the fetishistic transition from patriotism to pornography? Or indeed that which Marks had two years earlier offered anonymously to Lewis Gilbert's *Carve Her Name with Pride* (1958) with its story of brave Violet Szabo one of Marks's SOE agents dropped into France, the actual code-poem (a love poem) he had written for Szabo's use in the field? Gilbert's film is naturalist melodrama with a brilliant performance by Virginia McKenna as Violet, the young mother from Stockwell who gives up family life to parachute into France. *Peeping Tom* with its enveloping darkness and serial killings seemed like the downside of this reaffirmation of war pride filtered through a tough, self-sacrificing heroine. But it was more. Set at the start of a new culture in 1960s Soho, twin site of London prostitution and the British film industry, which Heller's garish Eastmancolor suits absolutely, Powell's imagination made it prescient about the growth of two things in a new consumerist age: the interwoven expansion of still and moving image, and as side-effect that has now moved centre stage, the spiralling of the nascent sex and pornography industries. In the twenty-first century they are vast and global: the critical horror that greeted Powell's film may well have contained a deeper fear about things to come, a repressed recognition of the horrors of anti-progress, how the toxic mix of culture and technology can set back the cause of civilisation in any shape or form. If there is a lineage in cinema's reading of this sidelined catastrophe, then *Peeping Tom's* true successor is David Lynch's *Lost Highway* (1996).

The other plus in Powell's narrative is the double-trauma. Infantile trauma in Mark is followed by its tragic effect – secondary trauma on the part of Helen (Anna Massey) as the loving girl who survives. Helen is the only one to survive the torture of the camera with eyes wide open. So it is that trauma repeats itself, and is transferred from victim-perpetrator to innocent victim. The closure may seem melodramatic but Massey's powerful acting leaves open the question of how Helen will be affected in future. Will it damage her trust in men and her capacity to love? Fascinated by Powell's film it is almost as if Roman Polanski has fashioned the image of Carole in *Repulsion* as a sequel to that of Helen in *Peeping Tom* in a film that invites us to conceive of a childhood trauma that is markedly absent, a mystery unrevealed. At the same time the victim's love for the killer gives Powell something of a pseudo-romantic get-out clause. Is he trying to lessen the derangement or draw its sting? Can any obsessed artist solemnly proclaim 'There but for the grace of God . . .?

A tantalising thought lingers. Is there an act of bad faith implicit in the filming of *Peeping Tom* in which Lewis is transformed though Powell's casting into a *German* obsessive played by Carl Boehm (against the wishes of Marks whose screenplay killer had been a middle-class Englishman)? One can argue that Laurence Harvey, the original choice and at that time a screen idol, would have been far better, not because of any deficiency in Boehm's acting, which achieves genuine pathos, but in the shock-value of turning round a handsome icon who represented at the time the quintessence of suave Englishness. And had Powell as the scientist-father in the film acted in good faith by using home movies of his own son for those of Mark the child? But the problem is not really this. It is that Carl Boehm's Mark comes across as Hans Beckert Mark II, a facsimile of Peter Lorre's child killer in *M.* The Weimar legacy looms large in Powell's cinematic unconscious. What originates in British wartime intelligence as an allegory of trauma and helplessness ends up onscreen as the resurrection of a Teutonic demon, the shy focus-puller as a new incarnation of the cinematic 'undead' of an earlier tradition. If German expressionism is Powell's estranged filmic father, then given his bizarre self-casting in this reflexive film, we can truly say the son is the father of the father. And Boehm as the child-victim 'turned' is the metaphorical son of Lorre the child-killer – and cursed with the same active-passivity.

## FEMALE 'MADNESS' AND MODERNISM: *THE INNOCENTS* AND *REPULSION*

These films of the early 1960s provide continuities backward and forward. They stand on the cusp of modernism, or rather the *return* of modernism in sound narration, as a neo-modern cinema. If, as Bordwell contends, one of the key features of an emergent art-cinema at this time is the *ambiguity of the image* and the questioning of causal motivation (Bordwell 2008: 156–8), both films do both but in different ways. In *The Innocents* the female subject follows a clear line of motivation for much (but not all) of the film with which audiences can identity. But what she perceives is ambiguous and the audience must share that ambiguity: it has no evidence or omniscience to move beyond it. In Polanski's film, by contrast, the process of Carole's disintegration can be mapped out by an observant spectator, but her motivation remains a mystery. Her reactions to events and people are largely affectless, her understanding of consequence disturbingly retarded. Let us consider each in turn. Deborah Kerr's great role in *Black Narcissus* was now to be bettered by her extraordinary performance for Jack Clayton in his adapting of the Henry James tale 'The Turn of the Screw'. Polanski, admiring the link that Powell had made between claustrophobia and sexual horror in *Peeping Tom*, created his own special variant on sexual disintegration in his English début film, also set in London. And *Repulsion* is one of the key examples of the expatriate eye that defined the new British modernism of the 1960s where other foreign directors – notably Joseph Losey, Otto Preminger, Michelangelo Antonioni and Stanley Kubrick – came to the fore.

Both films, like *Peeping Tom,* enter directly into Freudian territory. Yet, unlike Powell's film, both resist holistic closure and became key neo-modern texts in what is seen as the poetics of ambiguity. The term 'ambiguity' will be challenged later. But the word 'text' here means no arid narrative ripe for formalist imprimatur. These are both rich, enigmatic trauma-tales that break new boundaries – and defy categories – even though 'trauma-tale' is the imperfect category in which we place them. Clayton's modernist 'ambiguity' depends on a floating, shared uncertainty in which the fear of the distraught governess become a mirror for the uncertain reading of the film's audience. Polanski's use of 'ambiguity' depends on motivation withholding, on the puzzle and mystery of homicidal madness. Miss Giddens, the Jamesian governess, and Polanski's Carole (Catherine Deneuve), a Belgian hairdresser, are women of different epochs yet are equally torn apart: anxious about what threatens them but equally anxious about their own reactions to it. As spectators, moreover, we have no real vantage point from which to read objectively that trepidation's source or its outcome. Is the governess seeing in the figures of her predecessor, Miss Jessel, and of Peter Quint, the projections of her own imagination? Or are the living ghosts of Bly House's recent past really there? The doubt crosses our minds as it crosses hers. Neither subject nor viewer can escape the anxiety of uncertainty in the answer. Nor is the conceit just a Jamesian device in the house of fiction. William James (Henry's brother) had after all recorded in *The Varieties of Religious Experience* the numerous visitations of God and of Christ, of prophets, angels, ghosts and saints upon the nineteenth-century devout, or so they had claimed. In a devout culture, we could say, the paranormal becomes normal, just as in a scientific epoch many claim to have been abducted by aliens. Clayton has said that in his film he wanted to hold the stark alternatives of authentic sighting or of hallucination by the governess in balance throughout the film, and this he does triumphantly (Tippitts 2002: 105–8).

In Polanski's film, because we cannot truly read Carole's illness, any more than she can accurately read the perceived threats of the male sex, we share her uncertainty; but we are quickly distanced from her by the presence of her frigid body and deranged soul. From the start we are perturbed by a double malaise, her overreaction to male threat and lack of reaction to friendly reassurance. In *The Innocents* there is a more subtle gradation. With Kerr's governess, we are close at first because we too have at times been haunted by ghosts from our past and by unexplained happenings. In addition one of

**Figure 5.2** The Trauma Rapture: Deborah Kerr and Martin Stephens in *The Innocents*

our great collective fears is the sexual corruption of the young. But over-reaction and fixation on Miles at the expense of his sister make us doubt Giddens' motives and finally her sanity. It would be wrong to assume that both women, however, are icy, virginal men-haters. Both share a latent attraction to the unavailable, the governess to the children's uncle and guardian (played by Michael Redgrave), who shows no interest in her, and Carole to her sister's married lover (played by Ian Hendry), whose sexual effectiveness she hears through the wall in the couple's late-night lovemaking, sounds of lovers' ecstasy that signify both threat and attraction. Both men, in romantic melodrama, could well have been heroic figures poised to exorcise female fears. But one (the uncle) is indifferent and the other (the married lover) is patronising. These then are trauma-tales of women alone. In the prolonged absence of the secret object of desire (would that the uncle came back from London/would that the sister's lover came back from Italy!), terror ensues. This conceit Polanski surely took from *The Innocents* as a motor of narrative suspense for his own film, in a setting where cityscape takes over from countryside, the Kensington apartment overlooking the convent school from the rural Gothic of Bly House and its lush, cultivated gardens.

The *mise-en-scène* of threat creates interesting variation in both instances.

For the 'apparitions' of the departed at Bly House, Clayton and cinematographer Freddie Francis use long shots of Peter Quint on the tower battlements and Miss Jessel, Giddens' predecessor, on the other side of the garden pond in which the face is slightly out-of-focus and indistinct, or again when close at hand Quint's face pressed against the window of the living-room from outside, so that any act of seeing confronts both obstacle and slight distortion. Tantalisingly, confirmation is just out of reach, and since the servants in the house claim to have no sightings at all, doubt intensifies . . . Reflexively we might speculate that writer Truman Capote, who made the decisive contribution to the final screenplay, invested Giddens' obsession with the departed with an obsession in his own professional life. He was writing *In Cold Blood* at the time, his classic reconstruction of two criminal drifters who brutally murder a Mid-West farming family in their rural home. Now in Europe he may well still have been haunted by the two murderous 'ghosts' he had interviewed in their prison cells, where they were shadows of their former criminal selves awaiting execution. Did they inhabit his imagination as Quint and Jessel inhabited the waking world of the governess? Or had Clayton, who had just seen *Vertigo*, used the model of Scottie Fergusson's obsession with Madeleine Elster? Like all good writer–director collaborations it was almost certainly a fusion of both and elective affinity worked a treat.

While Clayton used predominantly POV shots for Giddens and at crucial moments rang the changes to call her vision into question, Polanski slowly shifts from objective to subjective mode, from Carol as the disturbed object of our clinical gaze oblivious to the rotting flesh of the rabbit long removed from the kitchen fridge, to the subjective hallucinations of rape, of the flat's expanding, agoraphobic rooms and of hands bursting through the walls of the corridor to grasp her. Some would argue that Polanski is best served by the clinical gaze of the film's first part, others that its true horror is heightened by hallucination in the second part, where Carol has been left alone by the holidaying couple. Polanski's strategy entails a slow-burn transformation so that the deranged subjective creeps up on us unawares. Though both favour wide shots in their cinematic staging with middle-range lenses that simulate the eye, Clayton's decision to shoot in black and white Scope with its large cameras created a powerful frontal lighting to sustain depth of field: it meant that his camera was often static. In a way this was suited to the formalism of his revisionist costume drama and the filmic convention of the haunted house. Moreover black and white Cinemascope, unlike its colour counterpart, avoided 'cinematic mumps' in facial close-up and allowed a simultaneous depth and width to the image (Bordwell 2008: 289–306). Polanski, equally a depth-of-field enthusiast, had begun to specialise in close-range following shots which made his camera more mobile. It would move with his female subject along streets, corridors and into rooms in over-the-shoulder shots that preceded Steadicam by fifteen years. And for a contemporary city film, this too suited Polanski perfectly.

*Repulsion* brought in its wake Polanski's anti-trauma comedy *Cul-de-Sac.* Yet the latter, in conception, had preceded the former. In order to bankroll the black comedy, a long-term project, the nomadic Polanski agreed with his London producers to shoot the former, a short-term inspiration, first. The industrial reality of film and good box-office returns thus reversed his chosen order, which in retrospect seems natural – a farce after terror, a comic rebound from deep trauma which nonetheless deconstructs trauma itself with amusing consequences. In a way it echoes *The Ladykillers* a decade on, a repetition of classic Ealing by modernist means. Two gangsters on the run after a botched robbery cross to Holy Island at high tide. One (Lionel Stander) is a parody of a New York gangster of the 1930s, the other (Jack MacGowran) a comic cast-off from *Waiting for Godot.* Both are reinventing the theatre of the Absurd for the big screen. Yet both discover the forbidding castle there to be occupied by an even wackier couple than themselves, an eccentric Englishman (played by Donald Pleasence) (an Englishman's home is . . .) and his young French wife (played by Françoise Dorléac), playing cross-dressing, sadomasochistic games to ease the boredom of solitude. The lonely wife has a young English lover with whom she cavorts half-naked in the dunes, the husband awful middle-class relatives who come to visit unexpectedly. Tough Yankee gangster Stander, trying to embark on a reign of terror, is traumatised by the eccentric idiocy of it all and fatally succumbs in a moment of weakness. First the failed robbery, then the mad flight to a mad island, then this . . .

If we can match the trauma-tale to the expatriate eye in Polanski we can do the same with Preminger in his modernist psycho-thriller *Bunny Lake is Missing* (1965). It too has non-Brits in its lead roles, this time Americans. Our bright-eyed couple Anne (Carol Lynley) and Stephen (Keir Dullea), both young and dynamic, represent on the face of it progress, modernity and Yankee know-how, frustrated by an eccentric, old-fashioned English culture which hardly seems to acknowledge their existence. Yet cracks soon appear in their brother–sister relationship, which had appeared at first sight that of husband and wife. Ann's four-year-old daughter Bunny disappears on her first day at a large Hampstead nursery, where the distressed single mother has to confront her neurotic teacher (played by Anna Massey) and reclusive headmistress (played by Martita Hunt), who claim to know nothing about the child. Atmospheric strangeness deepens with the appearance of Laurence Olivier as a dilatory police inspector who seems to have little interest in solving the case. Does the child actually exist or is she a figment of the couple's imagination? Matters are made worse by Ann's menacing landlord (Noël Coward), a drunken lecher harassing his good-looking tenant, a further milestone in Coward's acting career after *Our Man in Havana.* The turn-on for him is in treating the young mother as a girl-child, and her seduction as just one step removed from paedophilia.

Ann is not just traumatised by the kidnapping of her child but also by the refusal of all to believe her. True, this comes out of classical melodrama, but Preminger's modernist trope lies in his staging of *the absence* of anticipated response: none of the Londoners acts as you would expect them to. They behave in front of the traumatised mother not only as if no kidnapping has taken place but as if she too is unreal, a ghostly figment of their collective imagination. But if Preminger's London, this eccentric neo-Dickensian city with its Gothic Victorian architecture, seems a throwback to the past, then our American couple are out of the contemporary world of Freud and our vision of the damaged psyche, where Preminger unerringly replicates the Freudian division between psychosis as male and neurosis as female. Like many couples in the Preminger canon, Ann and Stevie appear to have an incestuous relationship. In a sequence in Ann's flat where they discuss Bunny's disappearance, Stevie is in the bath smoking, Ann is perched on its rim not two feet away: it is the intimate discourse of spouses or lovers. An official explanation is given for Ann's single motherhood – an unstable, no-good boyfriend back home, unfit for marriage or fatherhood. And yet as we regress into the fantasy childhood world of the strange couple, a more troubling thought crosses our minds: could Stevie, the deranged brother, be the unacknowledged father?

The cinematic challenge of London for Preminger lay in extending the range of one of his style trademarks, the long-take sequence-shot. Here his rapid, fluent camera is in full exploration mode, moving through London streets and the interiors of sinister Victorian buildings with a brio and virtuosity that makes it as much a part of 1960s innovation as the long-take aesthetics of Antonioni or Miklós Jancsó. The tracking shot near the end, where the camera moves from front to back through Stevie's Hampstead mansion and then shows us the menacing garden play of the reunited trio, in which the regressing Ann and Stevie are as much children as Bunny, is Preminger at the peak of his technical game, just as earlier is a key sequence in the toy repair basement where Preminger, critically, breaks with the long take. Ann discovers Stevie burning Bunny's favourite doll, taken from a shelf of repaired dolls, as the only 'evidence' left of the girl's actual existence. The unnerving track-in on his glistening eyes is followed by Preminger's first crucial reverse-shot of the film as he cuts to Ann at the foot of the stairs watching in horror before dashing towards her demented brother. The near-symmetry is perfect

**Figure 5.3** Welcome to the Dollhouse: Carol Lynley in *Bunny Lake is Missing*

– Stephen: medium shot track-in to extreme close-up, reverse-angle cut to Ann, then pan to medium shot as she dashes forward. Later, Preminger repeats single matching close-ups for the couple in the mansion garden: Stephen beside the shallow grave wielding the spade that can be used either to bury Bunny or kill Ann – or both: the reverse-angle cut to Ann's terror as the desperate look of a protective mother thinking on her feet about how to survive disaster. Because he uses the close-up reverse-angle so sparingly, Preminger the long-take specialist can truly freight it with the imagination of disaster.

*Bunny Lake* joins *Peeping Tom* and *Repulsion* in mapping out the menace of a cinematic London, doing for Hampstead what Polanski had done for South Kensington and Powell for Soho. It also extends the innovative range of sequence-shot inventiveness, the look of the London of the time in grainy detail but with a fluency and in-frame editing that in British terms was a cinematic first in 1965. As a whodunit thriller, expertly adapted by Penelope and John Mortimer, it resolves many of the ambiguities it sets up, like *Peeping Tom,* with an uncanny intimation of childhood trauma as the source of secondary psychosis. But Preminger's camera acts out in the final garden sequence the adult regression to childhood fantasy more convincingly as moving image, as visual enactment, than Powell's reflexive fix on home movies and tape recorders. And the mystery of the brother–sister liaison lingers long after the film has ended, as enigmatic as the look of the detached child Carole in the family photo which ends *Repulsion*. If *Repulsion* reveals too little, and *Peeping Tom* tries to reveal too much, *Bunny Lake* matches *The Innocents* in its architecture of ambiguity: it reveals much, but beyond a certain point it can reveal nothing.

## The trauma double bill: *Don't Look Now* and *The Wicker Man*

The key romantic element in trauma film is the linking of Eros to violent death, and this cult double bill, first seen late in 1973, was no exception. Like *Peeping Tom* and *Repulsion*, this entails the coupling of sexuality and murder. Indeed it may well be seen as the culmination of British achievement in this unacknowledged genre where British film was *de facto* a world leader for thirty years from the war's end. Let us take *The Wicker Man* first. When ready for release, the Scottish shocker (written by Anthony Shaffer and directed by Robin Hardy) was cut, then unceremoniously dumped by the new executives of British Lion and reinstated as a theatrical appendage to Nicholas Roeg's prestige project with big stars, where Lion hoped it would quietly die. But the film has come back from the dead to haunt them and us, and is now one of the most talked about Scottish pictures in the new century (Murray 2005: 11–34). While Powell sometimes played at paganism, the Hardy–Shaffer combination takes it head-on in this dark fairy-tale of a Scottish island community closing ranks against visiting Police Sergeant Neil Howie (Edward Woodward) determined to solve the mystery disappearance of a young girl, Rowan Morrison. In a way this is a darker version of *Whisky Galore* in which the English are no longer to blame as Howie, the devout Presbyterian Scot from the mainland, echoes the outsider role of the blundering Captain Waggett in Mackendrick's comedy. The chasm that widens in the course of the film is internal, the pagan strain in Scottish culture that simmers under the lid of the official Protestantism now in decline in a new consumer age. This is a country after all where, traditionally, the pagan ceremony of Hogmanay has counted for more than the birthday celebration of Christ (a celebration frowned on by Scottish Calvinism). Yet the feel of the film is also very contemporary, absorbing the new public hedonism of the late 1960s and the reinvention of folk music for an electronic age. Devoid of Powell's sporadic awkwardness, it matches the archaic to the contemporary and goes further by posing awkward questions about the sacred in a seemingly secular age. Is the alternative to Howie's devout yet dying faith the secular rationality acclaimed by atheists, or in a new consumer age is Christianity's loss paganism's secret gain? The film's finale provides a traumatic answer.

The story-concept is also *au courant* in echoing the paranoid strain of new modernist cinema, in *Blow-Up*, *Bunny Lake*, *Point Blank*, *Performance*, *A Clockwork Orange*, *Rosemary's Baby* (1968), *McCabe and Mrs Miller* (1971) and the American thrillers of Alan Pakula. Thus Hardy and Shaffer, who were fans of Roger Corman, Terence Fisher and Hammer Horror, wanted a new variation on horror for a new age they found difficult to categorise. The casting of horror specialist Christopher Lee as Lord Summerisle, laird of the island, is a clear pointer. Here Lee is a grounded, playful figure, a post-horror monster with a sense of humour who has come down to earth, a metaphorical vampire but also a figure of cunning who has resurrected, it turns out, a cult of human sacrifice. In his police variation on the Protestant work ethic, Howie defies all the sexual temptations put in his way by the locals and resolves to make the rational religious and the religious rational. There is a firm Scottish residue in this, indissoluble, which means he cannot be mocked and fobbed off lightly. It is the virtue of Shaffer's screenplay that he keeps in balance identification and separation. Howie is pompous, out of touch and old-fashioned, but also fair, tenacious and well-meaning, unjustly mocked not only by the locals but also in the uncut version by his fellow officers. Shaffer humanises him, resisting the lure of making him a soft target. It is because he wants to save the missing girl that he endures nightmare, just as Donald Sutherland in *Don't Look Now* suffers ultimate nightmare because he is devoted to the memory of his drowned daughter. Neither film follows the modernist trope of placing itself beyond good and evil: each evokes a sense of absolute evil that is read and felt without endorsing the supernatural at all. Thus there may be elements of the paranormal which we can all feel uncertain about at key moments in our lives, perhaps because we cannot explain sudden strangeness in habitual ways. Both films build on this but end by shocking us – truly shocking us – with tragic moments in which the seemingly implausible becomes horrifically plausible.

Hardy's film is complex and troubling. For Howie's investigation is a quest to save an innocent child from dire happenings, in the same way as the governess in *The Innocents* had nurtured her mission to 'save' the children. But from then on all is inverted: the salvation quest ends in disaster. In retrospect, *The Wicker Man* is a corrective to current hocus-pocus in high-end television, not an endorsement – and this is why. The film feels at the end like a deadly feint in a boxing match, faking to punch with one hand in order to set up the opponent for a deadly blow from the other. And the victim is not only Howie but the audience itself, since like him they don't see it coming.

*The Wicker Man* belongs tangentially to the lineage of the 'sacrificial unconscious' in modern cinema (Orr 1998: 32–43). It takes seriously the often unspoken links between 'the sacred' and 'sacrifice' as a powerful constant in the human condition. But it teases out its terror with unbearable articulation. The twist in its tale is well known by now, the young girl not kidnapped after all and not the intended victim but the bait to ensnare Howie and return his devout faith from its current orthodoxy to a primal scene of sacrifice and martyrdom. *He*, the suffering Christian, is the sacrifice to the pagan sun god, bound and thrust into the heart of the wicker man to be burnt alive and thus ensure the fertility and abundance of the island crops. The iconography of the ritual that fuses Eros and death starts off as pagan and then subsumes under it a pastiche iconography of the Passion in the figure of Howie, death by burning overriding death by crucifixion. Whereas Jesus foresaw his own crucifixion, Howie as habitual follower, a dogged, distant disciple and not a prophet, is blind to his impending fate. Here trauma is delayed recognition of what is latent in his predicament and his soul: repression of desire runs deep but suppression of recognition runs deeper. Faith has it that only the ascetic can attain true knowledge, but here Howie is left groping in the dark, blinded by the truth of daybreak.

In the myth of a secular – or is it a post-Christian? – culture, we complacently assume that faith is a way-station to secular enlightenment in which the model of Christ's compassion, his willingness to suffer for us all, will lead to an end-state where such sacrifice is redundant. Because we are now rational beings and can save ourselves, we do not need to be saved. And the Christian gesture of sacrifice was itself, as Girard has pointed out, a historical formula to end the blood-sacrifice of pagan ritual (Girard 1979: 39–67). The ending of *The Wicker Man* abruptly changes gear and shifts everything brutally into reverse. We scroll back from secular mockery through old-fashioned Presbyterianism to an archaic paganism, which may in fact be the consumerist successor to secularity rather than its primitive predecessor of long, long ago. In the ritual triumph of Fairisle, laird and island, and the ritual burning of the sergeant who calls, we may be speeding back to the future and all it holds.

## The neo-romantic turn and death in Venice: *Don't Look Now*

Roeg's early films represent a remarkable turn to the romantic after the modernist cool of the 1960s, while at the same time *advancing modernist innovation.* The latter is apparent in his virtuoso command of cross-cutting, rapid time-switches, bold zoom-shots and slow motion. The paradox seems at first sight scarcely credible: a renaissance of romantic sensibility, a mastery of modernist technique and the two perfectly intertwined. Roeg enhances the instability of the camera and by extension of our own powers of seeing, but also experiments with the time-image echoing the boldness of Chris Marker and Alain Resnais. In that sense he follows in the footsteps of Boorman's *Point*

*Blank* but his is an Anglo-European story, not Californian *noir*, and after the opening sequence of daughter Christine's drowning, it is based for most of its running time faithfully on Daphne Du Maurier's novella of the same name. The power of the fiction that is not his inspires the cinematic imagination that is his but also crucially structures it, so that what starts as an open, unresolved puzzle is transformed into what seems a predestined fate.

Here Roeg works through association and symbol, especially through the constant of water. John and Laura Baxter (Donald Sutherland and Julie Christie) will become aware of its presence recurrently throughout the film. The water of the daughter's drowning in their English garden is matched by the swirling liquid of the Venetian canals whose bridges they cross and recross. The whole film has an aqueous, tactile feel so that in the puzzle of possible sightings of Christine there is for the spectator a profound sensation of drowning in the image. The water-image also transmits and sustains the trauma-event. Just as the trauma of the drowning originates in water so it is sustained by water. For the grieving father (Donald Sutherland) as dedicated church restorer now to work in a city built on water is scarcely to provide exorcism at all. Here Venice in winter is a mixed blessing, a beautiful city that can distract the couple from their grief and enable them once again to make love after long abstinence, but also a city which haunts them and draws them into an impossible quest for contact with the dead. Indeed, the desire to exorcise the grief of family loss by wishing for contact with the departed may be part of that compulsion to repeat that draws death on more quickly. John the sceptic is at first immune to the murmurings and prophecies of the psychic sisters, Heather and Wendy, that so lift Laura's spirits. But when they do percolate through to him they bring in their wake hallucination, misjudgement and pure obsession.

The central fascination lies in the trade-off. The 'visit' of the dead Christine to Heather the blind psychic sister, a form of 'sightless seeing' that echoes the role of Mrs Stephens in *Peeping Tom*, is what brings Laura back to life and ends the period of mourning which had shaded off into melancholia. It is hope without evidence, but in her case it works. It makes her radiant and gives her a new lease of life, but ironically, only because she fails to recognise the downside, Heather's uncanny prophecy of John's eventual fate. Nonetheless the incident makes her immune to melancholia and obsession while her sceptic-husband, lacking the false fix of delusional 'vision', descends into obsession instead. Delusion restores normality in Laura but scepticism induces abnormality in John. It is he who 'sees' Laura and the sisters at his own water-borne funeral on the canal and stays on in the city for that reason. Sanderson has also pointed to Roeg's ingenious variation on the double-chase. The more the Baxters hunt through the city for the elusive sisters and rush to keep their

**Figure 5.4** Watching My Funeral Go By: Julie Christie, Hilary Mason and Clelia Matania in *Don't Look Now*

various appointments, the more they are running through a labyrinth full of dead-ends and ambiguous signs (Sanderson 1996: 25). As John finally changes after the fleeting figure in red, convinced it is the ghost of his daughter, Laura chases after him, the running man and the running woman, running away from as they run towards, trying to flee reality as they rush to capture it.

## Romantic symbol and modernist edit

In *Performance* and *Don't Look Now*, Roeg reinvents the romantic idiom for the modernist age. But the romantic core of the former film, where Roeg worked closely with Donald Cammell, is outlaw-romantic: the narcotic search for sexuality and exotica as a double-package of vision, of the seeing of the body from the outside induced by altered states. And it is destructive, literally, false transcendence a double-trauma of art and life. Traumatised by the hippie happenings at Notting Hill's Powis Square, Chas the south London gangster disintegrates. Traumatised by acting out the part of Chas in Powis Square in a kind of meta-*cinema vérité*, James Fox abandoned his acting career and became a reclusive and devout Christian (MacCabe, 1998: 47). Roeg's next film, without Cammell, reverts to the mainstream tradition of the romance by

**Figure 5.5** Hoodlum in the Age of Pop Art: James Fox in *Performance*

taking on board the story-structure of Du Maurier and adding symbolic flourishes. It combines the quest-narrative of mythic romance with the romantic love of the questing, grieving couple trying to uphold, in vain, the ideals of the nuclear family. That the best love-making sequence in all of British cinema is of a married couple rediscovering their love for one another after extended grieving shows how far from *film noir* British cinema really is. No fall guy, no *femme fatale*, no trace of seduction here. But the way in which Eros is composed onscreen, through temporal cross-cutting, has the resonance of pure association – imagistic and poetic, echoing the powerful opening and even more powerful ending, the fatal and beautifully rendered triangle of Death–Eros–Death.

How does Roeg undercut the romantic through the neo-modern and then triumphantly reinstate it? The Death–Eros–Death triangle works both as romantic feeling and a mosaic of inventive editing – Roeg's fast cutting integrated with zoom or slow-motion and sudden shifts in time. The cross-cutting of the drowning sequence is done through *spatial* juxtaposition – the children by the lake, the parents in the living room, finally broken by Baxter's despairing dash across the garden and into the lake after

Christine. The cross-cutting of the hotel love-sequence is done though *temporal* juxtaposition – the sudden, gradual acceleration of the erotic Event juxtaposed to the mundane dressing for dinner that follows it. In the film's climax, the fatal stabbing by the redcoat dwarf in the decaying, disused palazzo generates both *spatial* and *temporal* juxtaposition in one of the great montage sequences of the sound era. At first it is consecutive in its double chase pattern, John chasing the dwarf, Laura chasing John, but with the first blow of the diminutive killer Roeg expands the montage through space and time, a momentous collage of colliding and unifying images. Part are images lodged in the brain of a dying man: part are the autonomous images outside the brain though the dividing line is so fine it can never be clear which is which. Part are image-memories on the edge of consciousness and part are simultaneous 'elsewheres' in the broader life-world of a dying church restorer. Are these 'objective' elsewheres or 'imagined' elsewheres? Factual or paranoid? Spectators have to work out their own answer.

The montage triangle – drowning, lovemaking, dying – can be formalised as a pattern of separation, unity and final separation. The drowning separates the child from her parents, long-delayed lovemaking exorcises grief in the grieving couple, and sudden death finally separates them for ever, at the very moment when Baxter thinks they will be 'reunited' with their daughter. Diremption–Redemption–Diremption, a formal pattern with deep emotional underpinning, carried by the colour of red and the ubiquity of water: romantic symbols that Roeg turns into indelible images. Through the poetics of separation Roeg's film achieves artistic unity. But he also does it by more dramatic means which echo the endings of Oscar Wilde's *Dorian Gray* and Hitchcock's *Psycho.* As spectators Roeg has made us yearn for the metaphysical miracle of redness his ending hints at – the ghost of Christine returns to earth, a momentous reunion and homecoming. As the tiny figure turns round in the *palazzo* we yearn for impossible resurrection, the growing radiance of the young girl reborn. Instead, like Dorian Gray's mirror-image, we witness a ravaged and demented old age. Just like Hitchcock's rotating 'Mother' in the rocking chair, where face and flesh are reduced to skull and skeleton, we have a terrifying figure that intimates catastrophe. At that moment we too are as traumatised as Baxter and just as helpless. If Mark Lewis transfers to the escaping Helen through his gruesome death that quality of trauma that has disfigured his life, so Baxter makes his trauma ours. We are his collective double, horrified and wiped out by the travesty of resurrection which ends in the repetition of gruesome death.

# CHAPTER 6

# *Joseph Losey and Michelangelo Antonioni: the expatriate eye and the parallax view*

The expatriate eye is an outsider's gaze. Usually this means London from the outside looking in, as in *The Servant, Repulsion, Bunny Lake, The Deadly Affair, Blow-Up, A Clockwork Orange* and *Moonlighting*. The 1960s was the seminal decade, and 1960s London is now mythical in its status as a cultural magnet for the shock of the new in music, theatre, art, fashion, scandal – and cinema. Classical Hollywood joined in, dashing across the pond and modifying the old rules in the Old World: not only Otto Preminger, but Martin Ritt, Sidney Lumet, William Wyler, Stanley Donen, Joseph Mankiewicz, Stanley Kubrick, Sam Peckinpah and the returning Hitchcock, all making their 'British' movies. With the studios seeking to breathe new life into their projects, the Hollywood invasion pushed at the weakening boundaries of censorship and classical narration with freer visual styles, more location shooting and more explicit content. The results were mixed, for the most part *neoclassical*. At the same time this was the start of a new cinema in the UK, a neo-modern remake of 1920s modernism for the sound era: 1963 with the release of *The Servant* was as momentous as 1929, and the expatriate eye was an integral part of modernism's second wave, the aesthetic dominant in the rise of the British neo-modern an aesthetic which we shall call, more precisely, the aesthetics of *the parallax view*.

In general, the writing *is* native, and the fusion of expatriate eye and insider's text counts for so much – John and Penelope Mortimer with Preminger, Harold Pinter with Losey, Edward Bond and Mark Peploe with Antonioni, Anthony Burgess freely providing his brilliant novel for Kubrick, Ritt and Lumet with Paul Dehn adapting Le Carré; wider still in the sharing of the look we can cite Truffaut with the inspired photography of Nicolas Roeg on *Fahrenheit 451* (1966), Polanski with Gil Taylor's superb black and white lensing on *Repulsion* and *Cul-de-Sac* and a collaboration unequalled in film history, that of Kubrick and his English cinematographer John Alcott on *A Clockwork Orange* and *Barry Lyndon* (1975). This is not to deny the importance of *Performance* or Lindsay Anderson's *If*. . . (1969) in the modernist canon: they are immense originals. But they remain the major exceptions. After *Peeping Tom* and *The Innocents* the key innovators are nearly all incomers – Polanski,

Losey, Antonioni, Kubrick and Skolimowski. And among the native-born it is Nicholas Roeg alone who really matches them.

Having already looked at Polanski we start with that victim of the Hollywood blacklist Joseph Losey, who had been living in England for ten years before he directed *The Servant,* and showed himself the shrewd observer of a class culture that was not his own. Historically, it is this cool idiom of the 1960s that seems a defining moment in the break with classical narration. Sound-wise, it is a crossover for the musical score where modern jazz finally comes into its own – British, American and Polish. Johnny Dankworth composed and played some of his finest music for *The Servant* and *Accident,* Cleo Laine sings superbly in *The Servant* ('Leave it alone, it's all gone'), Herbie Hancock is at his distinctive best in *Blow-Up,* while Polanski is superbly served by Chico Hamilton on *Repulsion,* before reverting to his long-term Polish composer, Krzysztof Komeda, for *Cul-de-Sac.* All five features have an identifiable music that resonates in and through their images, plaintive, reflective, bluesy but also dissonant, shorn of the overripe orchestrations of 1950s melodrama, a breathing space before the age of stadium rock and synthesisers. Sonically, they urge us into an optical mode of detachment where feeling is still powerful, but we must judge what we see on the basis of ambiguous and uncertain evidence. Their sound supplements that uncertain evidence. Answers are not morally coded in advance but are contingent upon the spectator's response. We are out there intrigued and unsure, fascinated but stranded.

We can, I think, isolate nine films as vital to the expatriate eye and four more at the start of the 1980s, which appear as an epilogue for the series. *The Servant* and *Accident, Repulsion* and *Cul-de-Sac, Blow-Up* and *The Passenger* are all major moments. They are extended by Stanley Kubrick's dark visions, comically of the near-future in *A Clockwork Orange* and tragically of the eighteenth-century past in *Barry Lyndon,* where Kubrick discards American obsessions and studio staging to make two haunting location pictures. And we can also note that Anglo-French crossover, with its story-within-a-story and dark comic view of the near future – Alain Resnais's *Providence* (1977) using an original screenplay from Yorkshire's David Mercer. As a coda, we can take the expatriate fix on modernism forward to the start of the 1980s in the maverick work of Jerzy Skolimowski. After his blistering English début *Deep End,* we have an intriguing trio of features, *The Shout* (1978), *Moonlighting* (1982) and *Success is the Best Revenge* (1984), standing out at a time when the industry had slipped into the doldrums and 'swinging London' was a thing of the past, American studios packed up and gone, the old British studios all but defunct and television starting to pick up the pieces with its new funding packages. We could also cite by way of parenthesis the low-budget *Radio On* (1979), never an expatriate film since director Chris Petit, then a *Time Out* critic with no portfolio, was a début Englishman. Yet this unlikely feature, co-produced by Wim Wenders and containing cast and crew from Wenders' German pictures, is a black and white road movie that seems at times a vehicle through which New German Cinema traverses the terrain of southern England. Meanwhile *Moonlighting*, fronted by Jeremy Irons as the leader of a gang of Polish bricklayers dazed and confused in West London, imports the traumas of Solidarity and martial law in 1981 into the heart of the indifferent English capital.

*The Passenger* is very loosely but undoubtedly British. Produced by MGM as the last of its three-picture deal with Antonioni, this transnational film with European and North African locations and an American lead boasts an original story from Mark Peploe, a final screenplay from Peploe, Peter Wollen and Antonioni. Located in the ethics of BBC overseas reporting, it was intended by Peploe to be his directing début. With Antonioni coming late to the project as director (though he had discussed the story with Peploe much earlier) it was then subject to his expatriate eye. Antonioni, that is, was casting his visionary eye on a fleeing expatriate in a film which is also casting a documentary eye on a reporter making a documentary. A different form of reflexivity is to be found in *Providence*. Resnais explores the symbiosis of text and image through the nocturnal story-telling of a dying alcoholic writer (played by John Gielgud). With a mostly British cast, fronted by Gielgud, Dirk Bogarde and David Warner, a French crew and Belgian, French and New England locations it was also a new kind of cinematic mix, with Mercer's screenplay one of the best since Greene's *The Third Man* and with Gielgud's author vaguely resembling Greene himself.

The argument of these two chapters is roughly the following: the expatriate eye sources a parallax view of British culture where it provides antithetical readings of image, action and motive within a single narrative. We cannot read the image in one specific way without being aware of an opposite reading that seems to contradict it. *The Parallax View* (1974) is of course the title of Alan Pakula's paranoia thriller, but there is a strong case for viewing the UK modernisms of the 1960s and 1970s as stronger versions of the parallax view than the genre thrillers of New American Cinema. British film modernism is often stronger and more daring. Moreover, it would be wrong to reduce the parallax view to an aesthetic of ambiguity since the term 'ambiguity' is itself ambiguous. What is at stake is more than the 'ambiguity' of specific motive or action. Thus Bordwell's 'poetics of ambiguity' through which he tries to read the rise of what he calls 'art-cinema narration' is, in this instance, not far-reaching enough (Bordwell 2008: 156–8). We have already seen elements of the parallax view in the trauma-film from *The Innocents* and *Peeping Tom*, but here it crystallises into a new form. In *Accident*, *Blow-Up*, *A Clockwork Orange* and *Moonlighting* we can have parallel readings of the same narrative. We can hold them in balance, or oscillate between one and the other, or on reviewings of the picture opt for reading A as opposed to reading B. Both, or all, readings make sense in their own terms. Something more is at stake than psychological or perceptual ambiguity, of action that may be enigmatic – for this anyway has often been a feature of classical narration. While the reflexive strategies we see in *Peeping Tom*, *Blow-Up* and *A Clockwork Orange* that call attention to the presence of the camera also feed into the parallax view, something more is at stake. What is *new* is the structural alternation in seeing. The parallax view is a kind of bipolar vision converging on the same image which allows viewers to 'see' a film equally strongly in one way then in another that seems diametrically opposed.

Later, when Boorman, Russell, Jarman and Davies revive romanticism through the modernist looking-glass, they are building on this transformation, but also displacing it through the organic vision of the romance. The parallax view is still strongly rooted in *Point Blank*, *If* and *Don't Look Now*, but after that among native directors it largely tails away. And in the self-conscious postmodern fables of Lindsay Anderson and Peter Greenaway it is replaced by knowing manipulation of narrative and addiction to pastiche. Because the power of the parallax view has been neglected, the modernist moment of UK cinema has also been undervalued. And it barely features in Bordwell's study of art cinema or Gilles Deleuze's meditations on the time-image. The following two chapters attempt to correct this imbalance and remind us of an undervalued moment in film history, that is, *global* film history. *The Servant* is our starting-point.

The exiled Losey was a Brecht enthusiast and darling of the critics at *Cahiers du Cinéma* and *Positif*. Yet his 1950s films remain overrated and you feel that Losey's baroque dynamism, which follows in Welles's footsteps, would have benefited from the latter's gift for writing his own scripts. Instead, Losey gives us maverick variations on the moral melodrama that sustained much of 1950s British cinema. *Time without Pity* has great acting from Alec McCowen and Ann Todd and compulsive spatial rhythms, but the dialogue is clichéd and histrionic, the plot contrived. Meanwhile Losey's camera seems to have a momentum of its own, a sparkling virtuosity that often bears little relation to the story he is obliged to tell. Even after he has seen early Antonioni and Resnais, influences that feed into his Italian *Eva* (1962), the problem persists. Here his camera (courtesy of Gianni Di Venanzo) wheels and pirouettes with amazing grace and he elicits bravura performances from Stanley Baker and Jeanne Moreau. But camera and drama seem to exist in different worlds. There is minimal fusion. His tortured Venetian fable of Eros and death in winter compares badly with *Don't Look Now*. But Losey moved on: after *Eva* his cinema was on the verge of something special. Thank God, then, for Harold Pinter. And in retrospect, Pinter might have said, 'Thank God for Losey'. And both might have said, 'Thank God for Dirk Bogarde'.

## LOSEY AND PINTER: THE MODERNIST MOMENT IN *THE SERVANT* AND *ACCIDENT*

Losey made his best films with Pinter, and Pinter wrote his best films for Losey. How did this come about? As Pinter became the UK's major playwright of the 1960s he simultaneously transposed the power of his dramatic writing to the big screen. After Losey's location-shoot on *Eva*, *The Servant* was an interior film, a black and white chamber picture unlike anything previously to hit the British screen. In *Accident* Losey opened out again to film in colour in Oxford, Chelsea in winter, followed by Oxford in summer. Pinter had started his first 'Servant' draft in 1961 from Robin Maugham's 1948 novella which Losey had long wanted to film. Four years later he repeated the process with Nicholas Mosley's modernist novel, *Accident*. In both cases he takes a first-person narrator from the printed page and eliminates his onscreen voice. In a way, this is purification through elimination of the subjective persona. In Maugham's novella the narrator is an intermediary; in Mosley's novel he is the central subject. In Pinter's screenplays the former vanishes while the latter has no overt voice. The playwright forges the groundwork for a cinematic objectivity, which Losey's camera enacts with scrupulous precision by shifting from subjective to objective mode. We cannot identify with the narrator's account of events as in Maugham's novella because there no longer is one, we can no longer see the events of *Accident* exclusively through the eyes of Oxford philosophy don Stephen Jervis (Dirk Bogarde) because his musings and Joycean free associations are all *disparu*. True we are guided by Stephen's flashback after the fatal accident and he remains the focus of the picture, with Bogarde in nearly every scene: but the film is a commentary on him as much as it is on anyone else. We are on the outside looking in and Losey's *mise-en-scène* keeps us there, clinically distanced, deprived of identification, unsure of our sympathies.

Both films then function as an objectivist cinema of intimacy, close in that respect to Polanski's *Knife in the Water*, Bergman's *The Silence* or Antonioni's *The Eclipse*, all released in 1962 just prior to *The Servant*. *The Servant* is closest to Bergman because it is so interior and claustrophobic, yet, unlike Bergman, shot with a sharp eye to time and place. Bergman's studio location is a filmic imaginary, an unknown city in Eastern Europe. Losey's is distinctly Royal Avenue, Chelsea in the early 1960s with recognisable exteriors. Yet both black and white films excel in the use of extreme deep focus and high-contrast photography to evoke communication breakdown and febrile intimacy. Both are about intimate power-struggles and eschew the melodramatic fix of empathy. If Losey is neo-Marxian in his shrewd eye for the nuances of the English class system, he and Pinter are Nietzschean in the effect their film generates. No one is deliberately maimed or murdered, but the struggle for power still triumphs over compassion and kindness. It does so within the bounds of outward civility, beneath the veneer of bourgeois civilisation which from the outside seems intact. Speech, body language, spatial positioning are all ludic, elements in a game-playing scenario with deadly consequences. Possession and territory are matters of mimetic rivalry where Pinter and Losey spin out narrative tension through set plays for advantage and where understatement is always the key.

The feeling for the spectator is one of a privileged intimacy coupled with an icy sense of removal. We are in rooms, gardens and bars together with Losey's subjects, observing at close quarters but there remains something inscrutable. Not much is given away: reserve, that standby of the English middle-class culture of constraint in mid-twentieth century, is a weapon in the armoury of power. In *The Servant* that is expanded by the dynamics of master–slave dependency: in *Accident* status is finely nuanced and of equal measure to class. In both cases a pattern of order is disrupted by an outsider, an intruder, Barrett the new butler in the London film, Anna the Austrian aristocrat (Jacqueline Sassard) in *Accident*. In their narrative pattern, the films significantly diverge. *The Servant* is linear, *Accident* cuts back and forth between time past and time present. Yet in feel and framing they are close. As Losey told Michel Ciment: '*Accident* is confinement – Oxford is enclosed, the colleges are enclosed, the rooms are enclosed, the lives are enclosed . . .' (Ciment 1985: 269). The tightness of space, the tightness of culture, the tightness of mind: yet in *The Servant* the order of things seems transformed while in *Accident* it is preserved.

In *The Servant* Losey's insistence on studio design, on the fluidity of interior space in Tony's Chelsea town house (done expertly here by Richard Macdonald), is crucial. Macdonald invented the spiral staircase that is the spine of the film: Douglas Slocombe's deep-focus lenses and gliding camera enlarge the tight spaces of rooms and corridors and enhance their presence in long takes where Losey and Macdonald use mirrors as reflective spaces offering convex distortion. The house too changes identity. The opening sequence, where Barrett (Bogarde) discovers Tony (James Fox) dozing in the sunroom after a liquid lunch, finds it empty and cold. After decoration when the newly appointed Barrett starts to exert his influence, it is painted and beautiful. During Barrett's return in the second part of the film, it is crumbling and distressed, and then for the reassertion of the *ménage a trois* and the final 'orgy' sequence it is garish, vulgar, expressionistically lit (Caute 1994: 10–11). Yet the built set with ceilings entailed that no tricks were done with high-angle lighting. The look remains largely naturalistic with key variations, and that is essential to the tenor of the film.

Losey integrates the very essence of power into the dynamics of cinematic space. This is evident early on in the staging of three back-to-back sequences soon after Barrett's 'sister' Vera (Sarah Miles) has joined the household. In the first Vera unexpectedly brings Tony his breakfast in bed instead of Barrett. There follows the kitchen scene where for the first time it becomes clear that Barrett and his 'sister' are lovers. The third is the hallway–bathroom sequence where Tony unexpectedly discovers Vera naked using his bathroom, complains bitterly to his servant, then leaves for the morning, whereupon Barrett in the same continuous shot joins his 'sister' for a bath in 'his Lordship's bathroom'. In all three sequences the long fluent take and depth of field are vital. In sequence one Losey demonstrates Tony's awakening desire for Vera. In sequence two, Vera enters the kitchen frame right while Barrett with his morning shopping enters it frame left. The empty space becomes a two-shot with Barrett slowly advancing towards Vera as she perches provocatively on the edge of the kitchen table. Losey then cuts to a hand-held POV shot as Barrett moves tight in on her reclining body. In sequence three a single fluent take reveals the depth of the servants' contempt for their 'master'. After Tony storms out, Barrett moves forward up the steps to enter the bathroom, the camera panning with him, then following him in. He opens a side-door to wait for the sound of Tony closing the front door before starting love-play with his 'sister'. Three (plus one) long consecutive takes like the rhythmic unpeeling of three layers of an onion. Cinematic space is territorial space and the servants have expropriated it from the master.

This 'expropriation' is echoed and reversed in the set-up that follows, when Tony finds Vera alone in the house late at night after Barrett has gone to visit his sick mother in Manchester. In a series of repetitions, Tony 'seduces' Vera, though we know by now it is the other way round and he unknowingly imitates Barrett in forcing her back on the kitchen table. After Barrett's return Tony sends him shopping, then adopts his servant's ear for the sound of the closing of the outside door before starting in on seduction – this time in his swivel chair whose back discreetly veils us from the spectre of cunnilingus. Later, in a brilliant of touch of dramatic irony, Susan, Tony's girlfriend (played by Wendy Craig), who visits when Tony is out, humiliating Barrett with a series of commands and insults, spoils her triumph by slumping into the very chair on which her unlikely rival has been seduced.

But Losey's *tour de force* is soon to follow. When Tony breaks short a social visit with Susan to take her home and consummate their relationship, they catch the servant couple *in flagrante delicto*. Losey is too intelligent to film a crass bedroom discovery but astute enough to film the whole sequence in a single fluid take. This is the first encounter between the two couples and stage one of the rich couple's humiliation – the second encounter will occur at the very end, revealing the core symmetry in a film of symmetries. The shot starts in the hallway as the rich couple enter and hear intimate voices off, having outside spotted the light in Tony's bedroom. The camera backtracks and pans left, turning into low-angle deep focus as Susan stands foreground left, and Tony behind and above her right, on the first step of the stair. In silhouette we see a huge shadow of a naked Barrett by the banister rail on the landing, a telling effect that Losey and Slocombe created by mounting an arc light on a rostrum above the stairwell (Caute 1994: 17). With Vera's alluring bedroom voice in the background, his shadow bisects the couple beneath, literally and metaphorically coming between them, as Tony turns away in humiliation and rests his head against the wall. Barrett's shadow above turns back and closes the bedroom door. 'What are you going to do?' Susan asks Tony. 'This is your house. They're in your room, in your bed.'

The camera pulls back without a cut and pans further left 180 degrees, opening up the living room with a low angle, coming to rest on the convex mirror on the far wall in which the face of the crestfallen Tony is now reflected and distorted. The aesthetic of the mirror image as an aesthetic of damaged identity, the money shot of the whole picture. In a last desperate gesture Tony rushes back to the stair and shouts for Barrett to come down before joining Susan by the mirror. Descending, Barrett's distant image enters the mirror between them, perfectly bisecting them – earlier his shadow and now his reflected image. Losey then cuts for the first time to a full-length reverse-angle of Barrett at the door. He calls for Vera to join them. When she does, Losey cuts back to the mirror shot. This time the servant couple's image bisects Tony and Susan – the usurpers who are their lower-class doubles. We know now they will have to leave and that the rich couple's delayed consummation will be delayed even further, if indeed it ever takes place at all. As if to establish continuity through space and time Losey audaciously opens up the second part of the film, the 'reunion' sequence, with another mirror shot in a local pub after time has elapsed and both men, it appears, are solitary. Barrett looks towards the camera as a distant Tony enters the pub behind him on the other side of the partition. He looks up towards the camera lens in recognition, that is, as if he has eyes in the back of his head. The camera then pans 180 degrees, establishing the establishing shot as a mirror reflection and replacing with the direct image first the reflection, then the image. It is a pure symmetrical inversion of the 180 degree pan in the living room from stairwell to mirror and from image to reflection – Alice through the looking

**Figure 6.1** The Townhouse as Goldfish Bowl: Dirk Bogarde, James Fox in *The Servant*

glass. The film retains on the retina a double-image of figure and reflection, so that the status of the image and the state of mind remain always elusive, Losey's unique contribution to the parallax view.

There is a backstory to the film's origin, literary and fascinating. Robin Maugham lived and wrote in the shadow of his famous uncle, Somerset, who was influential in more ways than one – hence the title of nephew's 1972 autobiography *Escape from the Shadows.* Although Robin claimed the characters in his post-war novella were composites, the intertwined sagas of his own and his uncle's life were indirectly evident. A literary source for the masochistic dependency of Tony on Barrett – far more powerful in the film than the nephew's fiction – is the long tortuous relationship in uncle's *Of Human Bondage* where the cultured hero (Philip Carey, a close version of Maugham himself) becomes infatuated with Mildred, a London waitress who discards him for her own dependency on a married salesman. A personal source for the novella, candidly revealed in *Among the Shadows*, was the impact of his uncle's bisexuality and their joint 'corruption' by uncle's American secretary-lover, Gerald Haxton who weaned Robin off Gillian (his London sweetheart) by offering him a handsome beach boy at Cap Ferrat. Nephew duly noted uncle's extreme dependency on Haxton who had also destroyed the writer's marriage to Syrie Wellcome and later helped him in the gathering of material for his stories, especially the 'Far Eastern Tales' (Maugham 1972: 84-105).

The feel of Losey's film echoes this oblique personal history. It also lies at the English intersection of tradition and modernity, restraint and transgression, power and decadence. This is Chelsea in the early 1960s, on the brink of consumer transformation, yet the accretions of upper-middle-class Englishness are still present in which sexual transgression is veiled, understated or simply unspoken. This is also post-colonial England in which entropy has set in among the privileged, Tony a figure of lassitude and ripe for the taking. His talk of coming back from Africa and heading out to Brazil with a grand design for a new city sounds like a caricature of past imperial ambition and boomed out in his patronising voice lacks all conviction. The point is moot. As well as clear homology between Pinter's modernist objectivism and the *nouveau roman* writers in France – Alain Robbe-Grillet, Robert Pinget and Michel Butor – in their predilection for the 'thing-ness of things', the shrewd, pitiless dissection of English mores we find in Pinter's Losey screenplays echoes those to be found in the later writings of Somerset Maugham. A spare, minimalist dissection of the vanity and judgement of the British in the Far Eastern colonies in Maugham's tales and in his Chinese novel *The Painted Veil* are brought home in the figure of Tony. For Maugham the colonies exposed the moral shortcomings of the colonisers: with few colonies, if any, to go to Tony's weaknesses are exposed back home, at the heart of the metropolis itself.

The 'orgy' sequence is much criticised for being too tame in the light of scenarios soon to follow in *Blow-Up*, *Performance* and *A Clockwork Orange*: yet it has an unheeded strength in its staging. For sure, Losey, fearing censorship, was just as reticent to display drugs as he was homosexuality, though Tony is clearly spaced out during his long humiliation. While Susan's impulsive pass at Barrett momentarily squares the circle to complete the effect of a promiscuous quartet, we should not overlook the long shot of Vera at the back of the room, a lush recessional shot where she combs her hair in front of a mirror in her dressing gown, an idle narcissist and amused observer of the developing scene. She is in her element, a house fixture in a *ménage à trois* that places Susan as the new outsider. Losey's mirror-shot clinches the new arrangement – so it matters not that no real orgy takes place.

And yet . . . it is still possible to argue otherwise. Downstairs in the hallway before she leaves, Susan suddenly slips the bracelet from her wrist and slashes it viciously across Barratt's face. He reacts with genuine shock, and then with barely suppressed desire. The echo of the earlier scene where she has humiliated Barrett suddenly reverberates. Contemptuous of his master's commands, he is nonetheless responsive to hers. The upstairs reading where Vera laughs at Tony's humiliation and smiles in the mirror at the reflected image of Susan and Barrett embracing is undermined by this late counter-riposte. It may be a parting shot that confesses failure or it may be the new tactic of a virtuous lady who has decided to become a Sadean woman. Will she reinvent her sexuality to reverse expropriation? Will she contest the territory by changing identity? You sense that she has found Barrett's weakness, but will she try to exploit it? The future is open and the film has no closure. We can see it as a class expropriation that triumphs or as an episode in continuing sex-class warfare where masters and servants alike use Nietzschean means to retaliate. The choice remains: Marx (exploitation, conflict, expropriation) or Nietzsche (will to power, mimicry, repetition) – this is the pitch of the film's parallax view that is both abstract and concrete at the same time, and there is no final resolution.

*Accident* maintains the theme of mimetic rivalry in *The Servant* but forsakes couple symbiosis for the asymmetry of multiple desires. The aristocratic Anna is not only an object of desire for the aristocratic William (Michael York), but also for their joint college tutor Stephen and celebrity don Charlie (Stanley Baker), writer and broadcaster. Anna and William are an obvious social match, Stephen and Charlie older married men with transgressing impulses, the latter more successful than the former. While part two of *The Servant* discreetly intimates the sexual attachment of Tony and Barrett, here mimetic rivalry is even more ambiguous. For Stephen as a conservative family man living in the Oxfordshire countryside, William and Charlie are both attractive for different reasons, handsome youth (a bisexual element in Bogarde's chameleon gaze) and media man, qualities he envies but knows he cannot possess. But they are also rivals who induce jealousy and contempt in equal measure, and as lovers of Anna, which Stephen is not, they are each other's rivals. *Accident* matches *The Servant* in the plotline of its cognitive frame. Stephen, Charlie and Anna are the knowing threesome, William the unknowing fourth, just as

Barrett, Vera and Susan are a knowing threesome and Tony the unknowing fourth. Tony and William are upper-class variations on the male cuckold, but while Tony is destroyed by sexual truth, William remains blithely unaware of Anna's fling with Charlie. Knowledge of it threatens Stephen instead – until he gains unlikely revenge.

Mimetic rivalry, though central, never becomes formulaic because it flourishes and diversifies with the rich texture of Losey's locations, Canterbury quad at St John's College, the grounds of Magdalene College for the punting scene along the Cherwell, the isolated Surrey location (posing as rural Oxfordshire) for Stephen's farmhouse, and the classical proportions of Syon House in London's Brentford for the aristocrats' brutal ballgame in the Grand Hall, where William and Stephen test each other's physical mettle (Reeves 2001: 10–11). Cinematographer Gerry Fisher, himself a country boy, delivered the look of a languid and timeless summer and shaded it, as Losey wished, with a pointillist, painterly feel. Losey extended this look sonically with his striking use of live sound, atmospherically recorded on telescopic rifle-microphones and long booms (Caute 1994: 190). Even the weather seems cinematic, a verdant summertime slowed down to bask in its reflected glory. Time stands still but not quite: stillness is a *trompe l'oeil* as things shift beneath surfaces and games are played – formally with the Syon House ball game and the college cricket match to which Losey cuts immediately after, or implicitly with the jousting at Sunday lunch and tea, the 'meeting' charade at the BBC or the punt along the river where Stephen takes his involuntary plunge.

Here Losey opts for subtle variation of pace, languid in the Oxford summer, a quickening of the pace as Stephen returns from London to find Charlie and Anna unexpectedly in one of the farmhouse bedrooms when his wife Anna (Vivien Merchant) is away at her sister's and expecting her next child. The London visit is Stephen's big chance to make it at the BBC. But is it? Bell, an ex-college producer (played by Pinter), gives the hapless don the bum's rush: by way of compensation Stephen visits the flat of Francesca, an old flame. There is an intimate meal at a nearby restaurant, followed by a discreet one-night stand. But does it actually happen? The clue may be in the selection of Delphine Seyrig for the part of Stephen's old flame since Losey had admired her in one of his favourite films of the moment, that most unreliable of time-narrations, Resnais's *Muriel* (1963). Here Losey keeps the camera at arm's length. Conversations are held in long shot at the restaurant they visit, filmed through a rain-flecked window from the street with voices off. In Francesca's flat Losey uses sharp segmental cuts, mismatching continuity, sometimes in singles, sometimes in two-shots so that time and space are in momentary disarray. With the casting of Seyrig it is clear that *Muriel* had inspired both homage and pastiche. Nothing in the *Muriel*-style montage of the reunion in the apartment could be so *unlike* the long fluid interiors that follow when Jervis returns to his Oxfordshire home.

Yet this abrupt change in style for the 'lovers' reunion', accompanied by the disembodied voices of Seyrig and Bogarde whose conversation is never rendered by lip-synch or facial expression, suggests something else. The tripartite sequence, flat–restaurant–bedroom, separates sound and image entirely and the tempo of Dankworth's music alters abruptly to evoke the earlier, more dissonant soundtrack on Resnais's film. Is the extended sequence all in Stephen's mind, a wishful reunion and imaginary resurrection of the past? Or does it actually happen? When he goes back to Oxford he informs the absent-minded college provost of the 'visit' to his daughter. But that does not mean it actually took place. We are left in doubt. We can read the sequence, which ends with a high-angle shot of the couple lying side by side in bed, *either way* – as wish-dream or actuality. It is an embodiment of the modernist parallax. As Resnais has shown us, and Losey knows that Resnais has shown us, the ontology of the image is never decisive. Without violating its naturalistic frame, Losey makes the disembodiment of the lovers' voices a convention of remembering. But aren't the actions taking place in time present? After all, he gets home late at night. When then does he *have time* to remember before he opens the front door to find Charlie in *his* house wearing *his* dressing gown? The style of the love-sequence suggests time remembered more than it does time unfolding – time past, not time present. A memory-sequence flashbacked through the car journey home would be the obvious device. But Losey does not use it, and so like Resnais in all of *Muriel* he begs the question of certainty about the nature of time, memory and truth in this one extended sequence where he is paying homage to the French director. With his discovery of Charlie and Anna we are on more certain ground. His house has been used for a steamy assignation that he treats at first with contempt. But is there a hint of jealousy too? Whereas Mosley's first-person narrative allows us to read Stephen's thinking and moral anxieties explicitly, Losey–Pinter withhold the motivation to enhance suspense. His contempt could come from thinking he has just slept with a beautiful, sophisticated woman and not a crass college girl. But the tension he feels could *equally* have come from juxtaposing an adulterous fantasy against the actuality of his rival's affair with a younger woman they both desire.

In the omelette sequence, a virtuoso single take that starts with Bogarde cracking the eggshells by the cooker and ends with the loaded conversation at the kitchen table, the suspense of double-reading is sustained. This scene in the novel is fraught with Stephen's moral anxiety, but here morality is eliminated: the sequence follows the parallel lines of contempt (for the couple's rank sexual opportunism) and mimetic desire (a wish on Stephen's part to be as boldly opportunistic as they are). Bogarde's talk and body-language can be read both ways and neither violates context or staging. Stephen can be the put-upon don with 'ordinary' faults and temptations who still embodies the conscience of us all, especially since we cannot really identify with anyone else. Or he can be seen as just as ruthless but playing the longer game and who finally possesses the girl through blackmail after the accident when his rich student-rival is now dead and his lusting writer-rival has already been dumped by the conniving Anna. Convenient too, that his pregnant wife is elsewhere delivering their child. Thus Stephen can be read as the residual force of a besieged English liberalism, a man of conscience in a purely game-playing amoral world: or he can be seen as a man of no conscience at all, playing the game better than anyone else because he is so adept at hiding the fact that he is doing so. It is possible to view the film as a consistent artwork by adopting either of these antithetical readings. The choice between them is not so much Marx versus Nietzsche as Nietzsche versus John Stuart Mill. But still they are worlds apart and the spectator has to choose.

## CODA: *PROVIDENCE* AS RESNAIS'S RIPOSTE TO LOSEY

Just as Losey in his French period took screenwriter Jorge Semprun and actor Yves Montand from Resnais's *La Guerre est finie* for his 1978 film *Les Routes du sud*, so a year earlier Resnais had taken Mercer and Bogarde from the Losey file for *Providence.* In the 1970s Mercer had adapted *A Doll's House* for Losey, then worked with him on Patrick White's *Voss.* A further Mercer link lies in the casting of David Warner as Bogarde's brother Kevin since the character bears similarities with Warner's version of Morgan in the 1967 film which Mercer had scripted for Karel Reisz, *Morgan: a Suitable Case for Treatment.* But the real connection lies in making the case for *Providence* as the unofficial finale of the Losey–Pinter trilogy, the film they failed to make, as opposed to *The Go-Between*, the one they unfortunately did. Having deconstructed English class divisions with a distilled ferocity, Pinter and Losey sadly succumbed to the aura of the Edwardian aristocracy in their version of L.P. Hartley's novel. Viewed now, it is a sad travesty of their previous work – which makes the case for *Providence*, Resnais's first English language feature as the 'last' of the trilogy, all the more enticing.

Here Resnais almost deliberately and amusingly seems to replicate the Francesca effect in particular, which of course echoes *Last Year in Marienbad* (1961). Did it or didn't it happen? While Clive's nocturnal story (the writer seriously ill and drinking heavily to dull the pain) could be read either as stylised flashback and character-assassination of son Claude (Bogarde) persecuting son Kevin (reminiscence), or as virtual flash-forward (a fictional near-future nightmare in a police state), the sudden switch to 'time present' at the end of the film poses further questions. On one reading it clarifies Clive's nocturnal ramblings as a fictionally disguised account of the real family – perfectly normal and loving – who turn up to celebrate Clive's birthday the following day. The birthday party 'reality', the French country house, verdant lawns, the bright spring sunshine, the naturalistic acting and staging, the match-cuts and continuity – all contradict the deranged (though highly amusing) night-time vision. For the audience it is both revelation and reassurance. Yet Bersani and Dutoit have contended that Resnais subverts the 'natural' ending by making it just as artificial with its postcard beauty, its trees in bloom, its adoring circular camera, as the dystopian nightmare which had preceded it (Bersani and Dutoit 1993: 202). Might it not just be the instant daydream on the verge of death that follows the long nightmare of dying in the writer's final moments? There is no answer, no closure, and we, the audience, have to make up our own minds. Is Resnais offering through Gielgud's virtuoso performance a genuine compassionate reassurance? Or is he still playing with our uncertainty?

## ANTONIONI'S PARALLAX VIEW: *BLOW-UP* AND *THE PASSENGER*

*Blow-Up* offers us two ways of seeing anything and everything. A young fashion photographer Thomas (David Hemmings) thinks his snapshots of a couple in a South London park may show evidence of a murder. The film offers no conclusion to the mystery. There are good reasons for thinking that he has witnessed a killing and equally good reasons for thinking that he hasn't. And what sort of a photographer is the young arrogant Thomas, driving round London in a state-of-the-art Rolls Royce convertible? On one view, he is a top fashion photographer with a vanity sideline in photo-realism. On another he is the opposite: a suppressed photo-realist selling his soul to the consumerist devil in his smart, photo-shoot studio. He is a cocky hedonist who has risen without trace, or a working-class boy still troubled by the material world. How we see him, and how we see the film's mystery, is our choice. Antonioni in various interviews has intimated what he thinks but the achieved impersonality of his art always puts the onus back on us. And it makes us vaguely uneasy, as if we ourselves are part of the mystery that cannot be solved.

Identification is always unsettling in this picture – the casual cynicism of the photographer and his childlike drift towards distraction both draw us back. Yet the momentum of his investigation also carries us forward and makes us part of it. We may not particularly like him but we want him to succeed, to resolve the mystery of the incident in the park since it not only challenges his powers of perception, it challenges ours too. The visual aspect of the mystery in the film will never date because our audio-visual world has intensified in the forty years since this film was made. Technology now offers us a veritable feast of instant images, still or moving. Anything from the Abraham Zapruder recording of the Kennedy assassination to CCTV and cell-phone images of possible crime perpetrators have broadened the field of visual evidence and also raised in its wake a variety of new questions. As a cult film of its time *Blow-Up* now seems to lie at the very origin of all this, a cine-feature of uncanny prescience. The Zapruder recording may have preceded it by a few years but the endless re-viewing of that home movie footage on TV programmes that followed it, debating the assassination and finally spliced into Oliver Stone's sprawling paranoia epic *JFK* (1991), suggests something else. Through the medium of conspiracy theory, life appears to imitate art. After all *Blow-Up* has a blow-up of what appears to be the arm, face and gun of a gunman on a grassy knoll in a city park, about to pull the trigger on an unsuspecting victim, just as endless blow-ups from Zapruder's film and other photographic evidence sought the same, long after *Blow-Up* from the grassy knoll in Dallas opposite the president's cavalcade. In this copious conspiracy file no credible image of a second assassin has yet appeared after forty years: but in *Blow-Up* we do have one brief and indisputable shot in *one* of the photographer's blow-ups of an armed man pointing a gun out of the park bushes. It appears to offer clinching evidence of a killing in Antonioni's unassuming park, especially when another blow-up indicates the face and torso of a horizontal body at the foot of a tree. Yet at this point of frenzied visual detection in the studio we still have no final evidence that suggests the image is 'real'. We do not know whether we should take it as an objective fact, or whether it is a figment of Thomas's fevered imagination. Is it an 'objective' or a 'POV' shot? And what for that matter is an 'objective shot' or a 'POV' shot anyway? Antonioni never returns his camera to the same shot: none of Thomas's acquaintances ever see it. And if we believe naively that 'seeing is believing', then we really are in deep trouble. A typical style-trope of the maestro clinches the argument for the shifting sands of subjectivity. At night in the park when Thomas has discovered the corpse, the camera rests for what seems an eternity on the face and torso of the dead man. That stillness seems to seal the subjective shot, but then, at the last moment Antonioni pans away to show us Thomas watching at the side of the tree and now we are looking at *him*. It was not his POV shot after all. It is seen from our point of view, the audience. The subjective shot is objectified without a cut. The problem of what is seen segues into the problematic of who sees what.

Antonioni had upped the ante for his mystery by using bona fide photo-realism in the still images for his picture. Photographer Don McCullin took the remarkable photographs of the figures in the hostel for the homeless that Thomas shows his agent – they remain part of McCullin's life-long portfolio. He also took photographs (and blow-ups) which belong exclusively to the film, stills of the couple (played by Vanessa Redgrave and Ronan O'Casey) on the Saturday morning in the park where Thomas, attracted by the quality of the light after his visit to the antiques shop, stumbles on them by chance. In his autobiography McCullin also noted that the park (Maryon Park in south-east London) which appears to some critics to be 'natural' after the 'artifice' of the fashion shoot in the studio, was an invention of the director, made over quite specifically with painted grass and paths, its background framed by specially constructed neon signs and apartment façades (McCullin 1992: 87–8). The park on this reading is as unreal as the studio, which was a composite of two actual Holland Park locations, the studio interior being the working studio of John Cowans (Reeves 2001: 62–3). On this reckoning the park is no more or less made over than the studio interior. Both are real and reinvented at the same time.

Another double reading floats into view. Might *Blow-Up* not be as much a ghost story as *The Innocents* or *Don't Look Now*? Take the dishevelled figure of Hemmings we see emerging from the doss-house early in the morning with his fellow inmates. Should we take him at face value as he and they trudge sullenly away, barely talking on a street of industrial warehouses and crumbling wasteland? But then we don't know where to place this sequence as it is intercut with another one, of students in fancy-dress and white-face shouting and gesturing from the back of the van as it drives through central London streets framed by modern plate-glass buildings. We guess they are part of a student charities event, but since this is parallel cutting, which sequence (and group) merits our attention more? Cheery, boisterous students or sullen, silent homeless? The issue is decided when Hemmings furtively breaks away from the group of older men and sneaks along to a parked Rolls-Royce once they are out of sight. He gets in and drives away and this, we sense, will be the core of the film. The students of course will end up in the film twenty-fours later when they perform a mimed tennis match (no balls or rackets) on the court in the park where Hemmings has just failed to find the corpse that had been lying under a tree there the previous night. Separate fates are thus conjoined.

Yet this last scene is also the point at which the photographer himself disappears from the film. In the penultimate shot he is seen from a distant high angle, a human speck on a canvas of green park grass. A jump-cut to the final shot of the film removes him entirely. All we have is a grass landscape, depopulated. Thomas has disappeared from the face of the screen. In retrospect this disappearing act prompts us to further speculation about the film's opening. Is Thomas the photographer a virtual figure dreamed up by the young vagrant who leaves the doss-house in the first sequence? After all, half the people he sees in the tight time-span of 24 hours between Saturday morning and Sunday morning are dressed in white-face – the student mime artists, the fashion models, the audience in the rhythm and blues club, the girls at the party where he seeks out his agent. Are they all zombies . . . or ghosts? Is the gleaming white convertible parked by a warehouse the wish-dream of a young working-class guy down on his luck? And the smart dark blazer and white jeans into which he changes at the studio from his soiled and crumpled clothes the Mod dream of a 1960s *arriviste*? Is he just a dreaming loser who knows there is a new world he is missing out on?

This narrative book-ending of invention and extinction, the rise and fall of the virtual photographer, poses questions that it does not resolve. But, so then, does the whole film. Antonioni in effect creates a multi-parallax. Parallaxes overlap and fold in and out of one another. We assume that Thomas is genuine and that he disguises his identity to get into the doss-house. We assume later that he has inadvertently witnessed a killing in the park, which explains why a nervous Vanessa Redgrave is anxious to reclaim his roll of film and offers her body as a trade-off. His discovery of the corpse of her male companion, late at night in the park (another pale-faced ghost) seems to confirm the blow-up he has produced in his studio. The ransacking of his studio, the stealing of his prints and film stock while he is in the park, seem to confirm the desperation of those wishing to destroy all the evidence. But the disappearance of the corpse the next day with no crime scene in sight suggests the opposite: this has been a figment of his imagination all along. The blow-up of the man with the gun may well be an illusion that emerges out of the abstract pattern of dots on a flat surface, just like the canvases of the painter next door. When he starts to hear the sound of imaginary balls striking imaginary rackets in the students' mimed match on the tennis court in the park, he begins to doubt the evidence of his senses altogether. Moreover the division between the studio and the park, which some have taken as evidence of a genuine split between artifice and reality, culture and nature, is also a *trompe l'oeil.* The park, as we have said, was reinvented by the director, spruced up and made artificial with its painted paths, grass and tree trunks. The fashion studio was just as real but is similarly redesigned for the film. We want to believe the park is a natural 'outside' and the studio an artificial 'inside', but instead we have a uniformly phantasmagoric city inside and outside – an image-cameo of phantasmagoric modernity.

Make no mistake: the image in *Blow-Up* is always tactile. The locations existed there and most, including the park, still do. This is and was 1960s London. Yet the indelible real is at the same time ghostly and surreal, so that practically every image seems to operate on two levels, belonging to a surface world and a subterranean world at the same time. Given this is a mystery of

**Figure 6.2** Thomas the Vagrant: David Hemmings in *Blow-Up*

**Figure 6.3** Thomas the Magnifier: David Hemmings in *Blow-Up*

displaced meanings, Antonioni also sources the notion of displaced meaning ironically in the fine detail of the life-world. When Thomas buys the propeller from the antiques shop and has it delivered to his fashion studio, what looks in place as a lost plane part amidst a sea of junk looks totally out of place at his studio. Likewise the guitar fragment trashed by Jeff Beck in the R&B club that Thomas grabs when it is tossed into the audience has a transient iconic value. In the street outside it is reduced to a visual gag. Thomas, having escaped with it from a pursuing crowd, then looks at it blankly and tosses it into the gutter. The film replays the gesture after he leaves. A passer-by picks it up, looks equally blank, then tosses it back again. A fragment of Beck's guitar is, out of context and like the propeller, simply a piece of junk. The vagaries of sound suffer the same fate, haunted by uncanny absences. Thomas blasts his car horn in the deserted alley outside his studio and elicits no response. When he revisits the park at night, the only sound is that of the wind rustling the tree branches: no footsteps, no voices, no traffic nearby. At the R&B club a still and silent audience listen to the Yardbirds blasting out on faulty sound equipment, bursting into sudden life only with the guitar trashing. At the drugs party where Thomas tells Ron his agent about the corpse in the park, there is uncannily no music playing at all, only the live acoustics of floating voices, offscreen laughter and creaking floorboards. Particular sounds become conspicuous by their absence or, as in the case of the mimed tennis match, uncanny by their unexpected presence.

The deframing of the image complements the decentring of sound. Antonioni, valued in his Italian films for his adventurous use of the long take and the sequence-shot, develops here a style of jagged and angular cutting, especially in the studio sequences in which, however, depth of field and fluent camera movement are still retained. With its layered framing of objects – chairs, gauzes, screens, sloping roof beams to the fore and its placing of characters in middle distance, framing objects in front of and beyond the same time – Antonioni uses decentred reverse-angles in editing, often a slight mismatch or displaced eye-line cut, to stall easy familiarity. Moreover the plan of the studio-cum-apartment on two floors (groundfloor plus mezzanine) gives the interior space a labyrinthine quality where the relationship of rooms, and entrances and exits, become visually elusive. The editing exhibits and echoes the open-plan single-space virtuosity of Hitchcock's *Dial M for Murder*. but if anything, it is even richer and more complex. If we are perceptually puzzled by the mystery in the park and Thomas's photographic reconstruction of it, we are spatially disoriented by the studio in which the reconstruction takes place. The flat itself changes identity as well, fashion studio in the morning, editing studio in the afternoon, as the action shifts from ground to first floor. The fashion shoots are noise-events, Hancock's music accompanies Redgrave's visit, and the orgy is a sensory feast of rolling bodies crumpled backdrops, shouts and screams. But as Thomas 'edits' his film, silence prevails.

The photographic act made cinematic is itself chopped up and made tripartite. We see the prints of the shots that Thomas has taken in the doss-house but not his act of taking them. How did he manage to conceal who he was? We see the prolonged fashion shoots, first the close-in tangle with the model Verushka, then the multiple shoot where tempers fray. But we never see the results. First prints with no shoot, then shoots with no prints. Finally, we see both with photos from the park, the act of shooting and the act of printing – and finally of a kind of editing that tries to create a narrative out of still frames. But here the absences, the ellipses, are just as vital. What happened in the park between shots? Thomas, like us, must look at his washing line set of prints for key connections and make eye-line matches with his pointing fingers, knowing there are key absences. The two blow-ups of the arm with the pointing gun and the corpse's torso behind the tree should clinch it. Psychologically at this point we demand resolution, but this is *Blow-Up*, this is Antonioni, and none is given us.

## WHAT'S IN A TITLE? *THE PASSENGER* OR *PROFESSION: REPORTER*

This was a film with two titles and two released versions, the Anglophone *Passenger* and the European *Profession: Reporter.* Antonioni's failure to persuade MGM to release his own preferred cut for the Anglophone version helped create the division. Antonioni's cut, seven minutes longer, was released in Europe with the Italian title. (It is now available in the Sony Pictures 2006 DVD English language version with the English title.) But the titles are not even synonyms: if anything they are opposites. One refers to the TV reporter David Locke (played by Jack Nicholson), the film's central figure. The other refers to the Girl with No Name (played by Maria Schneider), who joins him late on in Barcelona and becomes the 'passenger' in the white Oldsmobile convertible with red trim which carries them from Catalonia to southern Spain. One title directs us to the main man, the other to the supporting actress. In the course of the film the former becomes a known quantity, while the latter remains a mystery. Do we thus focus on what Antonioni saw as the 'documentary' he was making about a fictional maker of documentaries? 'I tried to look at Locke the way that Locke looks at reality,' he claimed (Antonioni 2007: 342). Or does 'The Passenger' draw us to the figure of the Girl beside him in the car about whom we know nothing beyond her claim that she is an architecture student travelling around Europe? The answer is probably both at the same time. But from this very division of titles there arises all at once the germ of a parallax view.

The film is elusive in every way. Classified as American because of its MGM production and its starring role for Nicholson, it does not have one American-born character or New World setting in its story: its reporter's job and home are in London. If we take it as British, then why does it have an Italian director, a French female lead and a preference for European locations? But if we take it as European, what about the opening sequences in North Africa and the African documentary sequences thereafter? The film is everywhere at the same time. Like *Lawrence of Arabia* the virtuoso logistics of its multiple location shoot would be impossible in the twenty-first century. If it eludes national identity as a transnational film so its main characters elude our conventions of personal identity This is a love story between a man with someone else's name and a woman with no name and it may not be a love story at all, but a honey-trap setting up an assassination. Or it may not. Or it may be a film about love *and* betrayal. It may well be the existential love affair of a couple on the run it appears to be, and it may be that paranoid viewers – like the author – are paranoid in thinking otherwise. There is no closure and no answer. The film can be viewed either way with perfect consistency. The real subject of the film can either be the reporter of the European title or the passenger of the Anglophone title. Or there may be a cunning trade-off between actual and metaphorical meaning. We assume the Girl is there just for the ride because it enhances her sense of adventure. But since she seems to be driving Locke's destiny in Spain by prompting him to keep all the high-risk appointments in Robertson's diary, she may well be in the 'driving seat' and Locke the 'passenger' borne towards his own fate. Who knows? Well, critics are supposed to. But who really knows?

The film can be read quite consistently either way. But this means there is no division between surface account (political chronicle with existential love affair) and deep account (a study in betrayal). And there is no division in Antonioni's phenomenology of the life-world between 'surface' and 'depth'. In his vision the life-world itself is a mystery. *The Passenger*'s narrative logic allows for bipolar responses to that mystery which prompt us to reflect in turn on the limits of human thought, on how fragile our knowledge actually is, on how little we truly know. The world may perplex us but at least in reading movies we can be omniscient, or so the illusion goes. But we are not omniscient even in a cinema, we are nowhere near and it's no use asking the director because he doesn't have the answers either. In his various interviews, Antonioni seems to opt for the existential love affair and the unlimited freedoms it appears to offer Locke and the Girl. That is reassuring. But he is just interpreting the film like anyone else: the test of his artwork lies at the level of impersonal creation and this can make us feel very small, which is one reason why viewers often steer clear of his films. In watching this film we can only alternate between the horrors of the void (knowing absolutely nothing) and the parallax view (two contradictory versions of the same set of events). And then there are the cross-over speculations. If the Girl betrays him, does she not also love him at the same time, more in fact than he loves her? Is she not both angel and demon?

If Locke, in trading his identity as TV reporter for the dead Robertson's life as a gunrunner to African rebels, is accepting risk as part of the freedom of a false identity, is he also accepting that he will meet the same fate as his double, whose passport, likeness and profession he assumes. (As a reporter Locke in the opening desert sequence abjectly fails to make contact with the rebels who are the subject of his assignment. Later he realises that Robertson has already done so.) This is a film of endless duality and repetition in which destiny repeats itself just as cinematic staging repeats itself. Robertson dies mysteriously on a hotel bed in Chad; Locke as Robertson dies mysteriously on a hotel bed in Andalusia. The interior décor and design of both buildings, studio sets designed by Piero Poletto, curiously resemble each other – including the door panelling. The Girl he sees on a seat in the lobby of Gaudi's Palais Guell in Barcelona is the same Girl we saw earlier sitting on a public bench in London's Bloomsbury. She tells him later she is an architecture student so that she could well be researching at the British Museum and then travelling to Barcelona to study Gaudi's many buildings in the city. But then again she could be following Locke in conjunction with the secret agents of the African government who may already have assassinated Robertson in his hotel (did he really have a weak heart?) and have certainly kidnapped Achebe, the gunrunner's contact in Barcelona, who fails to show up for Locke's appointment in the Umbraculo.

Another approach to the film is to view it as a perfect hybrid of trauma-fugitive narratives. Locke's epiphany in the desert, reminiscent in tone and atmosphere of some of Albert Camus's North African stories (Orr 2007: 54–62), is a moment of nightmare under the desert sun in which Nicholson, marooned beside his broken Land Rover, slumps against a wheel, spreads his arms crucifix-style and yells 'I don't care! I don't care!' But he does. This is a moment of pure desert trauma, framed naturalistically against a deep-blue sky and sun-bleached sand. Antonioni has built up to it, as Chatman notes, through a series of spatial deframings in which the reporter's eye, like ours, is disoriented by the shifting relations of people and landscape in a terrain without landmarks (Chatman 1985: 198–9). Locke is led up a rocky outcrop by a mysterious guide who then deserts him at the sight of a distant police patrol in the valley below. Deserted in the desert and then on his return marooned in the soft desert sand. Back at the hotel, Locke's resolution of trauma is the switch in identities, wrongly seen by some critics as unmotivated. It is an over-coming through metamorphosis done with a still and steely calm, with a quiet desperation, creating a shield against despair. The freedom to move again as someone else seems to triumph, symbolically, in the cable car above Barcelona harbour where Nicholson leans out of the window into the open sky and mimics with his arms the action of a bird's wings. But to fly is also to take flight. Flying can not only be flying *towards* but also flying *from.* And before long Locke is in flight with the Girl, as his London colleague Martin Knight (Ian Hendry) catches up with him at his Barcelona hotel. Later, when his estranged wife, Rachel (Jenny Runacre), fears her trip to the Chadian embassy to reveal his true identity may have put in his life in danger, her arrival in southern Spain becomes the second instalment of the search and of the flight. The film repeats the motif of the hotel near-miss. This time the police are firmly on his track too and Locke has become a fugitive from those trying to warn him, the freedom of the open journey rapidly closing down on the dusty roads of Andalusia.

Much of the film was shot in the semi-desert terrain of Almeria, acting as a surrogate for many of the Andalusian and African sequences (the other Chad sequences were shot at Fort Polignac in southern Algeria). Its terrain stresses the crossover between southern Spain and North Africa, as does the Moorish architecture of the Seville hotel where Locke flees from Rachel. After the cool cloudy light of London and its muted colours, Locke gravitates to the original colours of the trauma imprint – deep blues and blinding yellows – on the walls of the room and the look of landscapes and also in the colour of clothes – the blue of the denim shirt he inherits from Robertson, the lemon-coloured bathrobe of the Girl at her most alluring. The arrow of escape becomes the arc of return as Locke plans to leaves the Girl and return alone to North Africa. But he is stranded in its Spanish simulacrum and to paraphrase the closing line of T. S. Eliot's 'East Coker', in his end is his beginning. His fate in the desert is repeated in the dusty town of Osuna in a hotel opposite the piazza outside a disused bullring where Antonioni's famous sequence-shot echoes the spatial deframings of the failed encounter with the rebels.

Let us reconsider that shot in which the camera moves from Locke's hotel room into the square outside and then turns 180 degrees to point back through the barred windows at his inert body discovered by his estranged spouse, his current lover, the police and the hotelier. It was a late afternoon shot and Antonioni says he was inspired by Ernest Hemingway's atmospheric story 'Death in the Afternoon' (Antonioni 2007: 338). In a bullfight we know the bull will die, but in Hemingway's story the matador dies too. The latter has a very good chance of surviving, the animal none at all. The bullring is an arena of death and you sense in this sequence that Locke's death is just as inevitable. What has started in freedom ends up in necessity. Antonioni preserves the paradox to the last – as sonic and optical image. This is a virtuoso seven-minute shot untrammelled by a cut, with the ingenious freedom of a gyroscopic camera running on wires: but what it finds as it explores the space in front it loses through the image it has left behind. Here the camera replicates a human dilemma – it does not have eyes in the back of its head. It does, however, continue to hear what it cannot see, out of frame. And yet with its fixed frame it still has an enclosed vision. The shot plays on the reverberations of offscreen space and offscreen sound. In a way it is also a virtual shot – what Locke might have seen if, like a bird, he could take flight and soar back to his starting point. The camera starts out as a virtual POV, but then becomes a disembodied POV which breaks through the barred window with the freedom to see, but still fails to 'see' with its rectangular frame the things that determine the fate of Locke himself.

*The Passenger* shares with *Don't Look Now* the double-chase climax that portends disaster. But while Roeg's film revisits its primal trauma, Antonioni's is now beyond trauma altogether, poised at the crossroads of existential risk and tragic necessity where fear of death has no dominion. At the end we could posit more clearly the contrast between the two women in Locke's life: Rachel, who now views him clinically as documentary subject '(I never knew him'), and the Girl, who claims she did know him. The irony is that the clinical and distant Rachel, who still has a morbid fascination with Locke's career and its limitations, tries to warn him of danger, while the Girl who is in love with him may have goaded him on to his final destination – death. But then maybe Locke knows he will die and wants to anyway. Part of their love may be exactly that – the romantic death-wish that Antonioni fractures through the parallax view. She may collude in his death, but then so does he.

## CODA: THE NATIVE EYE IN *RADIO ON*

While *Blow-Up*'s ocular power is clearly an influence on Greenaway's costume pastiche *The Draughtsman's Contract* (1982) and lies as a forerunner to the enigmatic feature documentaries of Patrick Keiller, both his British films are an inspiration to Chris Petit's unique, low-budget road movie, *Radio On*. In truth, Petit's native eye is bringing *The Passenger* back home while extending *Blow-Up*'s topographic mystery to all of southern England as it moves west out of the capital and ends up in Weston-super-Mare. Petit started filming under the conscious influence of New German Cinema and, as we have seen, his film also mimics the motion, the look and the mood of a Wenders' road movie: yet its native riposte to Antonioni is perhaps its most fascinating aspect and one that in the modernist idiom cannot be overlooked. The feature starts with a grimy Steadicam stair shot (natural lighting only), which spies a corpse in the bath of a grimy Bristol apartment only to pass on into the other rooms. But whose POV is it? Just anyone's? The director himself, perhaps, who seems as much interested in the motion of the camera through the cramped spaces of the flat as in the corpse it fleetingly captures? We never know.

We detect in the film's opening the story of a third corpse; after the corpse in the park in *Blow-Up* and the corpse on the bed in *The Passenger*, the corpse in the bath in *Radio On.* How this body, the protagonist's brother, ends up a corpse is also a mystery. Accident? Murder? Natural causes? Robert B. (David Beames), the diffident London-based sibling, embarks on a mission to the West Country to find out. Only it isn't a mission at all and he isn't really interested in finding out. It's an excuse for a Boston haircut, a trip in a clapped-out Rover and music cassettes on the car radio; an excuse for David Bowie, Kraftwerk and Ian Dury, for flyovers and hitchhikers, pin tables and jukeboxes in roadside pubs. The journey is everything, the goal nothing.

In this it has a fleeting resemblance to Wender's *Kings of the Road* (1976). Indeed, homage is directly paid. In Wender's lorry cab, driver and passenger sing along at one point to Heinz's *Just like Eddie*, in turn a homage to Eddie Cochrane. At a deserted petrol station in *Radio On,* near the site of Cochrane's fatal car accident, Beames meets Sting as a caravan nomad with a guitar who gives us a rendition of Cochrane's 'Three Steps to Heaven'. In giving this nod to Cochrane *and* to *New German Cinema*, Petit does a reflexive 360 degree turn and pays homage to the act of paying homage. The main hitchhiker interest on the trip is provided by a Scottish squaddie (Andrew Byatt) who has deserted after a gruelling tour of Northern Ireland that has clearly unhinged him. But this is not the male front seat bonding of Wenders. As the hiker's story gets more unhinged, Beames takes the opportunity to dump him without pity by the roadside. We sense that Petit is striving here for a pure cinema of disconnection. If *Blow-Up* was the city version, this is the cross-country version. DJ by trade, his young bourgeois misanthrope is averse to human contact, especially that of women. As Petit pushes for zero degree motivation and nil plot resolution, he provides us involuntarily with a sociopath at large, foreshadowing the articulate sociopath that Mike Leigh will give us in his inspired and apocalyptic *Naked.* But unlike David Thewlis in that dark fable, Beames is largely taciturn in this one – specialising in the occasional three-word sentence. The constraint has the awkwardness we recognise in the earlier middle-class heroes of Lean and Powell, but here there is something icy and cold, a post-romantic purgatory of the soul. Like Antonioni's photographer, Petit's DJ seems to meet everyone but is connected to no one, looking only for casual encounters with no repercussion or repetition. For him the end of the world is the edge of a vast, dirt-black quarry near Weston, where the sun does not shine and where his car finally claps out. This is a film we could say which has nothing to offer to anyone – which is why it remains endlessly fascinating.

CHAPTER 7

# *Expatriate eye 2: Stanley Kubrick and Jerzy Skolimowski*

On the face of it Kubrick and Skolimowski are like day and night. The American director had settled in England to film big pictures that revolutionised the genre and indeed cinema itself. He had easy relations with the chief studio executives of MGM and Warner Bros and a large country home in rural Hertfordshire from which he ran pre- and post-production on his projects with the special luxury of the final cut. Located in London, the self-exiled Skolimowski tended to live from hand to mouth, was nomadic like Polanski, and chased money and producers everywhere for independent, on-the-hoof projects. Kubrick took popular genre into new dimensions: at times Skolimowski seemed like a one-man Anglo-Polish option to the *nouvelle vague*. Yet both were to the 1970s what Antonioni, Losey and Polanski had been to the 1960s in UK cinema: visionaries with an expatriate eye who got under the skin of the indigenous culture and its many complexities. In addition, they were both masters of the film fable, more effective than Anderson after *If*, more urgent and alive than Greenaway in the 1980s. In 1968 Kubrick was able to use the expertise of British film technicians at Elstree Studios for his great science-fiction masterpiece, *2001: a Space Odyssey*, a futuristic epic that puts everything else in the genre into the shade. He followed it with his only two films that dealt precisely with the past, present and future of his host country, *A Clockwork Orange* for the world of the present and the future, *Barry Lyndon* for the world of the eighteenth century. The former is specifically English and shot in London and Hertfordshire locations: the latter is both Irish and British, shot on location in both countries and arguably the most powerful cinematic vision of their long, troubled relationship, With this scale of ambition Skolimowski and his makeshift 'poor cinema' could never hope to compete, and never wanted to. As we shall see, his value lies elsewhere. While Kubrick and Skolimowski are at opposite ends of the modernist spectrum, they both play a crucial part in the evolution of British cinema.

In the relativistic world of artistic modernism it is surprising that what drives Kubrick much of the time is something absolute: the existence in human affairs of Original Evil. In *2001* it is present at the dawn of human life in the predations of our simian ancestors (in which the more humanoid prey on the more simian) and, after a virtuoso jump-cut to time future in outer space, Kubrick charts the advent of the computer machine HAL, which absorbs evil from the organic human body into the techno-world on which that body is now so dependent. (Indeed, the primal aporia in this extraordinary film is the history of the human race to date – posted missing.) There is no Catholic residue in the Jewish-American Kubrick which would allow us to short-circuit this absolute vision by speaking of 'Original Sin': in *A Clockwork Orange* there is no Enlightenment critique of modern 'society'. Kubrick, who never realised his Holocaust film project, nonetheless had a post-Holocaust vision of the contemporary world. In interviews he exercised his artistic right to self-contradiction by adopting at different times both the liberal (code: totalitarian danger) and the fundamentalist (code: absolute evil) positions on the picture. But then again in interviews all good directors can do what they cannot do in their films – have their cake and eat it. Thankfully, in Kubrick's case his vision surpasses the discourse that always seems to follow, a discourse that is both necessary and misleading at the same time.

Between the ape that is almost man and the evil computer with crackling voice lies the missing link – the figure of Alex, leader of the Droogs, the organic summation of human evil, past, present and future but reserved for the next picture. The challenging feature of Alex, who Malcolm McDowell plays to perfection, is his star appeal. He is the most lovable rogue Kubrick ever created and yet also the most psychotic. Unlike Jack Nicholson in *The Shining*, McDowall extends and expands his body in the fictional pursuit of evil: Nicholson's later antics seem merely to betray his. Or rather, we could say, having embodied original evil so purely in the gaze of Alex in *A Clockwork Orange*, Kubrick's attempt to repeat himself in *The Shining* could only lead to impurity and to self-parody. If Nicholson looks like Kubrick on a bad day, that is because McDowell had already given us a mythic version of Stanley's staring eyes that was near-perfect. He may well be the most enticing screen figure that Kubrick ever created. And therein lies the rub. He is pure evil, the ignoble villain with, however, a noble flaw in his vicious make-up that almost puts him on the side of good – his undying love of Beethoven's Ninth Symphony. In modernism's post-jazz mode Kubrick's musical soundtrack goes forward not to rock'n'roll but to techno-classical, pure and high art in one sense but compellingly impure in another since one version of the soundtrack's Ninth Symphony and another of Rossini's *The Thieving Magpie* rely on newly invented Moog synthesisers. Hence Kubrick is classical and contemporary at the same time, traditional and state-of-the-art. During the Ludovico treatment, the film shows Beethoven's Ninth to be a Nazi favourite, a nightmare dilemma for the Jewish director since the worst enemies of his people liked the same music that he does. Alex adores the Ninth but shrinks from the greater evil of Hitler adoring it too. He becomes a pure embodiment of the twentieth-century dilemma, the coexistence of art and atrocity and in the process, since the dilemma is far bigger then he, his body is almost literally torn apart.

He is part-perpetrator and part-victim: in that respect the film is a deadpan Swiftian fable toying with the victimisation of a wilful perpetrator. We cannot hope to view the film naturalistically. It has poetry in its visual motion and in McDowell's Nadsat voice-over, which lifts the hypnotic invented language of Burgess from the novel's printed page with absolute conviction. It has an aesthetic beauty in much of its staging that is as breathtaking as *2001*. Impeccably, it stages evil with a clinical eye, yet is deeply and darkly funny. Like Skolimowski's *Deep End* (released in the same year), it is perverse tragicomedy, joking about things you are not supposed to joke about in the troubled arena of broken lives. In Part 1 of the film, the ruthless, amoral Alex creates a roll-call of victims; in Part 2 he becomes one himself. But he also survives to live another day and has learnt from his troubles one of two things depending on your point of view – how to be cured – or precisely nothing. Here there is no concession to reform in Kubrick's cinema, no wider vision of progress and no solution to evil. State 'reform' is a betrayal of human freedom, yet the Droog violation of the rights of others equally so.

Naremore contends with good reason that Kubrick is a late modernist who employs detachment and shock in equal measure, and that *A Clockwork Orange* with its menacing location shoots refracts the dark side of *2001*'s 'white modernism' (Naremore 2007: 3, 163–9). Detachment and shock in equal measure. It is a fine line – to err on the side of shock is to spill over into melodrama, to err on the side of detachment is to congeal into mannerism and petrifaction. But Kubrick here is the maestro of balance, the expert on equilibrium. The role of filmic evolution, in the formalist sense, cannot be overlooked either. Kubrick has absorbed and superseded key elements in British film of the 1960s: his fable contains a reflexive critique of the medium that becomes the starting-point for his own venture but not, thankfully, its object. At times McDowell and his family seem like a modernist parody of Kitchen Sink Realism – a northern parlour family thrust from their two-up two-down terrace into the bright, anaemic world of a London council flat redesigned as garish overkill. Alex's ageing mother, bedecked in red mini-skirt and white PVC boots, is proverbial mutton dressed as lamb with a new twist – the kitchen drudge of black and white cinema now dolled up in Mod-style futuristic costume more suited to the teenage sister Alex never had. In the family sequences McDowell's accent seems a near-parody of Albert Finney in *Saturday Night and Sunday Morning*. At another level Alex's picaresque persona seems to mimic that of Finney in *Tom Jones* yet endows it with chilling malevolence. The apartment interior, a modest flat near Elstree made over by production designer John Barry, has a material weight that empowers the satirical, manufactured image. And Kubrick uses the material weight of location just as effectively right through the film – South Bank, Thamesmead, Chelsea, the Brunel university campus in West London and the Elstree area for semi-rural stockbroker chic. This is England with a vengeance.

The challenge of complex locations made over and absorbed into the film's meticulous design may well have been Kubrick's riposte to *Blow-Up*. Antonioni's film involves a partial make-over of London locations but Kubrick's, you feel, is absolute. Every location becomes a constructed scene, a scenario, a spectacle, a tactic that Greenaway would later adopt for his inspired Rome shoot of *The Belly of an Architect*. The Korova milk bar is Kubrick's only big concession to studio design. Its artificiality is total, its well-heeled customers comparable to the white-face models in *Blow-Up*'s fashion studio. In the film's speeded-up orgy scene after Alex picks up two girls from the music store (filmed at the Drugstore on the King's Road, Chelsea), we also have a spoof on the orgy footage from *Blow-Up* which had cut abruptly (in the censored version) from the lusting trio (Hemmings and the two girls) ripping each other's clothes off to postcoital slumber. Here, five years later, three-way orgy is shown explicitly in a single long shot with no cuts but also lampooned by fast-motion editing which turns it into a comic sex cartoon. Gillian Hills, the naked unnamed girl in the *Blow-Up* orgy, reappears here as – yes – a naked, unnamed girl rolling around happily in a threesome with a rampant McDowell. Meanwhile the film also seems a response to the Pop Art adornments of Losey's *Modesty Blaise*. Where Losey had sought to appropriate Pop Art smugly into a chic vision of modernist cool and failed, Kubrick draws back to open a tension between his stylistic modernism and the sterile modernism, as he saw it, in the plastic arts of that time. Revealingly, he told Michel Ciment in interview, 'I think modern art's almost total preoccupation with subjectivism has led to anarchy and sterility in the arts' (Ciment, 2001: 149). Here Kubrick aligns himself with Antonioni, yet pushes things much further. The Korova bar, the Cat Lady's house and 'Home' are all sophisticated parodies of that sterility in a new sexualised age, rich and bourgeois, stuffed with soft-porn bric-à-brac yet aseptic and asexual.

As in *2001*, Kubrick becomes an artistic modernist by attacking plastic modernism, playfully biting the hand that feeds him. The ploy is fair game because the execution is so precise. The Droogs with their bowler hats, white catsuits and codpieces (cricket protectors), are a knowing party to this, forged by Alex into designer teenage wannabes making dodgy fashion statements, fomenters of anarchy and chaos craving for ritual being. Perversely, they are outlaws who blend visually into the over-designed bourgeois territories they

**Figure 7.1** One False Eyelash, One False Move: Malcolm McDowell in *A Clockwork Orange*

violate. Even more perversely their violence is attractive because it is staged and scenic, so that ritual destruction is a back-handed way of producing order out of chaos. Here Kubrick's great daring is to frame first-person voice-over within the audio-visual field of the cinematic body. The words of Burgess are made to sound seductive, alluring, simply by virtue of McDowell's presence, the voice, the look, the walk, the bearing, the all-conquering eye that stares out from beneath a strategic false eyelash, framed by the low brim of his bowler hat. We find this lovable psychopath hard to resist and Kubrick knows it. He is challenging us *not* to be lured in, and *not* to feel sympathy in the second half of the film when, metaphorically speaking, he replays the first half backwards as Alex's erstwhile victims get a tidy revenge and Droog No.1 receives a dose of his own medicine.

There is musical add-on too. The choreography of violence suggests a ballet or a musical, not a melodrama, but a musical seen through a glass darkly. Kubrick sets it rolling with a ritual gang-fight after an attempted rape, staged in an old East End casino, which violently mimics *West Side Story*, and then continues it with Alex's lakeside beating of Dim and the Droogs. He thus builds up to the shock use of Gene Kelly's 'Singin' in the Rain' for Alex's assault on the helpless husband Alexander (Patrick Magee) after the ritual clothes-ripping and rape of the defenceless Alexander wife (Adrienne Corri), filmed tight in by Kubrick himself with his trusty Arriflex. Meanwhile, the soundtrack defines itself through a Moog synthesiser makeover of Purcell which cues the title sequences and the entry of the Droogs into every menacing scene (LoBrutto 1998: 353–4). Thus Kubrick uses music to carve out further the subjective and objective realms of the tale, the personal and the impersonal. Or so it seems. Diegetic Beethoven blends in with Alex's voice-over, his beloved Ninth on his bedroom gramophone, on the Alexander family stereo and over the Nazi rally footage he is forced by lid-locks to eyeball during the Ludovico treatment in prison. Conversely, Rossini for Droog action and Edgar's 'Pomp and Circumstance' for prison ceremonies are key soundtrack accompaniments to the film's satiric tenor. Kubrick's statement on modern culture is damning. Self-indulgent subjectivism has a market value for the complacent bourgeois: artistic classicism (Beethoven) is now revered by a working-class psychopath.

A further thought presents itself here which contradicts the musical division between diegetic subjective and non-diegetic 'objectivity' in Part 1 of the film. All the music could be heard and seen as the monomaniac preserve of Alex, as an imaginary orchestration of the soundtrack, a 'soundscreen' which is totally subjective and enhances the power of Droog violation. This leads to a parallax soundtrack as complement to the parallax view. Either diegetic music and its opposite are a marker of the film's subjective/objective divide – Alex/non-Alex – or the music in Part 1 is *all* Alex *except for* his beloved Beethoven, and the visual choreography of music and image becomes the psychopath's special delusion of grandeur. Slow-motion, fast-motion, wide-angle – all act in sync, it can be argued, with Alex's soundscreen orchestration of violation and his Nadsat voice-over. The visuals of criminal violation are enhanced by symphonic orchestrations of the mind's inner ear. Thus musical reversal of the obvious might just as well be the case. Instead of Beethoven as the 'diegetic subjective' and the soundtrack as the 'impersonal objective', the soundtrack could be the orchestrating Alex; conversely, his beloved Ninth could be so great, so awesome *that it lies beyond his control* – it is out there in the open on his gramophone, on the soundtrack of the Nazi film he is forced to watch with lid-locked eyeballs, and in the living-room below on the Alexander stereo that booms through the ceiling and drives him in despair to jump out of the window. On this reading he cannot control what he truly loves while lesser music pumps his adrenalin and puts him on a roll. On one viewing, the Ninth is the one thing that is truly his: on another it is the one thing that truly eludes him.

The Droogs' invasion of 'Home' as a prelude to balletic rape and beating, perhaps the film's most controversial sequence, came to haunt Kubrick in a way he never envisaged. British tabloid accusations of copycat rapes and murders rained thick and fast as the notoriety of the film spread and audiences increased. Unsettled, the reclusive director also, reportedly, had to endure threatening phone calls and unwelcome stalkers near his country home. We can only speculate about his fear of life imitating art. If the rural household of the Alexanders with its neon 'Home' sign at the roadside entrance and interiors shot in a designer Radlett house were too close for comfort to Kubrick's nearby domain, comparison went further with the large painting of his wife Christiane – 'Seedboxes' – which was placed by Kubrick on one of 'Home's' interior walls. Perhaps, subconsciously, he had turned the Alexander home into a simulacrum of his own. There is no single answer. Was his decision to withdraw the film from the UK alone the admission of a complex fear or a gesture of self-censorship, or a mixture of both? One thing is certain: the Droogs' invasion of the Alexander household is a choreographed violation of home, territory, culture and finally the human body unparalleled in cinema, the true forerunner to Michael Haneke's 1997 shocker *Funny Games*, which it still surpasses. Had this, the end of domestic sanctuary, become Kubrick's worst nightmare? His one truly English film was pulled in the UK by its director in 1974 and only released again after the end of his life. Was his host country now being punished as Alex had been in Part 2 of the film? The vexed relationship of life and art remains an enigma: the jury is still out.

Debates about the social meaning of the film will run and run. We can see it as a fable about serious personal vice outmatched by the institutional vice of a society priding itself on authoritarian therapy in which state criminality exceeds the criminality of its victims. And as a bonus we can see the ending as one in which a docile Alex finally succumbs to the Ludovico effect, all his individuality drained out of him by a horror story of cruel mechanical programming and its monstrous destruction of 'Ludwig van'. Or we can see him in the opposite light. His opting for the 'scientific' treatment of lid-locked eyeballs and its bait of early prison release is a Machiavellian wager on survival through faked deference, cunning and braving the pain barrier. He has not reformed at all since he has not been brainwashed by an omnipotent totalitarian state but mangled by a motley bunch of misguided paternalists using him as a pawn in their political infighting, conservatives versus liberals, 'scientists' versus priests. On this reading, Orwell and *1984* are nowhere in sight. The whole prison sequence looks instead as if a strong dose of Michel Foucault had been injected into a *Carry On* movie. In any case, whichever way we go in this film's parallax view of the nature of evil, no one can deny its pure ocular vision, unmatched in modern cinema of its time. No one, that is, can deny the menace in the eyes of Alex the Droog or deny the fear imprinted on the eyeballs of Alex the prisoner.

## FREEDOM AND FATE: *BARRY LYNDON*

Kubrick wrong-footed everyone with his next film. From *A Clockwork Orange* to *Barry Lyndon* is a quantum leap, a bigger leap into the past than Kubrick had ever made before, to the pre-revolutionary Europe of the late eighteenth century. After the surfeit of publicity and controversy over *Clockwork Orange* he shrouded preparations for his period epic in secrecy. As a result it was admired on its release but prompted no critical buzz and was soon forgotten. Yet it was the greatest history film in British cinema since *Lawrence of Arabia* and sadly the débâcle of Lean's *Ryan's Daughter*, also set in Ireland and made several years earlier, was to highlight just how good it is. In it Kubrick continued his inventive experiments with naturalistic location lighting. In *A Clockwork Orange* he had consistently used single-source, on-set lighting: in *Barry Lyndon* he tried to replicate the low-light levels of eighteenth-century living through the use of a special Carl Zeiss lens and the strategic use of candlelight. He tried specifically, that is, to convey the look of that century through the lives of its wealthier beings and used the many drawings and paintings of the time as mediate pointers. It was thus a challenge for the ex-photographer to capture the century before the invention of photography, to become painterly in his framing, since painting was the true portal to discovery. In that respect the film resembles another history film made at the same time, Terrence Malick's *Days of Heaven* – but with a crucial difference. Set in Texas at the start of the twentieth century, Malick's film is set in the age of photography and starts accordingly with a montage of Western photographs from its period. Kubrick by contrast starts through painting, the great visual art of his earlier epoch, especially in English life where Constable, Stubbs and Hogarth had all come to the fore so memorably.

Another contrast is apparent. Malick was an American romantic, Kubrick anything but. Or was he? This is the one film he made that begs the question. But in a way Kubrick draws back for he has no romantic answer, he poses the question with the balance and poise indicative of his best films. Is Ryan O'Neal's Barry Lyndon an opportunistic rogue as he is in Thackerary's picaresque tale, or is he Kubrick's version of a one-note Irish romantic trying to survive in a dangerous, unromantic world? Not only did Kubrick want to pose this question for his audience to answer, he wanted to do it through understated performances and a history without melodrama, a tragic personal history with a sense of slow-burning fate. Like Alex the Droog, Barry experiences both rise and fall, conveyed by his critical change of name, from Redmond Barry, his Irish birth-name, to Barry Lyndon, his adopted British one. The change suggests triumph, usurping through marriage a titled British name and leaving his Irish past behind him. But the change is also the beginning of the end, the start of his fall from grace where the arc of destiny seems preordained. Kubrick is a witness, not a moralist, not asking us to judge the moment where everything goes wrong but rather challenging us to realise that no such moment can be isolated, that there may in fact be no such moment at all.

The sense of destiny is as strong here as it is in *Don't Look Now* or *The Passenger* – an accretion of moments that compel in the one direction. At the same time, Barry's trajectory is a personal one in which he must live by his wits. The Irish dimension here is crucial. A misty-eyed, melancholy dreamer, Barry is twice cheated in his native country before he heads off to war, once by the duel that is faked in favour of English officer-rival Jack Quinn (Leonard Rossiter) by his local cousin and again by highwaymen on the rocky road to Dublin. If this opportunist is a rogue and a fraud, then he starts off as an Irish holy fool. Yet as Newman has stated, Kubrick's hero makes a key transition from 'romance to ritual' (Newman 2009: 22–3). He survives through the mastery of ritual where he failed in the duplicities of romance. Kubrick is fascinated by ritual violence, but also by games and gambling, and the period is made for him. Barry's father is killed in a duel: the son wrongly thinks he has killed Quinn in his first duel; He finds favour in the British army by winning a boxing match against a bigger opponent and ends up a card sharp in Berlin, working in partnership with another exiled Irishman masquerading as a French chevalier (Patrick Magee). Meanwhile he becomes a servant of two masters, the British with whom he enlists, and then their ally, the Prussians, after he is caught impersonating a British officer in an attempt to get out of the Seven Years' War. When the chevalier is forced by the Prussians to leave the country Barry impersonates him and books his passage to freedom. Caught out in maze of duplicity, Barry is the reverse of Alex. He starts out as victim then becomes an instigator. His subsequent flirtation with the beautiful young wife of the ageing Lord Lyndon becomes his *coup de grâce*, a superb piece of sexual *Realpolitik* that is rendered by Kubrick as a moment of pure aesthetic beauty.

Yet you would not know it. Barry looks the same anxious holy fool that he was in the Irish countryside. When he first kisses his bride-to-be, he does so with a concerned longing that betrays no bodily sign of scheming or duplicity. Kubrick objectifies his hero through the consistency of the look just as he objectifies the film by transforming Thackeray's first-person narration into the impersonal third-person of Michael Hordern's voice-over, a voice that comments omnisciently and with quiet gravitas on events as they unfold. The objectification pattern echoes that of Losey–Pinter in *The Servant* and *Accident*, or the objectification of the reporter-subject in *The Passenger*. We experience the world through the eyes of the subject but we also judge, quite clinically, the experiencing subject himself. The juxtaposition of the romantic look with

**Figure 7.2** The Rogue as Holy Fool: Ryan O'Neal in *Barry Lyndon*

the ritual or the instrumental act – this is how we see Barry through most of the film, as a living contradiction. He connives in his name being turned inside out because he has turned his identity inside out. So the question of identity can be read in contrary ways. Does the consistency of look guarantee the consistency of being in spite of the vagaries of fortune? Or is the look itself the visual sign of monstrous self-delusion, the desperate clinging to a self-image of authenticity amid consecutive acts of bad faith?

As Redmond or as Lyndon, Barry remains an enigma, to us and to himself. In the misty-eyed image of the Irish-American O'Neal, he does not seem to have the secret fermenting chamber of the corrupted mind that Bogarde intimates so well in his Losey pictures. If he becomes corrupt, which he does in the film's latter stages, it is because corruption steals up on him unawares. Occasionally, Kubrick intimates change through the powdered face that offsets the flesh tones of the early Irish look, or the elaborate wigs that conceal his chestnut hair. But all dolled up to mingle with the English aristocracy, O'Neal still seems possessed of a dreamer's oblivion. After his marriage to the widowed Countess Lyndon (the silent and beautiful Maria Berenson) he does not see the red sail (warning sign: red for danger) of the boat that glides behind their own as they float lovingly along the river. He simply cannot read the signs and this we can happily interpret either as lingering naivety or as wilful self-denial.

Just as the boat floats along the river Barry seems to float too, floating into infidelity and debauchery, skimming along the surface of things while his stepson sees him as an interloper and plots revenge. The insolent boy may be chastised by his new master but he still has the upper hand – a title (Lord Bullingdon) – while Barry has none, and after the riding accident that kills his own son, no true heir either. When Barry tries to kill Bullingdon with his bare hands at a select gathering of the eminent and titled, we know he has crossed the line and blown it. Kubrick also plays cleverly with the divide of mother–son couples, English versus Irish. As his problems increase Barry becomes more dependent on his Irish mother who has come to live with them: the adolescent Bullingdon is just as protective of his own mother to whom he displays near-oedipal affection. Barry spends his wife's fortune on fruitless ploys to gain public recognition: at a brief audience with the king, the latter is told of Barry's willingness to raise a volunteer army to fight the American rebels. The king seems to imply that Barry should go with them as a 'noble' gesture – that is, he should die there and there will be no question of him getting a title. Even before the fateful duel with Bullingdon he is already lost. He has fallen between two stools by falling between two names. He is no longer 'Redmond Barry' but he has yet to become accepted as 'Barry Lyndon', and never will be. Bankrupt, his leg amputated after the duel, he ends up in his mother's care – as no one at all. He remains in fact, involuntarily, a colonial subject who has failed to shed his skin.

If Kubrick is fascinated by contest and ritual, he is equally fascinated by the visual field of domination. Onto the hilly emerald landscape of south-east Ireland floods a sea of scarlet right across the screen as Kubrick films in splendid wide-angle the marching Redcoat army and its booming drums recruiting for the Seven Years' War. Barry's woes and his opportunities stem from that moment. Robbed by a highwayman and penniless he joins as a mercenary not a patriot, but when he switches to the British ally you feel it is the lesser evil – shedding Union Jack scarlet for Prussian blue. Just as he has no name that is truly his own he has no uniform that is truly his either. He is caught between a rock and a hard place and Kubrick, you feel, is putting an ironic gloss on Joyce's 'silence, exile and cunning'. Except that Barry then makes his move to recognition within the Old Order and it is the wrong move for someone who cannot truly anglicise himself. The American Revolution has started, the French will follow and Ireland is just two decades away from Wolfe Tone. Barry is a man out of time but also out of place in the exquisite interiors across southern England that Kubrick used for the Lyndon abode – Longleat, Wilton, Petworth and Corsham Court. Ostensibly the master of this composite house, he is as much in control of it as Charles Foster Kane is at 'Xanadu' as the end approaches. And like Welles whose film he admired,

Kubrick aimed high for a sense of tragic destiny in recreating a past cinematically with a visionary attention to detail equalled only by Luchino Visconti. On British costume drama the film would have little impact apart from its immediate take-up by Ridley Scott in *The Duellists*, but its long-term effect is now showing elsewhere – in Martin Scorsese's *Age of Innocence*, in Andrew Dominik's *The Assassination of Jesse James by the Coward Robert Ford* and in the successful HBO mini-series *John Adams*. Kubrick had revolutionised cinema's way of looking at history and that transformation is still being felt.

## SKOLIMOWSKI AND RUNNING WATER: OR, *DEEP END* AND *CUL-DE-SAC*

Jerzy Skolimowski had come to international attention for his screenwriting on Polanski's *Knife in the Water* (*Nóż w wodzie* 1961), a film which is the true predecessor to both *Cul-de-Sac* and Skolimowski's *Deep End*. In the past his pre-British career has often been seen as superior to his English films. But Ciment, the French critic and supporter of the Polish director, estimated that *Deep End* was more accomplished than his francophone début, *Le Départ*, and that by 1982 *Moonlighting* was his best film to date (Ciment, 1984: 507). Certainly Skolimowski's journey from east to west was just as significant as that of Polanski's. The latter of course had shown impressive topographical continuity; from the Polish Mazurian lakes (*Knife in the Water*) to the shoreline of the North Sea on Holy Island in Northumbria (*Cul-de-Sac*). Both films have complex location shoots that make atmospheric use of nature's givens. *Deep End*, on the other, hand, deals less with nature and more with culture. Its running water is confined to that of a London public baths constructed and filmed in a Munich studio, a double artifice signalled by its Anglo-German co-production. In *Cul-de-Sac* the flooded causeway at Holy Island is a recurrent force of nature that has unfortunate consequences: the water in Skolimowski's swimming pool is humanly controlled but also turns out to have tragic consequences. At the start of his film Polanski shows us the causeway flooding with the gangster's car and the hapless Jack MacGowran stuck in the middle, an ominous through amusing sign of things to come: towards the end of his film Skolimowski shows us the public pool drained and emptied for the first time. The sea that daily floods the causeway we can take as a fact of nature. A swimming pool emptied of water after a film in which it has always been full bespeaks an uncanny absence. It becomes the visual sign of premonition. We cannot guess how or why, but as pool attendants Mike (John Moulder-Brown) and Susan (Jane Asher) head back out of hours to melt the snow that might contain the missing diamond from Sue's engagement ring (a beautifully surreal touch in a film full of them) we fear the worst. Why so? It is the sudden shock of the pool's emptiness that increases our foreboding, the absence of water that plays on our fear. It is not 'rational'. After all we cannot control the tides but know we are subject to their regularity. Yet public baths are humanly controlled: a mechanic pulls levers and flicks switches to drain them and fill them again. In *Deep End* the culture of chlorinated water is more unpredictable than the nature of the sea around the English coastline.

If *Deep End* were solely a comedy, a *rite de passage* film about an awkward fifteen year old trying in vain to lose his virginity, we should feel fine and after a number of comic sequences in the first part of the film that is what we expect. The film is hilarious at times. Skolimowski sets the tone by casting Diana Dors, a cine-diva of 1950s British film, as a lustful woman of a certain age demanding special favours in her changing cubicle from her naïve attendant. Moreover, he makes it something of an oedipal gag by staging the encounter like infantile regression, as Dors grabs the 'boy' to her bosom. At first sight the bemused Mike is forcibly 'breastfed' against his will and then, in a brief enticing shot, seems to looking for re-entry head first into the womb. Except that the bathing lady is treating the contact as highly agreeable friction while providing a running commentary on a boy's first love – football – where George Best, in her words, is 'forcing the ball between the goalposts'. It is a standout audio-visual gag, one of the very best in British cinema, carried out with panache by actors and director alike. Others follow during Mike's sortie into Soho with his first week's wages as he stalks the alluring, auburn-haired Susan and her flash fiancé. Unable to enter their pricy club he wiles away the time eating hotdogs from a Chinese pavement vendor and idling up and down past strip-joints. To his horror, he spots a life-sized cardboard cut-out of a half-naked Susan outside a club – 'Angelica from Manchester', he is told – snatches it and runs in blind panic into a brothel where he sees a middle-aged prostitute reclining on a bed with her leg and thigh in plaster. She offers him a reduced rate and places Susan's cut-out over her broken leg to encourage him to 'express' himself.

Skolimowski's gift for the surreal is often underestimated. But he is always good on the dream logic of events with their juxtaposition of unlikely objects, and equally good on the cruel wonder of discovery that this intersection of life and dream creates. His gags are never dated. For TV viewers his London coppers would seem like *Monty Python avant la lettre* and his public baths an aqueous version of *Fawlty Towers*, again before its time. But his values are instinctively cinematic. His camera roams with a nervous but observant restlessness; like Polanski he specialises in following semi-subjective shots. But while his compatriot is technically more disciplined, Skolimowski provides a kinetic energy we associate with Jean-Luc Godard or Federico Fellini. That is why here and in *Success is the Best Revenge*, the male teenager presents him with an ideal subject. There is a kind of anxious, directionless quality, matched by a mixture of naivety and perverse cunning that Skolimowski captures so well with the eye of an outsider looking in on the canvas of London culture where his teen dramas are acted out. But with Mike the drama acts itself out with women, not girls – two of them old enough to be his mother and the other, Susan, a foxy twenty-five year old who teases him then pretends to act like a concerned older sister; at the same time being 'engaged' to an older rival while having a furtive affair in a swimming cubicle, of all places, with Mike's old sports teacher. For thin-skinned Mike it is the stuff of nightmares; for his hardened director a comic feast.

Yet Skolimowski has the power, which many British directors do not, of switching gear from the comic to the tragic without a sign of effort. In this he is aided by surreal logic and overt symbolism. His visuals are daring – washed-out monochrome shading into colour but not quite, with primary colours foregrounded at critical moments, red, yellow and, sparingly blue. Jane Asher's lemon designer raincoat seems a fashion pastiche on the yellow oil-skins of fishermen at sea, the colour of protection against waves and storms. In the drained pool where she fatefully takes it off, it is a portent, an ominous sign that her protection against running water is gone entirely. Equally the painting of the walls around the pool red is another portent, realised when the paint pot tumbles into the water simultaneously with the blood flowing from Asher's head wound. The symbolic mix of redness, water and drowning would be echoed a year later in the tragic opening and finale of *Don't Look Now*. Roeg would separate out Eros and death, but Skolimowski conjoins them. The naked couple fail to make love in the pool as its starts to refill with water. After Susan's tragic death Mike becomes conjoined in the film's last shot with her floating body, her blood like a red dye on rippling liquid. Is this then consummation in death and consummation *through* death? On a modernist plane both films, his and Roeg's, echo Eliot's imagistic invocation of 'Death by Water' in *The Waste Land* and create new versions of it out of their cinematic imagination. But Skolimowski's film echoes too the ambiguous ending of *Vertigo*. How far does Mike connive in Susan's destruction? How far are obsession and the desired act of love a desire for revenge? Scottie and Madeleine, Mike and Susan: an ending open, enigmatic and mysterious.

We also have to admire Skolimowski's stylistic daring here and continuing in *The Shout, Moonlighting* and *Success is the Best Revenge*. In this Anglophile quartet he crosses the elusive boundary between the real and surreal, rhythmically oscillating between mimetic and surreal modernism, sometimes provoking a clash of styles, more often transcending it. At times, he can be self-indulgent. Yet there is one constant. He freights the image with a material presence then renders it uncanny. We think we know where we are and then he shifts the ground from under our feet. In *Deep End* he even achieves this through dubbing German actors with English voices in the pool sequences, so their spoken words seem to bear little relationship to their body language or indeed anything else. Sometimes the effect is comic, sometimes disturbing: unease and laughter mingle. Skolimowski shares with Luis Buñuel, Polanski and Lynch the knack of endowing a chain of material events with a dream logic that remains this-worldly: nowhere does this show more clearly than in the narrative chain that leads to the climax of *Deep End.* His powerless male subject also resembles Polanski's very English George in *Cul-de-Sac*, helpless before the Sadean tactics of a beautiful blonde wife. But whereas George is too old to please his young bride who amuses herself with toy-boys, Mike is too young for a much older girl engaged to someone else and who also amuses herself with married men. The difference between black comedy and tragedy then becomes apparent. Marooned alone at the film's end on his unforgiving island, on a rock perched above the rising tide, Polanski's George has literally nowhere to go. Skolimowski's fifteen-year-old Mike still has everything to play for, but it is abruptly taken from him and he is complicit. In the fate of both males, water is the mediating factor. But it is also a formidable hurdle for their female counterparts. In *Cul-de-Sac* the cruel Teresa survives it and escapes: in *Deep End* the equally cruel Susan is an unlikely victim and her virgin lover may well be her unlikely killer.

Let us return to the surreal logic of *Deep End*'s finale. It starts in winter snow. Determined to show his prowess and to spite the teacher who is Sue's lover, Mike cheekily enters his old school's cross-country race with Sue watching and wins – but only the first lap of the course. Cheated, he then punctures the tyre of the teacher's car, provoking Sue to punch out one of his teeth in the snow. Embedded in the missing tooth is the diamond from the engagement ring on her guilty fist. They search for it in the snow but to no avail, then heap the substance into bin-liners and take them to the baths where Mike plans to melt the snow with hot water from an electric kettle he attaches precariously to a dangling light socket. The surreal logic of this transition combines dream, daily life, a meticulous eye for objects and a reflexive eye cast on the exigencies of film plot. And there is more to come. The pool has been inexplicably drained so they are framed in high-angle long shot performing the tortuous ritual of melting snow with hot water from a kettle on its dry concrete floor. The pool is now a deep pit and once there, we sense they will never exit it. And does Mike want to? He finds the diamond, hides it under his tongue and lures his *femme fatale* to make love to him as a trade-off as the pool begins to fill. Except that he finds he cannot deliver. Skolimowski romanticises this moment of non-consummation with a 360-degree overhead whose lyricism of naked bodies induces both irony and pathos. The logical non-logic of the sequence ends in nightmare for its main subject. He has reached the end of his journey but remains a virgin and then becomes, against all odds, an involuntary killer. But how involuntary is that?

There is a nightmare logic that gets the hapless teenager to this point of no return but it is a logic that cannot be explained. There is consistency of action, consistency of motive, consistency of staging but a helplessness of consequence, a chain of events in which the links appear to uncouple. No one knows the full reason for the blood-filled predicament in which they find themselves, neither us nor them. Mike's final attempt to conjoin himself with the dying drowning body of his beloved is a defiant romantic gesture in the face of a modernistic fate. It is one of the most powerful moments in Skolimowski's cinema and equally in the British cinema of its time.

## RISE AND FALL: *THE SHOUT*, *MOONLIGHTING*, *SUCCESS IS THE BEST REVENGE*

There is a gap of seven years between *Deep End* and *The Shout*, but then four films in six years before Skolimowski left for America. (In between *The Shout* and *Moonlighting* he returned to Poland to re-edit the censored 1967 feature *Hands Up! – Rece do Góry*.) *The Shout* was a commercial and critical success, *Moonlighting* a critical success because of the performance of Jeremy Irons and the topicality of the Solidarity movement, and *Success* no success at all, the most autobiographical of his English films which bankrupted the director and prompted him to leave the country. In critical terms there is little to choose between them: none is as good as *Deep End*, which remains one of his truly great pictures, but all four excavate different elements of his modernist mindset in unexpected ways. *The Shout*, based on the famous story by Robert Graves, was a project he came to after it was lined up by producer Jeremy Thomas for Nick Roeg, who then passed on it. Skolimowski adapted the story with Mike Austin, used an electronic score from two Genesis musicians and the new forty-track Dolby optical stereo sound system introduced the previous year on *Star Wars*. Given the theme of the film embodied in the title, sound experimentation seemed natural: Skolimowski made it bold and compelling, and it remains so. Its clarity and multiplicity are still unnerving and while the insane Crossley (Alan Bates) shouts acoustically to kill, Anthony (John Hurt) experiments creepily in his edit suite with electronic surrogates that jar and menace the ear. Which, we might ask, is the lesser evil?

Yet the sound production of the Crossley shout is itself electronic – for Skolimowski one of the big challenges which attracted him to the film. In fact, this is a film in which sonic invention often outstrips visual invention as Skolimowski provides us with a variation on the horror movie where sound unnerves us more than image. The film's play on the ambiguity of the supernatural puts it in firmly in the lineage of *The Innocents* and *Don't Look Now*. Its mimetic elements and literary sourcing echo the partnership of Losey and Pinter. The *ménage à trois* in the Graves story in which Charles Crossley is a wrecker of marriages could well have been based on the female poet Laura Riding who had invaded Graves' personal life, just as the bisexual dramas of the Maughams, uncle and nephew, fuelled the household dynamics of *The Servant*. The outsider as destructive intruder is also a theme that Skolimowski and Polanski had developed in the yachting threesome of *Knife in the Water* so *The Shout*, with its haunting seashore sequences, is an echo of that and of the coastline insanities in *Cul-de-Sac*. And while Losey had already given us an expatriate view of cricket as life on Mars in *Accident*, Skolimowski takes it further in what is literally a saga of village idiocy. With his actress-wife Joanna Szczerbic as an unlikely umpire, heifers grazing on nonexistent boundaries, mad fielders crashing into cowpats at cover point and a distant peacock producing offscreen cries that act as ominous prelude to Crossley's apocalyptic shout, you feel this could well be life on another galaxy.

This acid but affectionate parody of English rural life (to match the urban parody of the London pictures) is shot with great verve on location in north Devon. Yet unlike Losey or Polanski, Skolimowski relegates the sexual triangle of this film to a secondary role as he plays on the narrative dynamics of enframing, of what enframes the story and what is being framed within it. It seems this is a *Cabinet of Dr Caligari*-style meditation on madness in which Crossley, the asylum inmate, tells the unreliable 'tale' of his life and his magic Aboriginal 'shout' to Robert Graves (Tim Curry) within the sanctuary of the scoring hut behind the scoreboard during the match between inmates and locals. Is the story we see and hear the truth of his supernatural powers or a delusion framed through his insane imagination? Or does the initial sequence of the film, repeated at the end, where Rachel (Susannah York) drives through a storm to find the corpses of Crossley, a fellow inmate (Jim Broadbent) and the chief asylum doctor (Robert Stephens) laid out side by side by side in the building's main hall, constitute the main narrative frame which then subordinates Crossley's framing to its own? It could go either way. Notably, Rachel is seen only once in her nurse's uniform. Is Crossley's story then one in which the nurse, *not* the doctor, is the visual synonym of Caligari? Is the evil Weimar hypnotist feminised and turned from a paranoid's demon into a middle-class English object of desire? Crossley's fantasy, on this reading, recasts his attractive nurse as the comely but childless wife of Anthony (John Hurt), the local batter hitting boundaries during the opening cricket sequence. He tells Graves: 'It's always the same story but I change the sequence of events.' But then the death-scene is the shot that ends the film too, where Rachel looks down at Crossley's body with a hint of triumph in her eyes. Is this a sign of *her* final revenge over the madman who has seduced her and sought to destroy her marriage?

The last paragraph was a string of questions because the film provokes questions without giving final answers, gives any number of alternative answers which contradict one another. We can take yet another enframing, which follows the first cricket sequence. Sunbathing on the sand dunes near their isolated cottage, the childless couple (Anthony and Rachel) seem jointly to conjure up the bone-pointing figure of an Aboriginal advancing towards them. Does this dark figure from the other side of the world then morph into the pale, bulky carcass of Englishman Alan Bates, he of *The Go-Between* and a very recognisable figure in British films of the time? Is Crossley their shared nightmare, the one who has come to conquer and cuckold and destroy? Is he the imaginary intruder by which they objectify guilt about their childlessness, refracted through his outrageous claim to be the righteous killer of the children he has conceived with his Aboriginal wife? Is he then their imaginary double from a primitive culture who questions their right to civilisation? Is he the spectre of their imagination, or are they the spectre-couple *in his commentary* to the hapless Graves? In *The Shout* the parallax view loops into endless playback with no final resolution.

The mimetic rivalry of husband and intruder for comely Rachel is filtered through rivalries over sound. Crossley claims to have taken eighteen years to perfect the 'terror shout' by which he can kill humans and animals alike. Meanwhile, Anthony's sound experiments seem to be countering the acoustic threat by electronic means. We see and hear him in his edit room miking close in the unnerving sounds of water on rolling marbles, a cello bow playing the edge of a sardine can and a bee trapped in a jar buzzing furiously on the surface of the microphone. The diffident church organist seems to change character as he turns up the volume on multi-track to breaking point, producing ear-piercing sounds. It seems like sonic counter-terrorism, trying to manufacture the electronic answer to the acoustic terror shout, almost as if the besieged husband is trying to get his retaliation in first. At the same time there is a reflexive fix here on the film's own reproduction of the terror shout. For the spectacular coastal scene where the power of Bates's shout forces Hurt to crash down in the sand dunes and also instantly kills a shepherd and one of his nearby flock, Skolimowski is mixing acoustic and electronic sound in post-production on forty-track stereo. The film thus conveys the raw power of the human shout by state-of-the-art technology. Here the mimetic split between the acoustic Bates and the electronic Hurt is a reflexive meditation on the film's own conundrum. Just as they compete over sex, so they compete over sound. Yet in the production of the 'shout' the acoustic and the electronic must combine. At the same time *the look* of the Crossley shout is based on a painterly image. It resembles one of Francis Bacon's Head versions of the Velásquez Pope which glitters with the menace of its bared teeth and beams down from a wall in the couple's cottage – Crossley's shout framed via Bacon and Velásquez. And maybe the sound we hear fills in the silence of the cry from that other great visual source that so inspired Bacon, the cinematic one of Eisenstein's unnamed woman on the Odessa steps shrieking from the pain of splintered spectacles on her bloodstained face. It is as if over fifty years later Skolimowski has finally given us what we always yearned to hear (but the silence of early film prevented). And if you want a reprise of the image we are given that too, in the contorted face of the asylum doctor in the scoring hut where he dies in agony and open-mouthed terror from the full force of the Crossley shout during the storm.

## BRINGING IT ALL BACK HOME: *MOONLIGHTING* AND *SUCCESS IS THE BEST REVENGE*

Skolimowski's homecoming from Devon to his house in West London meant abandoning experiments with the supernatural in favour of something more familiar, but the familiar made uncanny. In both films, the familiar is the family home in Kensington, a 'character' in its own right. After all, it saved studio costs and cut down on locations, a prime consideration for a director with little money. In the case of *Moonlighting* he could also save money by casting as Polish builders the very builders who had been working on his home and were caught out by the sudden imposition of martial law in their own country. This was a typical case of Skolimowski's art imitating Skolimowski's life at very short notice. In *Success* he could economise further by casting his own family as a Polish family in West London, though modestly removing himself as head of household in favour of Michael York, who plays a theatre and not a film director. And if you feel *Success* has a sense of *déjà vu* you're right. It is set in the same house as *Moonlighting* after the house has been renovated, a design sequel to the previous picture. A good solution you might think, except that the house had been remortgaged to pay for the film and when the film failed, said house was repossessed. Kubrick may have worried about the fate of his family after *A Clockwork Orange* but he never had to worry about the financial fate of his Hertfordshire mansion in which he lived until his death. And he never had to economise by using it in his films either.

In *Moonlighting* a story that Skolimowski wrote and filmed quickly in the middle of a London winter, Jeremy Irons plays Nowak, the leader of a building workers' quartet paid on the cheap by a Polish diplomat (Skolimowski himself) to renovate his London home and brought in from Warsaw to undercut local labour costs. Filmed soon after Christmas, the film uses

Christmas motifs with carol singers, Christmas trees, Christmas Mass and shoplifted turkeys. In much of British cinema, the world of work is usually real in a documentary sense: but here it seems both documentary and surreal, a form of daily wonder that is cruel and forbidding yet whose insane contradictions are a source of uneasy laughter. In Skolimowski it is the surrealism of the material image that triumphs. Part of that lies in the workers' daily grind of knocking through interior walls and rewiring rooms with primitive tools brought in from Warsaw amidst an endless dust storm and failing to get a signal for their junk shop TV, their only leisure activity. But the surreal image is sonic as well as optical and lies equally in the use of language, or indeed its absence. The director uses Irons as an English actor playing a Pole but speaking nearly always in English (he frames the narrative through Irons' voice-over). In his brief and terse exchanges with his fellow Poles we have Irons talking English-accented Polish: in his substantial voice-over and frequent dealings with the locals we have Irons mimicking Polish-accented English. The dominant Polish voice is thus English, a device that Skolimowski plays up by almost never having the other Poles talking to each other. As part of their bafflement at this strange new world where they sleep rough on the floor of the house, understand not a word of English, eat starvation rations and have no money to spend, they are struck dumb. Their silence suggests their language itself has been taken from them.

Yet the film also intimates that what happens in London runs parallel to what happens over there, in Warsaw. The official's cheapskate deal means the workers are no better off in London than in their own capital: his clear liking for Anna, Nowak's attractive wife, means that Nowak's stay is dogged with anxiety and suspicion about what is happening behind his back – back there. Skolimowski plays on the anxiety by parallax means, filming a secret assignation, witnessed by Nowak that takes place in the house opposite, between a young woman who looks like Anna and a visiting lover who looks like 'Skolimowski'. Not only has 'Skolimowski' not given Nowak enough money for building materials and living expenses, he has left a different kind of question hanging over their relationship. Yet all this pales before the politics that is set to unfold. In newspaper headlines one morning Nowak reads of the imposition overnight of martial law in Poland; on TV screens in shop windows he sees armed police manning barriers and tanks rolling along the streets of the capital. A film about the surrealism of work suddenly becomes a film about the trauma of politics, but as events progress it becomes impossible to disentangle them. Nowak decides to conceal the awful truth from his unsuspecting workers until the contract is completed.

Like *Cul-de-Sac, Moonlighting* aligns itself right on the trauma/anti-trauma divide. Events that horrify become funny; events that might cause permanent damage lead to behaviour that is faintly ridiculous. In order to protect his workers from the trauma of knowing the worst, as he now does, Nowak shrouds them in the veil of ignorance. He tears down Solidarity protest notices on street walls so they will not see them, ushers them quickly past TV shop windows, leaves them at home on shopping trips, prevents them from trying to phone home from the local call box, intercepts their intercepted mail (the Polish authorities first, Nowak second) and finally stops them from attending mass. They become virtual prisoners in their chaotic workplace. Thus he inadvertently repeats in miniature the strictures of silence, curfew and house arrest the new regime has imposed in Poland. His trauma response to the unexpected Event leads to a compulsion to repeat its worst effects. In order that they do not suffer the knowledge that he has suffered, they are made to suffer a version of what all Poles are suffering even though in London they are ostensibly in a free city. Their space-capsule London, where they see and understand nothing, becomes a surreal version of Warsaw under curfew. Meanwhile, Nowak can only sustain this elaborate pretence and get them to finish the work on time by shoplifting instead of paying grocery bills for which he no longer has any money. Inside the house he is a devious autocrat, outside a petty criminal and pilferer.

The second part of the film consumes itself with Nowak's tortuous cover-up in which the received idea of workers as heroic dissidents, seen in Wajda's didactic pro-Solidarity film *Man of Iron* (1981), never materialises. But that is because Skolimowski is supremely unpredictable. At this point we can contrast his use of political trauma with that of another low-budget feature of the same period, Jordan's *Angel*. Traumatised by witnessing a paramilitary killing of a deaf-mute girl, Danny (Stephen Rea) the sax player himself turns into a brutal avenger, a killing machine hunting down murderers. Traumatised by the military crushing of Solidarity, Nowak turns into a petty dictator in exile. In both cases, extreme revulsion results in a compulsion to repeat. But unlike *Angel*, *Moonlighting* ends on a note of surreal farce. On the first stage of their journey home, a six-hour walk to Heathrow pushing shopping trolleys full of luggage, the bemused Polish trio finally hear the truth from their duplicitous leader about events in their homeland. Nowak ends the film bruised and beaten on the tarmac of an anonymous car park, getting his just desserts. It is a defiant, anti-heroic ending redolent of human frailty.

The second of the brace of English auto-home movies, *Success is the Best Revenge*, transforms 'home' out of all recognition. For a start there is now a family in it, Skolimowski's own with actress-wife Joanna Szczerbic as the wife, and sons Michał and Jerzy as the director's sons. The director, however, is a theatre director called Alex Rodak played by Michael York and older son Michał, who wants to return to Poland in the film, appears in the credits under the pseudonym Michael Lyndon. Only from the outside is the house recognisable. The interior has been transformed from the wrecked hovel of *Moonlighting* into an elegant townhouse. Rodak, however, is still being harassed by building officers who claim he has made the roof too short in what they insist is a listed house. Another piece of autobiography? We never find out: the director resolves the issue with a visual gag worthy of silent cinema but too explicit to be in it. A young female inspector enters through the bedroom window determined to upbraid Rodak for breaking building regulations, but somehow ends wrapping her thighs around him to facilitate her entrance. Once safely in the room she protests but doesn't unwrap them. The couple shuffle like a couple of mating crabs into the sanctuary of a bedroom wardrobe and rooftop regulations are soon forgotten; a surreal riff on bureaucracy and desire that is reminiscent of Buñuel at his driest.

Rodak is really a director stranded between stage and screen – a self-styled maestro of performance spectacle, and as the film shows at the start an artistic celebrity in Paris and a hustling nobody in London. His staged street Happening with clashes between Solidarity protesters and Jaruszelski's militia (shot at Stonebridge bus depot) appears to have a cast of hundreds (Polish expatriates who are never paid) but no visible audience, which is actually lodged in a fleet of red London buses dodging in and out of the street confrontations and fitted inside with banked screens showing a recent Polish football win over England plus, even more bizarrely, cartoon illustrations of the betrayal of Yalta. Like Fellini's Guido in *8½*, Rodak is the maestro of the incomplete project, of a stillborn spectacular financed by seedy producer John Hurt who wants him to lure him into making porn-shows instead of political theatre that no one understands. And by way of homage (and reversal) the film includes Anouk Aimée (Guido's long-suffering wife in Fellini's film) as Rodak's stage designer and covert lover, who turns 'home' into what seems to be a cosy *ménage à trois*. Skolimowski's film comes to us at the end of the reflexive cycle of European modernism, whereas Fellini's masterpiece is at the beginning.

Skolomowski's 'happening' still presents us with a razor-sharp, doubled-edged sword. While it codes the Warsaw conflict between Solidarity and a militarised regime at a time when no Polish-based film would be able to do so, it simultaneously codes the tensions between London Poles and their indifferent hosts who care not a fig for Poland. In the end, is it more important for Poland to beat England at football than for Solidarity to beat martial law? In both *Moonlighting* and *Success* we have an Anglo-Polish parallax, the surreal uncanny sense that Poland bleeds into England and England bleeds into Poland, that one moment we are witnessing Warsaw-on-Thames and the next London-on-Vistula; while at the same time Poles and Londoners are separated by a cultural abyss. And of course this *is* location Kensington, this *is* London, this is the Skolimowski habitat, the remortgaged house that will have to be sold to meet the costs of a film which makes no money and prompts the director to leave the country, exiled from Poland by politics and censorship and now from England by lack of money and indifference. The two 'my house' films echo the earlier autobio modernism of his 1960s Polish period in *Identification Marks: None*, *Walkover*, *Barrier* and *Hands Up!* (Mazierska 2008: 3–6) and in a way complete them. And *Success*, brilliant and ridiculous by turns, completes the twenty-year cycle of the expatriate eye which transformed the nature of British cinema.

CHAPTER 8

# *Terence Davies and Bill Douglas: the poetics of memory*

In the latter part of the twentieth century we could argue that two indigenous visions dominate: in Scottish cinema that of Bill Douglas, in English cinema that of Terence Davies. That is to say, they dominate in terms of *vision*, not in terms of output. Both careers were haunted by failure to realise key projects. Douglas had devoted much of his time to a screen version of James Hogg's classic Scottish novel *The Confessions of a Justified Sinner*, for which there exists an extant screenplay but little more; Davies has tried for many years to bankroll a version of Lewis Grassic Gibbon's *Sunset Song* – two great Scottish artworks but neither in the end brought to the big screen. Uncannily, Douglas shared a desire to bring Hogg's classic to the screen with Ingmar Bergman, but in the end Bergman decided it was unfilmable. Douglas, with hand-to-mouth funding courtesy of the British Film Institute and then Channel 4, never had the luxury of making such a decision. What links Davies and Douglas in the UK films they did make is, loosely speaking, fictionalised autobiography – Davies in Liverpool, Douglas in Newcraighall, just outside Edinburgh. But these films are something much more: memory-films that forge a virtual history out of their own lives, fragments of a life that are remade and reworked, first through the medium of memory and then the medium of film itself. And both directors worked through overlapping trilogies – Douglas with *My Childhood* (1972), *My Ain Folk* (1974) and *My Way Home* (1976); Davies with *Children* (1976), *Madonna and Child* (1980) and *Death and Transfiguration* (1983). We could argue in fact that Davies produced a *double trilogy*, the first of these early short films, the second of the features which have made his critical reputation. His recent (2008) documentary *Of Time and the City* seems the unofficial third of a trilogy begun in 1988 with *Distant Voices, Still Lives*, followed by *The Long Day Closes* (1992). It is a documentary made as much by chance as by design after the director's quest for broader projects had crumbled. Or rather a window of opportunity opened up as Liverpool became Europe's 2008 City of Culture and Davies took his chance with an unexpected commission.

Douglas and Davies provide us with a cinema of memory which is also a virtual history of self, place and family, an audio-visual mosaic of time past.

The second Davies 'trilogy' – the unofficial one – is in fact a broader trilogy of family, self and city which may be unparalleled in its scope and ambition. The class dimension is crucial here. Both directors reveal, contest and revere their working-class origins while pinpointing the force of circumstance that caused them grief: their narratives of pain and redemption otherwise make no sense. In Douglas the pain is more harrowing, but equally the personal redemption (in Egypt) is stronger. The Douglas persona has no home to speak of and his life is spent searching for one. The Davies persona, by contrast, is rooted in home but despairs of losing it through the passage of time. Whether time corrodes or heals is the elusive mystery that lies at the heart of their work and we would have to say that it does both at the same time. The memory that starts in pain and loss ends in the healing art of film itself, the exorcism executed through the camera lens. Both re-enact the Proustian conquest of suffering through art, that is through an art-form that has to reveal suffering in order to transcend it. But since the kind of filming they engaged in was never easy, we could say it is a double transcendence, first of the pain and difficulty of the world the film portrays, and second of the difficulty of the film form itself, of the very act of filming – the shoot – which in the case of Douglas was particularly acute (Noble 1993: 119–24).

For his period, Douglas was a clear anomaly in Scottish cinema. He had no real ties to the documentary tradition instigated by Grierson and certainly none to the romantic tradition of the Scottish feature film. Having fallen in love with 1950s Hollywood and Doris Day, as Davies would do, but also with silent cinema, the next revelation for him would be the European modernism of the 1960s – Bergman, Truffaut, Antonioni. All three are present in his film school short *Come Dancing* (1970) – Truffaut's lyricism, Bergman's tight framing, Antonioni's spatial tension – and all feed into the trilogy, though in Truffaut's case the theme of forlorn childhood in *The Four Hundred Blows* (1959) has a special resonance. At the same time Douglas's strict adherence to the still frame would place him closer stylistically to Carl Dreyer, Yasujiro Ozu or Robert Bresson. Indeed, the unique Douglas 'way of seeing' almost puts him outside of UK cinema altogether. At the same time the internal break with previous Scottish cinema specifically is the most poignant aspect of the trilogy. It represented a modest, single-handed alternative to the whole of the romantic tradition rooted in what we might call island landscapes, in Powell's *The Edge of the World* (1937) (Foula) and *I Know Where I'm Going* (1945) (Mull), in David Macdonald's *The Brothers* (1947) (Skye) and in Mackendrick's *Whisky Galore* (1949) (Barra). Metaphorically speaking, with their tropes of suppressed love, we might want to call them, as Petrie does, 'islands of desire' (Petrie 2000: 35–2). To this we might add Lean's romantic melodrama *Madeleine* (Glasgow) as a townhouse history film featuring

Madeleine's 'basement of desire': for the trilogy was light years away from this too. Whereas *The Wicker Man* (contemporaneous with *My Childhood*) is a dystopian inversion of the island melodrama that works through its ingenious variation on trauma, it was still, as we have seen, an island film in the earlier tradition, which works through shore and cliff and sea. Douglas is a world apart. Unlike *The Wicker Man*, the trilogy helped to change the nature of film language itself, a unique example of mimetic modernism not only in Scotland but in the UK as a whole. Topographically too the sea is conspicuous by its absence. Douglas filmed dry land, the small and shabby mining village of Newcraighall, set amidst a landscape of flat arable fields and lumpy slag-heaps flanking the local colliery; and in the last part of the trilogy he switches to the RAF camp in the Egyptian desert – no Nile, no water. And, unlike Davies who followed him, there was no musical soundtrack either. The image was on its own, spare, unflinching, rendered without compromise.

Douglas and Davies both start with images of childhood towards the end of the Second World War, a looking back that spans twenty years. Air raid sirens sound in *My Childhood* and in *Distant Voices* and families huddle in bomb shelters. In the Douglas film, German POWs work the nearby farm fields: in the Davies film the family's Liverpool neighbourhood is heavily bombed. In both, family life is central, but in the work of Davies there is richness in the home as well as pain, which contrasts with the bleak, empty rooms in the tiny cottages that young Jamie (Stephen Archibald) inhabits in *My Childhood. Distant Voices* starts with the nuclear family; *My Childhood* is a world without parents, a dislocated world of grannies and young boys. Davies gives us recurrent music and song, Douglas neither, unless it is at school assembly or rare festive celebration. Davies gives us the rich rites of ceremonial; in Douglas they are conspicuous by their absence. Coming after Douglas, we could say, Davies supplants Calvinist absence with Catholic presence. But there is also a different kind of difference. In *Distant Voices* the wartime memories are mediated (strictly *the director's memories of his sibling's memories* who had told their young brother many tales of their own childhood which he then absorbed into his own imagination). The father's kindness on Christmas Eve, for instance, followed by his violent rage on Christmas Day is the *mise-en-scène* of the memory of a bitter memory. The childhood 'memories' of Davies thus have a broader mediate remit as family and collective memories, while *Of Time and the City* is a collective visual memory that goes beyond family, period footage compiled by Davies not so much as *his* memory but as his selective palimpsest of the common visual legacy of Liverpool at that time. By comparison Douglas had a tight, restricted focus – his early life within a semi-isolated mining village filmed twenty years later when it was still thriving, filmed that is, a few years before it was swallowed up by Edinburgh's urban sprawl and the colliery closed for good as the mining industry there was shut, as it was in the 1980s throughout mainland Britain, by a Conservative government at Westminster.

## MIMETIC MODERNISM AND FAMILY MYSTERIES: THE DOUGLAS TRILOGY

We can call the trilogy an example of mimetic modernism – it shoots on location and tries to be true to a life remembered. It is, then, a poetics of memory. It composes narrative as a mosaic of fragments, fragments of time remembered, selected, isolated and recomposed. It illuminates through visual language and precise editing, keeping dialogue to a minimum: for the most part Douglas makes no attempt to write naturalistic conversation. The fragmented nature of narrative is identical to young Jamie's fragmented experience of family, first one grandmother and then, after she dies, another in a cottage round the corner, and a father who lives opposite the second granny (his father's mother it transpires) and who appears to have a wife or girlfriend living with him, while his absent mother lies incarcerated in an asylum and his father's mother is consumed with jealousy of the paramour opposite. Family life is a riddle that has to be solved, step by step. It is one that can be solved in terms of lines of lineage, though not in terms of meaning. That lineage is organic and can be exposed: there are no parallax views here like the ones we have seen attached to modernism's expatriate eye. Lineage is opaque but organic, and Jamie is a reluctant detective, forced to be precocious to resolve the riddle of his own life.

Family dramas on screen are usually predicated on key events which happen early on: but that assumes some knowledge of the family by the main protagonist, and the spectator. The protagonist must know who they are and we must know who they are. It is a starting point often given us in the first five minutes of a Hollywood film where we can roughly label people and events. But in *My Childhood* we cannot figure out exactly who is who, and neither can young Jamie. That, more than anything, constitutes the early drama of the story – the quest to know what we normally expect to know in the first place. In *My Childhood* there is no primal knowledge. We as spectators are as much in the dark as he is. Where are his mum and dad? Who are they? Who is the ageing black-shawled lady he lives with in that tiny upper flat and who is the father of his older brother Tommy (Hughie Restorick), who also lives there? Things that normally unfold 'naturally' in childhood refuse to unfold at all. We see village houses within a stone's throw of each other, a neat and tight topography in Jamie's life that should give us the usual clues and cues of lineage, but instead give us neither. We face the same battle of recognition he does. We are not omniscient and given licence to detect the natural mistakes of a child. In viewing the narrative we are in the same bewildering position. 'Seeing' here is equivalent to exploring the hidden labyrinth of parentage (of absent parents) where nothing is made explicit and where a culture of silence prevails. The maze of meaning is identical to the maze of lineage.

The culture of silence here can be seen as the offshoot of a culture of shame and secrecy. In an early sequence Douglas shows a solitary Jamie searching for coal on a slagheap and looking down as miners, their shift over, are welcomed by their children coming up from the village. Excluded, he finds a surrogate father in the figure of Helmuth, a POW working on the fields, but as the war is ending Helmuth will soon leave for Germany and leave him stranded. Isolated, Jamie identifies with the foreigner, the prisoner, in effect, the enemy. Unlike the young subjects of Bresson and Rohmer whose search, subconsciously, may be a Catholic search for grace, Jamie's instinctual search is a search for meaning, any meaning, to his diminished life. In that respect he is a mix of Rossellini's Edmund in *Germany Year Zero*, especially in his search for fuel and other bare necessities, and of Bergman's Johan in *The Silence*, who cannot figure out the unnerving relationship between the two sisters, mother and aunt, in their mysterious journey to a foreign city. Neither Jamie nor Johan, that is, can read the adult signs. In Bergman's film the title refers not only to the near-silent relationship between the sisters but also to God's 'silence' where the state of human affairs is devoid of his intervention and hence of any imposed meaning. In the Douglas trilogy this works as a post-Calvinist conceit where the religious signs of meaning – salvation and damnation, humility and good works, modesty and the suppression of desire – are left stranded and devoid of faith. No minister, no kirk, no service, no devotion. The austere, the sparse, the minimal that in faith might be the signs of devotion and good works are here signs of the winter of the soul and the stretch of the void. Redemption, if it is to be found at all, is in the singularity of simple but precious objects, ordinary, profane things that have a transient sacredness for the outcast and the abject. They are precious because of their value and their value lies both in their use and also in the surplus value of possession and belonging in a child's world where there is no sense of belonging and precious little to be possessed.

The first part of the trilogy then is a parable of small things, simple but precious objects, the coal fire, the cat, the canary and the apple. In Jamie's grandmother's house (the house of his mother's mother) there is scant furniture and nothing much else at all. The scarcity of material things reaches down to degree zero, but uncannily in Douglas this also seems the true state of the post-Calvinist soul, its scarred psyche, and material lack seem doomed to reflect it in perpetual bleakness. In the first household the cat is the fireside companion of the granny and the two young brothers. Douglas uses simple objects as tokens of (potential) symbolic exchange. The brightness and heat of the fire around which the three huddle give them silent solace. One day, Tommy finds some dying flowers outside and puts them in a teacup to brighten up the shabby table in the cramped living-room. Jamie tips out the flowers, fills the cup with boiling water and puts it between the hands of his sleeping grandma to warm them – consecutive gestures of affection about which she knows nothing. Tommy's birthday present from his absent dad, who suddenly appears one day and gives him a canary in a cage before being shown the door by the irate grandmother, gives a focus to his life. Some time later he returns to find the bird's remains being eaten by the cat – has granny in spite deliberately left open the door to the cage? Tommy snatches up and kills the cat, Jamie's constant companion, in bitter revenge. Both brothers have had creatures to comfort them, now they have none. Yet the symbolic object can also offer a transient hope. Just before Helmuth is due to leave the village he flies a kite to Jamie's delight: its free upward movement suggests hope in a bleak landscape and is a portent perhaps of the hope that surges forth at the end of the trilogy. And the other thing the figure of Helmuth cues is the saga of the apple.

The solitary apple is the film's main symbolic object of exchange, an object for Jamie that was a rare treat. In the film it literally becomes word before it becomes object. Jamie tries to teach Helmuth English through the use of his school picture book, especially how to say 'apple' just as Helmuth teaches him in turn how to say '*Apfel*'. This, the moment of true exchange, before the picture in the book then becomes an object in the film. When the apple is real, however – and no longer an image – its exchange-value is lost. Granny gives Jamie one on the bus journey to see, for the first and only time, his mother in her hospital bed in an asylum. We find out about her just as Jamie does, starkly and suddenly in the midst of a conspiracy of silence. The mutual stare of non-recognition between mother and son as the sick woman lies motionless on her bed is perhaps the most harrowing moment of the trilogy. Just before, Jamie has placed the apple (as a gift?) at the end of the bed. A nurse pockets it and takes it away: 'You stole my apple,' the boy says. Not only has he been deprived of a precious moment of recognition but also of his modest act of giving, and both reduce him to nothingness. Before he has had no mother and afterward he will have no mother either. The second instance of the apple is with the second grandmother. He steals an apple from the dish on her table, he thinks unnoticed, as she sleeps by the fire. A few days later she asks him if he wants an apple, but this time the apple in the dish is flanked by a mousetrap, so Jamie declines. Later when the teenage Jamie leaves his care home to be fostered by a respectable middle-class lady in her Edinburgh home he is offered an apple from a full dish as his foster mother listens, eyes closed, to a classical symphony. Instead of accepting, he proceeds to steal the apples one by one from the dish and stashes them inside his zipper jacket. Soon he will flee, homeless, into the bowels of the city. All the apple exchanges are non-exchanges, instances of the breakdown of reciprocity, the dissolution of trust. And Douglas forges a near-silent visual language to illustrate it, creating multiplicity out of the minimal, complexity out of simple things.

Later there are other objects of symbolic non-exchange. With his second granny, Jamie the errant truant comes back one day via the back window when his erratic carer is out and drinks from a milk bottle in the larder. He then tries to top up the bottle with tap-water but the kitchen tap is dry. So instead he urinates, offscreen, into the bottle and onscreen into the dog litter by the fire so that that granny will assume the smell is from her beloved pet on which she bestows more affection than on her grandson. Later at the care home the boys' single Christmas present is a gift transformed into an object of non-exchange through its multiplicity. Douglas shows the care home supervisor, Mr Bridge, popping identically shaped presents into each of the Christmas stockings of all shapes and sizes that the boys have hung up in expectation. But the cultural importance of the gift (at birthdays or at religious festivals) would usually be in the uniqueness of the gift. Here each boy, including Jamie, gets an identical harmonica and at Christmas dinner Bridge is greeted by a cacophony of sound from identical musical objects. Boys taken from failing homes to a uniform life are thus made more uniform by this standardised act of giving that is near Dickensian in its reflex.

Halfway through *My Way Home* Douglas jump-cuts from the rail lines outside Edinburgh's Waverly station to the tyre tracks of a lorry travelling through the Egyptian desert. Offscreen is heard a new voice and a new friend, that of Robert (Joseph Blatchley) at the RAF camp where Jamie discovers at last the meaning of authentic exchange. The older English conscript, handsome and well-spoken, joins Jamie for breakfast one morning and both have kippers on their plates. Since Jamie's fish is untouched, Robert shows him how to bone it: Jamie tries to copy and fails miserably, and pushes the plate aside. Robert swaps the plates and they begin to eat, Jamie sampling at last the miracle of true exchange. He has made the transition from apples – sweet and succulent but which don't function – to kippers – tart and salty which do. The swap, we might say, is the start of a beautiful friendship, but one edged with tension and indirection. It is a modest male romance fraught by uncertainty and social difference – the raw, working-class Scot and the older, assured Englishman, in a way a romance that cannot find an easy label any more than Jamie's opaque family relations can. It is a romance because of place and difference – the leap to Egypt and the empty desert, then Cairo and bustling crowds – and it happens because of the transporting of self from one world to another. The uneasy, ineffable nature of the friendship that Douglas charts through spatial tension within the still-frame where the men talk and sit and fool around on empty desert landscapes framed by the camp's wire fence is the key. So modernist *mise-en-scène* firms up continuity with the earlier parts of the trilogy, but romantic feeling rips the canvas and the world starts afresh. Modernist poetics has an unlikely romantic coda and bears within it future hope of a true way home.

## Davies: the romantic imagist and the poetry of memory

For Davies memory is poetic and elliptical, visual and musical. It has rhythm and structure in its imagistic recall. And for Davies, the symphonic music lover, the ear must hear as the eye sees. If British cinema has produced one filmmaker who truly echoes the imagistic poetry of Eliot earlier in the century, he is it. In that respect he is as close to Eliot as Resnais is to Marcel Proust. For modern poetry is itself audio-visual: you simultaneously see the words and hear them: part of the greatness of Eliot's *Waste Land* lies in its spatial arrangement of free verse on the printed page which draws the eye to line endings in the way that modernist montage draws attention to the cut between shots. And yet autobiographical Davies is an unashamed romantic. He inherits from 1940s England the romantic realism of Jennings, Hamer and early Lean, matching that tradition to the abstract intimacies of the chamber drama he finds in later Bergman. He also fills that out, it has to be said, with the lush romanticism of the Hollywood musical and 1950s melodrama of Douglas Sirk and Max Ophuls. His use of realism is thus neo-romantic, matching the absorption of classical genre to the absorption of modernist abstraction where style is a constantly innovating force, especially in its rendering of time and memory. Davies embodies, then, a fertile contrast, a creative contradiction: stretching the point, you could say his best films are modernist musicals or conversely, romantic abstractions from family life.

*Distant Voices, Still Lives* is a memoir-musical, his musical but not his memoir, but instead a compendium of memory-fragments of his older siblings framed by his own memories in which there is no central autobiographical persona. Reared in working-class Liverpool, the youngest in a family of nine living siblings, Davies chooses three for his fictional family, two sisters and a brother, and excludes himself. His 'autobiographical work' – so-called – demonstrates the weakness and not the strength of the literal 'auto-bio' persona. It is everywhere but also nowhere: the memory films disperse it into a wider net of memories with many filaments – parents, siblings, school, church, pub, community and city. Just as Davies has difficulty with his adult persona on screen, so too he has problems with the present-ness of things, with the living or the recent present. Usually the two difficulties go hand-in-glove. You sense that in the hiatus between extended childhood and incipient filmmaking he is uncomfortable in his own skin. The past as cyclical and recurrent magic is a source of redemption sought out of desperation and, in one agonising projection, the future is imagined as the opposite, the hell of dying without God, central to *Death and Transfiguration*, Part 3 of the early trilogy where Robert, the Davies persona, confronted by the death of his mother, imagines his own death, the portrait of a repressed artist as an old man, encapsulated in the superb performance of the veteran Wilfrid Brambell.

In that short film trilogy (1976–83) the first and last parts – *Children* and *Death and Transfiguration* – work better than the central part, *Madonna and Child.* But the latter boasts the trilogy's most powerful sequence. It is very near the end. In the remarkable double-pan, left to right and then right to left across the local church altar flanked by its mosaic of the Stations of the Cross, the moving image is juxtaposed to a soundtrack of two men, tattooist and client (the distressed Robert), negotiating a genital tattoo in profane language over the telephone. The image is sacred, the voices profane. The slow camera pan is hypnotically poetic: the conversation shockingly naturalistic. At one level it is aural-visual blasphemy; the image captures the frieze of the Saviour's crucifixion while the conversation substitutes another form of crucifixion that can only be imagined. But in the mind of the believing persona haunted by his unalterable sin – desire for the muscular male body – he is substituting his own symbolic crucifixion for that of the Saviour. According to doctrine Christ died an agonising death to save the world. Robert desires a symbolic death (painful in a different way) in order to save himself.

The double pan also keys in a critical break with the still frame of Douglas – Davies' teacher and inspiration at National Film School – which had marked *Childhood.* Here, and in the flowing forward track where Davies frames the work canteen attached to Robert's office by placing him in long-shot behind a busy snooker table then moving the camera forward across the table until the shot is a composition of an excluded figure eating sandwiches alone, Davies shows his virtuosity for camera movement that flows and glides through space without drawing attention to itself. The Davies camera takes the spectator with it, a feature of effortless movement the director would use with even greater subtlety and daring in his later work. If the director's confidence in the exploration of space increases towards the end of the trilogy, then his explorations in time work right the way through it. As Davies' work progresses, movement in space becomes crucial to movement in time. Time 'jumps' in the memory, and in film the abrupt transitions can be simulated through montage. But Davies also wants to make it float through space; to make a film a transcendent moment in which the contingent barriers of space and time in the life-world are transcended. This is the great accomplishment of *The Long Day Closes.*

## FLOATING THROUGH SPACE AND TIME: *THE LONG DAY CLOSES*

An early matrix of conjoined sequences in the film shows the power and poetry of a trademark Davies' inventiveness. It is sustained by music soundtrack but ends with the solo acoustic singing voice of Bud's mother (Marjorie Yates). What flows sensuously through non-diegetic sound ends in poignant diegesis. Time, space, image and sound work in poetic interplay. The impulse is romantic but the nocturnal ending with the mother singing to Bud (Leigh McCormack) as he perches on her knee is wistful and forlorn, the long romantic moment capped by the unromantic *durée* of the domestic world. The editing allows time to flow through space across division. The single, concentrated movement of the camera is a time-image which flows through space and duration so that with the magic of the cinema, the discontinuous becomes continuous. It compares with a similar sequence in *Distant Voices, Still Lives*, again a cinema sequence that ends in a family sequence but with different consequences. In the earlier film Davies starts with an upward tilt from opened umbrellas in pouring rain outside the Futurist picture house, then brings up the soundtrack of 'Love is a Many-Splendoured Thing' from *Guys and Dolls*, cutting to a frontal shot of sisters Eileen (Angela Walsh) and Maisie (Lorraine Ashburne) inside watching the screen in tearful rapture. It is a romantic moment shattered by the sudden cut to the figures of their brother Tony (Dean Williams) and Maisie's husband George (Vincent Maguire) hurtling from collapsed scaffolding and shattering a factory's plate glass roof with their sudden fall. Romantically, Eileen and Maisie respond to the Hollywood screen image: materially they are brought down to earth by the horrific fall. And the Davies staging makes it seem as if the men are falling not merely through glass but through the cinema screen we never see, shattering the illusion. In both films Davies associates the cinema in general and Hollywood three-strip Technicolor in particular with the romantic nourishing of the soul. But outside the cinema, the world intervenes and the moment of nourishing cannot be sustained.

*The Long Day Closes* sequence starts with Bud watching from his bedroom window the Guy Fawkes bonfire in the street below. The soundtrack fades up the contralto Kathleen Ferrier singing 'Blow the Wind Southerly'. The song overlaps the time intervals that follow – the cut to Bud walking to school the following morning (right to left tracking) past the ashes of the bonfire, and then to his school desk where Davies brings the down the lighting of the

**Figure 8.1** Snug and Cosy: Alyse Owens and Leigh McCormack in *The Long Day Closes*

**Figure 8.2** Out in the Cold: Stephen Archibald in *My Childhood*

room to leave him alone illuminated in the classroom. Isolation by light amid darkness prompts a song–vision matrix. Bud looks right out of the classroom window and sees the sails of the schooner that the song evokes (left to right pan), as Davies fades up the imaginary sound of wind and waves. A reverse angle to the turned head of the watching boy suggests hair soaked by the spray. A frontal shot of the classroom increases illumination: Bud is sharply backlit now amidst other desks and pupils dimly lit. The camera pans right and down amidst the desks and a dissolve brings us out of darkness to a cinema balcony as Bud, again backlit, sits forward in the front row, flanked by mother and sister, looking down at the screen. They are watching the film of the *Carousel* waltz and the music is briefly diegetic before another dissolve to the neon star of a big wheel in a fairground as the erstwhile screen-gazers, mum, son, daughter, are walking in single file (left to right) through the fair. 'John! Kevin!' they call out to Bud's older brothers ahead of them at the rifle range chancing their arm. The music has changed once more to a timely, traditional ballad 'She Moved through the Fair'. The left–right track continues with Bud now eating candy floss and the music continues over the final cut to mother and son at home in a fireside armchair. Davies fades out the soundtrack as he brings up the mother's voice to complete the song that ends in marriage – the happy marriage we might guess from the earlier films that she never had. The camera tracks in and then holds on the mother–son couple for an eternity after the song has ended: tears begin to roll down her cheeks. The past for her is both nostalgia but also what might have been. 'My dad used to sing that,' she tells him, and her voice has already turned to lament.

In this form of time–space image the continuity is not so much dramatic as poetic, floating through sound and space. As in *Distant Voices* cinema becomes both subject and object as Davies conjures, like the magician he is, time–space images of the floating world. The right–left track or pan (as at the start of the sequence) is usually a visual trope for a return to the past. It echoes the right–left track down the deserted street to the derelict family house (now awaiting demolition) that had begun the film. There a subsequent dissolve to Bud sitting on the doorstep takes us further back in time to where the story begins. Thereafter the left–right track (the more usual convention in film) cues movement *forward* in time, but of course always in time past and time remembered. So it brings with it its own ellipses. For Davies, the spatial consistency of the camera movement bridges the memory ellipsis and turns it into visual poetry. But so does music. Musical cadence ushers it forward at the same time – of necessity. There is no pause here for non-musical sound. The three music pieces he uses merge into each other, and each has a distinctive, tangy association with the time in which the film is set. In the mid-1950s 'Blow the Wind Southerly' was a radio favourite, *Carousel* (1956) a lush Fox musical about a fairground barker with lyrics by Rodgers and Hammerstein and 'She Moves through the Fair' a popular 1950s revival ballad. Davies integrates thematic elements from all three sources diegetically into the *mise-en-scène*. For him, these are also sounds and images before the corrupt age of television and rock'n'roll, from his two beloved media, cinema and radio. Yet the momentum of the whole sequence is created by moving from a *division* between the romantic and the mundane – Bud daydreaming the schooner of the Ferrier song out the classroom window – to the *fusion* of film, music and the mundane, the film of *Carousel* about a fairground as a preface to the fairground sequence, the 'fair' ballad as the postscript that invokes the mother's memory of unrealised hopes in her own marriage.

The director's evocation of his past blends romantic sensibility with the reflex of modernist style. His cinematic references merge precisely with his themes of loss and separation: voice-over excerpts from *The Ladykillers* and *The Magnificent Ambersons* are truly self-conscious but for that reason *in place* rather than out of place. The film references are also visual – the posters, the cinema, the crowds, Bud's hustling for an accompanying adult in pouring rain, the auditorium: but at the same time Davies rightly withholds the screen image itself. As Bud watches from the balcony in the single auditorium shot, flanked by mother and sister, there is no reverse-angle. The film's persistence of rain may well come from *Singin' in the Rain*, an early Davies favourite; Davies' fixation for front door and hallway blends perfectly with the start of Mackendrick's *The Ladykillers*. Moreover the memory shot that seals the reflexive fix is a double act. In the classroom sequence Davies brings down the lights to leave a single, perpendicular spot backlighting the deskbound Bud. This is *before* the balcony shot where the same perpendicular light becomes metonymic: it stands in for the projector's beam thrown down at the screen. Thus Bud is backlit and bathed in the magic light which delivers the onscreen image that entrances him. It is because the stylistic device segues into metonymic illumination that the continuing sequence gathers strength. Style precedes substance but substance then becomes the revelation of style. This is not just a film bathed in the poetics of memory but a film about a cinematic childhood. Just as *Death and Transfiguration* had been a fleeting portrait of the future artist as an old man, so *The Long Day Closes* is a full portrait of the current artist as a young boy, breathing new life after the death of his tyrant-father, not yet facing the solitude and troubled sexuality of later youth when brothers and sister have left home. It is a blissful interlude as if the way-marks of the future artist's life were inferno, paradise and purgatory – in that order.

## THE PAST AS PRESENT: *THE HOUSE OF MIRTH* AND *THE WINGS OF THE DOVE*

Although *The Long Day Closes* can be seen as the middle film in the unofficial Liverpool trilogy, it also has an uncanny connection with his 2000 adaptation of Edith Wharton's *The House of Mirth*, which acts perhaps as the psychic counterpoint to the earlier dream-memoir. Davies, we could argue, turns to fiction and history for the disconnectedness that had marked his early adult life and which had featured as near-contemporary and autobiographical in the short films. It was his second venture into American fiction and history after *The Neon Bible* taken from the novel of John Kennedy Toole; but this time there are no children or teenagers to speak of, no mother–son relationship and no centredness on family life. For Davies, in that sense, it was a first. The American films also show his flair from creating, like Bergman, powerful and imposing women on screen. In *The Neon Bible* the superlative Gena Rowlands as the itinerant Aunt Mae was still family. Lily Bart (played by a superb Gillian Anderson) is a lone figure, very much detached from *la vie en famille* and with her failure to marry, unable to establish her own. Disconnection, exclusion, abjection, Lily Bart shows them all in her fall from social grace. When word spread that Davies was shooting a period film with East Coast American settings in the west of Scotland, eyebrows must have been raised. But his bold location shoot in Glasgow, standing in for New York with its extant and coherent Victorian architecture for an early century film, proved to be inspired. The architectural harmonies of his staging are crucial to the deft coherence of narrative and his imagining of social milieu with all its nuances. The move from working-class mid-century life to upper-class early century life (1905–7) is flawless. And as a 'Scottish-American' picture this is a triumph.

The other difference from his earlier films was, as he told Wendy Everett, the challenge of tragedy the novel presented (Everett 2004: 223–4). This is not a chronicle of survival but a complex fable of failure to survive. In this it differs from most British period films with their eventual romantic triumphs, or, conversely, failure and death that tend to be overly melodramatic. In this film Davies is neither romantic nor melodramatic. There is a steely austerity in tone plus a delicate shading of emotion in close-up which recalls Bergman at his very best. It also makes an apt contrast with the extravagant gestures and sumptuous décor used by Scorsese in his adaptation of Wharton's *The Age of Innocence.* Although Davies admires the lush melodrama of the lone heroine perfected by Sirk and Ophuls in the 1950s, he remains a very European director – perhaps the one moment of melodrama in his work is the killing at the end of *The Neon Bible.* His film stresses precision of design and costume and also the Jamesian side of Wharton – nuance, understatement, implied meaning. This is as far from the explicit sexuality of the early trilogy us can be imagined. Thus the blasphemous shock ending of *Madonna and Child* which broached the tattoo taboo is replaced at the start of this picture by the tea taboo, ostensibly trivial but still in its own way a deep transgression of milieu. It was simply not done for a single woman of means at the time to take tea, as Lily does, unaccompanied in a young bachelor's apartment. It is because Davies understands transgression so well that he can make a scene that should seem slight so deeply dangerous and reverberative.

Let us now look wider. In the close relationship between Wharton and Henry James we can note that *The Age of Innocence* has great plot kinship with *The Golden Bowl* since both texts deal in the subtle exclusion of the 'amorous foreigner'. Conversely, we can link *The House of Mirth* to *The Wings of the Dove* since both are novels about social predators in an age of etiquette where the act of predation remains something seemingly unnoticed and largely unspoken. A British version of James' novel had by chance come to the big screen in 1997, three years before *The House of Mirth*. Directed by Iain Softley and scripted by Hossein Amini, Amini has claimed his screenplay was mediated by cinema itself. He had consciously adapted the novel through the lens of *film noir* with its lexicon of passion, conspiracy and betrayal (Amini 1998: vi–viii). The results startle with their anachronism. The film is the most overt erotic costume drama in UK film to date, in which sexuality floats with a fluid ease between James' three main characters, Kate Croy (Helena Bonham Carter) Merton Densher (Linus Roache) and Milly Theale (Alison Elliott). Moreover, the elimination of Kate's sister from the story, the greater sordidness of her father, the invention of Densher's political radicalism, the overt sexual encounters of Kate and Merton are all major inventions of the film (Wood 1999: 22–7). This was poetic licence taken to the edge. By contrast, Davies is faithful to plot, faithful to costume and convention, faithful to milieu. Unlikely Softley's film, there are no opium dens, no sexual couplings and no revolutionaries. Davies has been criticised for eliminating Wharton's occasional anti-Semitism but that is answered by his conscious soundtrack inclusion of Jewish songs and music, as if to stress the only possible grounds for his contemporary makeover of the text. And the wider vision of Wharton's novel goes beyond her own narrowing of it. The film, like the book, is about the power of money and marriage to make or break – and without either, Lily is broken.

Both films divide their main characters into predators and unwilling victims. In Softley's film predation backfires: the trauma of Millie's death has damaged the conspiring couple irreversibly. Softley reserves his most sexual scene between Kate and Densher for the final moments where passion freezes and fire turns to ice. Davies, by contrast, reserves the most passionate moment of his film for the stolen half-kiss between Lily and Lawrence Selden (Eric Stoltz) at Bellomont, a passion made stillborn by milieu where no romantic transcendence is available. Selden is too weak to follow his passion for Lily and does not have the money to buy her through marriage: an affair with a married woman is instead an acceptable dalliance in a society where not only the rules but also the hypocrisies of the game have to be obeyed. The film then follows Lily's fall from grace and is uncompromising in its refusal to be over-emotional or sentimental about the terrors of isolation. This makes finally for a comparison between the end of the Douglas trilogy and the end of Davies's feature-film career to date. The austere modernism of Douglas allows itself at the end a glimpse of future hope through male romance. Conversely, in Davies the promise of romance gives way in the unfolding of Lily's fate to the austerity of isolation and the nearness of death.

CHAPTER 9

# *Conclusion: into the new century*

One of the striking features of the new century is that three major UK films to date (June 2009) are identical in two ways. All three are biopics and all are dèbut features by visual artists who have come from outside cinema. They are Douglas Gordon's *Zidane: a 21st Century Portrait* (2006), Anton Corbijn's *Control* (2007) and Steve McQueen's *Hunger* (2008). Gordon is a famous Scottish installation artist, Corbijn a highly regarded photographer and director of music videos, and McQueen a Turner Prize-winning video artist (Gordon and McQueen are also ardent cinephiles). A third element is common to all three films: they combine a British dimension with a non-British dimension. *Zidane* is about a famous French footballer and co-directed by Gordon with Frenchman Philippe Parreno, while photographer Corbijn is Dutch not British, and *Hunger*, co-written by Irish playwright Enda Walsh, is set and shot with Irish cast and crew in Northern Ireland. This duality is partly because film, especially in Europe, can move easily across national borders but also because, generically speaking, outstanding British cinema has always been enhanced by crucial elements of 'non-Britishness', and many would argue, anyway, that *Hunger* is, apart from its director, a completely Irish film.

*Zidane*, using multiple camera set-ups in real time to capture Zidane in action in a Madrid football match, has been impressively analysed by Beugnet as integral to a contemporary cinema of the body, 'as a moving sculpture of audio-visual matter' (Beugnet 2007: 171–5). The other two films are less experimental, but historically, I would argue, more ambitious. In revisiting the divide and crossover between romantics and modernists I want to look at *Hunger* and *Control* and especially the way in which their contrasting nature shows the legacy of both romantic and modernist forms. They are biopics of the same period, the start of the 1980s when the modernist period of UK cinema was coming to a close. They have real-life protagonists who both killed themselves. But they are differently conceived in terms of cinema in ways that are fascinating. *Control* reworks through Joy Division singer Ian Curtis the mythos of the doomed young artist and *Hunger* through Bobby Sands, the IRA hunger striker, the mythos of the doomed young activist.

Both are powerful, emotional pictures. Yet in *Control* romantic feeling is primary and modernist staging secondary: in *Hunger* it is the other way round. *Control* tells continuously the story of a troubled life that ends in personal tragedy: *Hunger* tells the immediate story surrounding the life before entering the life itself. In one film Curtis (Sam Riley) is the life; in the other, Sands (Michael Fassbender) enters the life some way into the film, a life which is the world of the Maze prison, its warders and its Republican prisoners.

Here it helps us to illuminate these features by looking at films that stand close to both of them. Two years before *Hunger* won the Caméra d'Or for first feature at Cannes in 2008, Ken Loach's *The Wind that Shakes the Barley* (2006) took the coveted Palme d'Or, a rare honour for an English director. For *Control* the doomed romance of the artist is prefigured in British film way back in Powell and Pressburger's classic melodrama *The Red Shoes* (1948). So let us start with this (unlikely) pairing of ballet and post-punk artistry first. In the earlier film Vicky Page (played by 21-year-old Moira Shearer) is a talented young dancer who literally dies for her art. Her fate is foreshadowed in the story through the extended ballet sequence, a *tour de force* in cinematic staging that dominates the picture. Here, in the Hans Christian Andersen fable the ballet enacts, the red shoes fitted to her agile feet to aid her artistry, prove fatal. In a sacrificial dance of death the shoes force her into perpetual motion where she literally, and very beautifully, dances herself to exhaustion and oblivion. At the end of the film, the sting in the tail of its romantic irony, life eerily imitates art and then merges with it. Vicky is torn between the love of her new husband, the precious Julian Craster (Marius Goring), and the demands of her ruthless impresario Lermontov (Anton Walbrook) for which she can find no resolution. Performing on the Côte d'Azur she dances the Red Shoes ballet in public for the last time, rushing from the stage and jumping from a balcony onto the railway track below. The imaginary onstage death has turned into an actual, offstage suicide.

Destructive propulsion was also integral to the stage performance of Ian Curtis, singer with the post-punk Mancunian band, Joy Division. (In the film the band performances are live and often electric, using Riley's own voice.) Moreover Riley, a singer himself, captures the essence of the Curtis performance. Curtis had developed epilepsy during his brief career and at times his uncontrollable seizures became a disturbing climax to his shamanistic onstage projection. The lyrics of his song 'Control', which give us the film's title, are precisely about the loss of control through epilepsy that he had first witnessed in a disabled client during his day job and which, suddenly and unexpectedly, would take over his own life. His artistic power to attract and express is inseparable from his power to destroy – destroy that is, himself, body and soul. Just as Vicky Page is torn between the conflicting demands of two men, so Curtis is torn between the conflicting demands of two women, his young wife (played by Samantha Morton) and his Belgian lover (played by Alexandra Maria Lara). These are classic romantic dilemmas evoked in *The Red Shoes* by stunning three-strip Technicolor and in *Control* by high-contrast black and white cinematography. The triumph of Lermontov's ballet is a riot of rich colour: the triumphant moment of the Manchester cult band is as dark as charcoal. But though the context of each film is as different as day and night, the quest for self-expression as an exalted art takes its doomed artist to the edge and then into the abyss. If this contrast is a world apart in terms of class and culture, a contrast between refined Southern ballerina and Northern city boy singer, it is also very English, evoking that irreducible romantic residue still immanent in a national culture which now prides itself on kitsch irony and upfront cynicism.

If this contrast convergence over decades is very English, then the key contrast convergence of this decade is very Irish, the delicate difference between *Hunger* and *The Wind that Shakes the Barley*, both directed by Englishmen. The veteran Loach, usually revered as a contemporary social realist, in fact reserves his two best films, *The Wind that Shakes the Barley* and *Land and Freedom* (1995) about the Spanish Civil War, for the genre of the revolutionary romance where the quest for a better world is upended by recrimination and betrayal. This is both Loach's strength and his weakness. For revolution he has to look beyond the British mainland where he is on less firm ground and also look away from the present towards the past. But here he finds strength in depth and a perspective with which to look at the revolutionary quest for liberation from oppression, in the earlier film the fight against Franco's fascism by the International Brigades, in the later film the fight by Irish Republicans in Cork against British colonial rule in 1920. Loach is naturalistic by inclination with an occasional touch of melodrama, but in *Barley* his naturalism has a steely precision. What strengthens his work in both these history films is the way in which he coaxes his acting group to establish a camaraderie that re-enacts the historic camaraderie of the revolutionary group, the subject of his film. Hence the masterly casting of Cork actors, including Cillian Murphy, to re-enact triumphantly the saga of the Cork Republicans who join the join the fight against the British and then, tragically, after the signing of the 1922 Treaty, turn on each other in the civil war that convulsed the new Free State. Some may say the film is a political riposte to Jordan's spectacle recreation *Michael Collins*, but in a way it is better seen as atonement for *Ryan's Daughter* – an English director and his Scottish screenwriter, Paul Laverty, getting Irish history and culture right where Lean had got it so disastrously wrong. Yet despite its atmospheric photography and strong acting, Loach has made a fairly conventional film which follows general continuity guidelines about history drama.

McQueen, by contrast, does nothing of the sort. His film starts with the life of a prison guard before switching to young Republicans even before Bobby Sands (Michael Fassbender) enters the frame for the first time. The film is thus a biopic which poses the question: who is the subject of this film? It then becomes polyphonic, changing its cinematic style in a three-act format. The first, long section of the film, the section of physical conflict between guards and inmates over cell defilement, is done almost without dialogue. The middle section contains a twenty-two-minute two-way conversation between Sands and priest Dominic Moran (Liam Cunningham), most of it in a backlit profile two-shot, and the third section, of Sands' starving-unto-death, the motif of 'hunger' is done again largely without words, with at times a steely silence that contrasts with the first act's tumult of noise and movement and the second act's conceit of continuous talk. The three-act narrative is thus a model of abstract lyricism with its own interior rhythms, like an audio-visual symphony. In this way McQueen extends, enhances and redefines the modernist heritage.

This abstract lyricism of ritual and repetition is unusual in films about Ireland and *Hunger* compares most strongly with Alan Clarke's taut, short film about endless killing, *Elephant* (1988). Clarke conceived of a sequence of killings that are repetitive but without apparent connection and in which both killer and assassin are anonymous, in which no dialogue (with one fleeting exception) ever takes place and in which Clarke shoots with live sound on exterior Belfast locations using a series of Steadicam long takes for killer and victim following shots. *Hunger* of course is largely interior, ingeniously shot in a derelict Belfast sports centre made over as the Maze Prison for the shoot. It is ironic that its only killing should be outside the prison when Ray Lohan, the warder (played by Stuart Graham), whose life it highlights in the first 'act', is suddenly assassinated in a care home where he is visiting his elderly mother. Like Clarke, McQueen shocks us through unexpected killing in an unexpected place – the experience, in fact, of many involuntary witnesses and surviving victims throughout the long period of the Troubles. He also makes sure that the rituals of everyday life loom large – the attention to small detail that obviates melodrama and places the extraordinary event, the Hunger Strike, in an ordinary context. We eat our food, wear clothes and generally observe rules of sanitation and hygiene. But in the Maze, they are shed one by one in the constant battle between guard and prisoner, between purity and defilement.

A prison movie with its immovable walls, ceilings and floors can be a limitation on shared vision, and the film's immense variation in style is in part a response to this. Like *Dial M for Murder* and *Blow-Up*, *Hunger* uses sharp change of angle and focus range in confined physical spaces to enhance the image through abrupt edits and extend the range of cinematic possibility. But this applies equally to the staging within the frame. One thinks of that harrowing sequence where naked prisoners (during their 'on-the-blanket' protest) are forced to run the gauntlet between lines of warders striking them with batons. McQueen here extends the range of the spectator's eye through a split-screen effect: a medium long shot shows the line up and the vicious blows on the left of the frame while on the right, slumped against a wall, is the shattered figure of a young warder crying himself into complete crack-up. And it is not only width but also depth in which McQueen excels. A wide-angle corridor long shot that follows the twenty-two-minute conversation shows in a single take a cleaner brush-washing urine with disinfectant as it seeps from the cells, washing that which defiles with that which cleans back into the cells from whence it came. The camera frame is perfectly still: brush and sweeper zigzag forward inexorably towards it, and towards us; there is no escape. As the film moves towards its end through segmented shots of Sands' dying emaciated body there is a sense of fatality, inevitability. Made about the final stages of the twentieth century in the early part of the twenty-first century, this is a film about tragic destiny which, on viewing again, still manages to surprise us.

# *Select bibliography*


Amini, Hossein (1998) *The Wings of the Dove: A Screenplay*. London: Methuen

Anthony, Scott (2007) *Night Mail.* London: British Film Institute.

Antonioni, Michelangelo (2007) *The Architecture of Vision: Writings and Interviews on Cinema* (ed.) Marga Cottino-Jones. Chicago: University of Chicago Press.

Armes, Roy (1978) *A Critical History of the British Cinema.* London: Secker & Warburg

Ashby, Justine and Higson, Andrew (eds.) (2000) *British Cinema, Past and Present.* London: Routledge.

Barr, Charles (1998) *Ealing Studios.* Moffat: Cameron & Hollis, 3rd edition.

Barr, Charles (1999) *English Hitchcock.* Moffat: Cameron & Hollis.

Bersani, Leo and Dutoit, Ulysse (1993) *Acts of Impoverishment: Beckett, Rothko, Resnais.* Cambridge, MA: Harvard University Press.

Beugnet, Martine (2007) *Cinema and Sensation: French Film and the Art of Transgression.* Edinburgh: Edinburgh University Press.

Bordwell, David (2006) *The Way Hollywood Tells It: Story and Style in Modern Movies.* Berkeley, CA: University of California Press.

Bordwell, David (2008) *Poetics of Cinema.* Berkeley, CA: University of Californian Press.

Brownlow, Kevin (1996) *David Lean: A Biography* London: Faber & Faber.

Caughie, John (1992) 'Halfway to Paradise'. *Sight and Sound* May, 11–13.

Caughie, John (1993) 'Don't Mourn – Analyse: Reviewing the Trilogy'. In E Dick, A. Noble, and D. Petrie (eds.) *Bill Douglas: a Lanternist's Account.* London: British Film Institute, 179–204.

Caute, David (1994) *Joseph Losey: a Revenge on Life.* London: Faber & Faber.

Chatman, Seymour (1985) *Antonioni: or, The Surface of the World.* Berkeley, CA: University of California Press.

Chion, Michel (2001) *Kubrick's Cinema Odyssey* (trans. Claudia Gorman) London: British Film Institute.

Christie, Ian (2000) *A Matter of Life and Death.* London: British Film Institute.

Christie, Ian and Moor, Andrew (eds.) (2005) *The Cinema of Michael Powell: International Perspectives on an English Film-Maker.* London: British Film Institute.

Ciment, Michel (1984) 'Skolimowski'. In Christopher Lyon (ed.) *International Dictionary of Films and Filmmakers*, vol. 2. London: St James Press.

Ciment, Michel (1985) *Conversations with Losey.* London: Methuen.

Ciment, Michel (2001) *Kubrick: The Definitive Edition* (trans. Gilbert Adair and Robert Bononno). London: Faber.

Coates, Paul (2006) '*Cul-de-Sac* in Context: Absurd Authorship and Sexuality'. In John Orr and Elżbieta Ostrowska (eds.) *The Cinema of Roman Polanski: Dark Spaces of the World.* London: Wallflower Press

Crowdus, Gary (2009) 'The Human Body as Political Weapon: An Interview with Steve McQueen'. *Cineaste*, Spring, 22–5.

Deutelbaum, Marshall and Poague, Leland (ed.) (2009) *A Hitchcock Reader* Chichester: Wiley-Blackwell, 2nd edition.

Dick, Eddie, Noble, Andrew and Petrie, Duncan (eds.) (1993) *Bill Douglas: a Lanternist's Account*. London: British Film Institute.

Dixon, Wheeler Winston (1994) '*The Long Day Closes*: an interview with Terence Davies'. In W. Dixon (ed.) *Reviewing British Cinema 1900–1992: Essays and Interviews*. New York: State University of New York Press, 249–59.

Drazin, Charles (1999) *In Search of The Third Man*. London: Methuen.

Drazin, Charles (2007) *The Finest Years: British Cinema of the 1940s*. London: I. B. Tauris.

Durgnat, Raymond (1970) *A Mirror for England: British Movies from Austerity to Affluence*. London: Faber & Faber.

Elsaesser, Thomas (1993) 'Images for Sale: The "New" British Cinema'. In Lester Friedman (ed.) *British Cinema and Thatcherism: Fires Were Started*. London: UCL Press, 52–69.

Everett, Wendy (2004) *Terence Davies*. Manchester: Manchester University Press.

Farley, Paul (2006) *Distant Voices, Still Lives* (London: British Film Institute)

Freud, Sigmund (1967) *Moses and Monotheism*. New York: Vintage Books.

Freud Sigmund (1984) 'Beyond the Pleasure Principle'. In *Pelican Freud Library Volume 11: On Metapsychologyi*. Harmondsworth: Penguin Books, 269–338.

Frye, Northrop (1976) *The Secular Scripture: a Study of the Structure of Romance*. Cambridge, MA: Harvard University Press

Gardner, Colin (2004) *Joseph Losey*. Manchester: Manchester University Press.

Girard, René (1979) *Violence and the Sacred* (trans. Patrick Gregory). Baltimore, MD: Johns Hopkins University Press.

Horne, Philip (2000) 'Beauty's Slow Fade'. *Sight and Sound*, 10(10), 14–18.

Horne, Philip (2005) 'Life and Death in *A Matter of Life and Death*'. In I. Christie and Andrew Moor (eds.) *The Cinema of Michael Powell: International Perspectives on an English Film-Maker*. London: British Film Institute, 117–31.

Jackson, Kevin (2004) *Humphrey Jennings*. London: Picador

Jackson, Kevin (2007) *Lawrence of Arabia*. London: British Film Institute.

Kaplan, E. Ann and Ban Wang (eds.) (2004) *Trauma and Cinema: Cross-Cultural Explanations*. Hong Kong: Hong Kong University Press

Kelly, Richard (ed.) (1998) *Alan Clarke*. London: Faber & Faber.

Kermode, Frank (1968) 'Modernisms'. In Bernard Bergonzi (ed.) *Innovations*. London: Macmillan.

Krohn, Bill (2000) *Hitchcock at Work*. London: Phaidon Press.

Kynaston, David (2008) *The Smoke in the Valley: Austerity Britain 1948–51*. London: Bloomsbury.

Leigh, Mike (1995) *Naked and Other Screenplays*. London: Faber & Faber.

LoBrutto, Vincent (1998) *Stanley Kubrick*. London: Faber & Faber.

MacCabe, Colin (1998) *Performance*. London: British Film Institute.

Macnab, Geoffrey (2009) 'Interview with Skolimowski'. *The Guardian* 11 March, 24.

Marks, Leo (1998) *Peeping Tom*. London: Faber & Faber.

Marks, Leo (2000) *Between Silk and Cyanide: A Codemaker's War 1941–1945* London: HarperCollins, revised edition.

Maugham, Robin (1972) *Escape from the Shadows*. London: Hodder & Stoughton.

Maugham, Robin (1973) *The Servant* London: W. H. Allen.

Mayer, Geoff (2003) *Guide to British Cinema* Westport, CT: Greenwood Press.
Mazierska, Ewa (2008) 'From Participant to Observer: Autobiographic Discourse in the films of Jerzy Skolimowski'. *Kinema*, Fall. www.kinema.uwaterloo.ca/mazi082.htm. Accessed 07 March 2009.
McCullin, Don (1992) *Unreasonable Behaviour: an Autobiography*. London: Vintage.
McGilligan, Patrick (2003) *Alfred Hitchcock: A Life in Darkness and Light.* Chichester: John Wiley.
Mee, Jon (2003) *Romanticism, Enthusiasm and Regulation: Poetics and the Policing of Culture in the Romantic Period.* Oxford: Oxford University Press.
Mosley, Nicholas (1991) *Accident; a novel.* Elmwood Park, IL: Dalkey Archive Press.
Mulvey, Laura (2005) 'The Light that Fails: A Commentary on *Peeping Tom*'. In I. Christie and A. Moor (eds.) *The Cinema of Michael Powell.* London: British Film Institute, 143–15.
Murphy, Robert (2000) *British Cinema and the Second World War.* London: Continuum.
Murray, Jonathan (2005) 'Straw or Wicker? Traditions of Scottish Film Criticism and *The Wicker Man*'. In J. Murray, L. Stevenson, S. Harper and B. Franks (eds.) *Constructing The Wicker Man: Film and Cultural Studies Perspectives.* Glasgow: Crichton Publications.
Naremore, James (2007) *On Kubrick.* London: British Film Institute.
Newman, Kim (2009) 'From Romance to Ritual'. *Sight and Sound*, 19(3), 22–3.
Noble, Andrew (1993) 'The Making of the Trilogy'. In E. Dick, A. Noble and D Petrie (eds.) *Bill Douglas; a Lanternist's Account.* London: British Film Institute, 117–72.
O'Pray, Michael (2003) *Avant-garde Film: Forms, Themes, Passions.* London: Wallflower Press.
Orr, John (1998) *Contemporary Cinema.* Edinburgh: Edinburgh University Press.
Orr, John (2000) 'The Art of National Identity: Peter Greenaway and Derek Jarman'. In Justine Ashby and Andrew Higson (eds.) *British Cinema: Past and Present.* London: Routledge, 327–38.
Orr, John (2002) 'Traducing Realisms: *Naked* and *Nil by Mouth*'. In (Julian Petley and Duncan Petrie) (eds.) *Journal of Popular British Cinema*, 5, 104–13.
Orr, John (2003) 'New Directions in European Cinema'. In Elizabeth Ezra (ed.) *European Cinema.* Oxford: Oxford University Press, 299–317.
Orr, John (2007) 'Camus and Carné transformed: Bergman's *The Silence* versus Antonioni's *The Passenger*'. *Film International*, 5(3) 54–62.
Orr, John (2006) *Hitchcock and Twentieth-Century Cinema.* London: Wallflower.
Orr, John (2008) '*Control* and British Cinema'. *Film International*, 6(1), 13–22.
Palmer, James and Riley, Michael (1993) *The Films of Joseph Losey.* Cambridge: Cambridge University Press.
Pasolini, Pier Paolo (2005) *Heretical Empiricism* (trans. Ben Lawton and Louise Barnett). Washington, DC: New Academia Publishing, 2nd edition.
Petrie, Duncan (2000) *Screening Scotland.* London: British Film Institute.
Reeves, Tony (2001) *The Worldwide Guide to Movie Locations.* London: Titon Books.
Richards, Jeffrey (1997) *Thorold Dickinson and the British Cinema.* Lanham, MD: Scarecrow Press.
Rohmer, Eric and Claude Chabrol (1992) *Hitchcock: the First Forty-four Films.* Oxford: Roundhouse Publishing.
Rosenbaum, Jonathan (2004) 'License to Feel: *Distant Voices, Still Lives* and *The Neon Bible*'. In *Essential Cinema: On the Necessity of Film Canons.* Baltimore, MD: Johns Hopkins University Press, 386–98.
Ryall, Tom (1993) *Blackmail.* London: British Film Institute.
Ryall, Tom (1996) *Alfred Hitchcock and the British Cinema.* London: Athlone, 2nd edition.

Sanderson, Mark (1996) *Don't Look Now*. London: British Film Institute

Silver, Alain (2004) 'David Lean'. www.sensesofcinema.com/contents/directors/04/lean.html. Accessed 15 February 2008.

Silver, Alain and Ursini, James (1992) *David Lean and his Films* Los Angeles: Silman-James Press.

Street, Sarah (1997) *British National Cinema*. London: Routledge.

Tippetts, John C. (2002) 'The Old Dark House: the Architecture of Ambiguity in *The Turn of the Screw* and *The Innocents*'. In Steve Chibnall and Julian Petley (eds.) *British Horror Cinema*. London: Routledge, 99–116.

Truffaut, François (1984) *Hitchcock*. London: Paladin.

Turner, Adrian (1994) *The Making of David Lean's Lawrence of Arabia*. London: Dragon's World.

Wapshott, Nicholas (1990) *The Man Between: a Biography of Carol Reed*. London: Chatto & Windus.

White, Rob (2003) *The Third Man*. London: British Film Institute.

Wollen, Peter (2002) *Paris, Hollywood and other Writings*. London: Verso.

Wollen, Peter (1993) 'The Last New Wave'. In L. Friedman (ed). *British Cinema and Thatcherism: Fires Were Started*. London: UCL Press, 35–51.

Wood, Robin (1999) *The Wings of the Dove*. London: British Film Institute.

# *Index*

*Accident* 3, 116, 117–20, 125–8, 149, 157
*Ae Fond Kiss*, 16
Aimée, Anouk, 162
Alcott, John, 115
Amini, Hossein, 178–9
Anderson, Gillian, 177–8
Anderson, Lindsay, 115, 118
Andersson, Harriet, 64, 77
*Angel*, 87, 161
Antonioni, Michelangelo, 1, 41, 79–80, 102, 106, 115–17, 119, 129–40, 141, 144, 165
*Apocalypse Now*, 84–5
Archibald, Stephen, 166–71
Arnold, Andrea, 4, 16
Asher, Jane, 152–6
Asquith, Anthony, 5, 7, 11–14, 28–9
Attenborough, Richard, 45
Auden W. H., 10, 12
*Aventure Malgache*, 31, 39–40

Bacon, Francis, 159
*Badlands*, 30
Baker, Stanley, 118, 125
Balchin, Nigel, 93
Balcon, Michael, 7, 35
Banks, Leslie, 72
Baring, Norah, 12, 14, 15
Barr, Charles, 24
*Barrier*, 163
Barry, John, 144
*Barry Lyndon*, 115–16, 141, 148–52
Bates, Alan, 156–9
*Battle of Algiers, The*, 26
*Battleship Potemkin, The*, 8
Bazin, André, 76
Beethoven, Ludwig Van, 142–7
Bennett, Arnold, 14
Bennett, Compton, 65
Berenson, Maria, 151
Bergman, Ingmar, 64, 77, 119, 164, 165, 168, 171
Bernstein, Sidney, 33
Bevan, Tim, 16
*Beyond the Pleasure Principle*, 87–8
*Birds, The*, 16
*Blackmail*, 5, 7, 12, 18–23, 41
*Black Narcissus*, 3, 21, 45, 91, 94–7, 101
*Bloody Sunday*, 25
Bloom, Claire, 25, 58–60, 63
*Blow-Up*, 3, 41, 109, 115, 117–18,124, 129–35, 139–40, 144, 183
*Blue Lamp, The*, 46–7
Boehm, Carl, 101
Bogarde, Dirk, 45, 117–29
Bolt, Robert, 68, 81
Bond, Edward, 115
Bonham Carter, Helena, 178–9
*Bon Voyage*, 31, 34, 36–40
Boorman, John, 1, 3–4, 58, 63, 87, 97, 111, 118
Bordwell, David, 101, 117–18
*Bourne Supremacy, The*, 25–6
*Bourne Ultimatum, The*, 25–8, 63
Brambell, Wilfred, 71
Brecht, Bertolt, 118
Bresson, Robert, 165, 168
Breton, André, 24
*Bridge on the River Kwai, The*, 64–5, 69, 78–9, 83–5, 94, 97
*Brief Encounter*, 11, 44, 64–5, 70
*Brighton Rock*, 30, 46–7
Brisson, Carl, 18
Britten, Benjamin, 10
Brosnan, Pierce, 58

*Brothers, The*, 165
*Bunny Lake is Missing*, 105–8, 109, 115
Burgess, Anthony, 115, 143–5
Burton, Richard, 58, 63
Butor, Michel, 124
Byron, Kathleen, 91, 95–8

*Cabinet of Dr Caligari, The*, 7, 157–8
Caine, Michael, 58
Cammell, Donald, 112
Camus, Albert, 137–8
Capote, Truman, 104
*Captive Heart, The*, 30, 54
*Caravaggio*, 17
*Carousel*, 176
Carroll, Madeleine, 25
Castro, Fidel, 61
Cavalcanti, Alberto, 9, 29–30, 34–5, 37, 46, 61, 90, 92–3
Chaplin, Charles, 6
*Children*, 164, 172
Christie, Julie, 111–14
Ciment, Michel, 120, 144, 152
*Citizen Kane*, 57, 66–7
Clarke, Alan, 16, 183
Clayton, Jack, 101–4
*Clockwork Orange, A*, 3, 109, 115, 116, 117–18, 124, 141–8, 159
*Colditz Story, The*, 30
*Come Dancing*, 165
*Confessions of a Justified Sinner, The*, 164
Connery, Sean, 58, 62
Considine, Paddy, 26
*Control*, 180–2
Coppola, Francis Ford, 84
Corbijn, Anton, 180–2
Corman, Roger, 108
Corrie, Adrienne, 146
*Cottage on Dartmoor, A*, 5, 11–14,
Cotten, Joseph, 54–6, 58–9
Coward, Noël, 60–1, 70, 106
Craig, Wendy, 121
*Cul-de-Sac*, 105, 115, 116, 152–3, 155, 157, 160
Currie, Tim, 157
Curtis, Ian, 180–2

*Dambusters, The*, 78
Damon, Matt, 25
Dankworth, John, 116
Davies, Terence, 1, 3, 45, 97, 164–7, 171–9
Dawson, Anthony, 22
*Days of Heaven*, 148
*Deadly Affair, The*, 58, 62–3, 99
*Dead of Night*, 21, 36, 49, 89–93
Dearden, Basil, 30
*Death and Transfiguration*, 164, 172, 176
*Death in the Afternoon*, 138
*Deep End*, 116, 143, 152–6
Dehn, Paul, 116
Deighton, Len, 58
Deleuze, Gilles, 66, 118
*Deliverance*, 63
Deneuve, Catherine, 102–4
*Départ, Le*, 152
*Dial M for Murder*, 13, 22–3, 134, 183
*Diamonds are Forever*, 58
*Diary for Timothy, A*, 44
Dickens, Charles, 45–6, 64–5
Dickinson, Desmond, 59
Dickinson, Thorold, 34–7, 88–9
Dietrich, Marlene, 15, 40, 66
*Dirty Pretty Things*, 16
*Distant Voices, Still Lives*, 164–6, 171, 173, 175
Dominick, Andrew, 152
Donat, Robert, 26
Donen, Stanley, 116
*Don't Look Now*, 4, 21, 88, 108–14, 118, 131, 139, 149, 154, 157
Dorléac, Françoise, 105
Douglas, Bill, 3, 164–71
Dovzhenko, Alexander, 6
Drazin, Charles, 54, 56
Dreyer, Carl Theodor, 165
*Drifters*, 5, 7–10, 17
*Duellists, The*, 152
Dullea, Keir, 105–6
Du Maurier, Daphne, 111, 113
Dupont, E. A. , 5, 14–16
Durgnat, Raymond, 2, 29, 90

*Edge of Love, The*, 93
*Edge of the World, The*, 93
*8½*, 162
Eisenstein, Sergei, 6–9
Ejiofor, Chiwetel, 16
*Elephant*, 183

Eliot, T. S. , 154, 171
Elsaesser, Thomas, 1–2
*Emerald Forest, The*, 63
*End of the Affair, The* 30
*Escape from the Shadows*, 123
Evans, Edith, 89
Everett, Wendy, 177
*Excalibur*, 63

Fairbanks, Douglas, 6
*Fallen Idol, The*, 31
Farrar, David, 91, 96, 97–8
Fassbender, Michael, 181–4
Fellini, Federico, 153, 162
Ferrier, Kathleen, 173–6
Finch, Jon, 14, 41
Finney, Albert, 143–4
*Fires Were Started*, 9, 44–5
*Firm, The*, 16
Fisher, Gerry, 126
Fisher, Terence, 108
*Fish Tank*, 16
Ford, John, 79–80
Foster, Barry, 42
Foucault, Michel, 147
Fox, James, 112, 120–9
Francis, Freddie, 104
Frears, Stephen, 16
*French Connection, The*, 26
*Frenzy*, 14, 40–3, 79, 93
Freud, Sigmund, 86–8, 102
Frye, Northrop, 45–6
*Funeral in Berlin*, 58
*Funny Games* (1997), 147

Gabin, Jean, 29
Gance, Abel, 6
Garmes, Lee, 65
*Gaslight* (1940), 21, 88–9
*Germany, Year Zero*, 168
Gielgud, John, 117, 128–9
Gilbert, Lewis, 100
Girard, René, 109
*Go-Between, The*, 128, 158
Godard, Jean-Luc, 153
*Goldfinger*, 58
Gordon, Douglas, 180
Grant, Cary, 33, 67

Graves, Robert, 156
*Great Escape, The*, 30
*Great Expectations*, 44, 64, 69, 72
Green, Guy, 45, 66
Greenaway, Peter, 3–4, 139, 141, 144
Greene, Graham, 11, 30–2, 35, 54–8, 60–2, 117
Greengrass, Paul, 25–8, 63
Grierson, John, 5–11, 165
Griffith, D. W. , 6
Guinness, Alec, 49, 61–2, 78–9, 93–4
*Guys and Dolls*, 173

Hamer, Robert, 1, 29, 44–50, 92, 93–4, 171
Hamilton, Chico, 116
Hamilton, Guy, 58, 110
Hamilton, Patrick, 88
Hancock, Herbie, 116
*Hands Up!*, 156, 163
Haneke, Michael, 147
Hardy, Robin, 108–9
Harrison, Rex, 34
Hartley, L. P. , 128
Harvey, Laurence, 25, 101
Heller, Otto, 45, 100
Hemingway, Ernest, 61, 138
Hemmings, David, 129–35
Hendry, Ian, 103, 138
Hening, Ugo, 12
Hitchcock, Alfred, 1, 3, 5–7, 12–34, 44, 62–4, 66, 69–70, 92, 98, 114, 134
Hobson, Valerie, 49
Hogg, James, 164
Holden, William, 79
Hordern, Michael, 149
*House of Mirth, The*, 3, 117–19
Howard, Trevor, 14, 29, 55–6, 66–9
*Hunger*, 50, 180–4
Hurt, John, 157–8, 162

*I Confess*, 16
*Identification Marks: None*, 163
*If*. . ., 115, 118, 141
*I Know Where I'm Going*, 165
*Innocents, The*, 21, 87, 101–5, 115, 117–18, 131, 157
*In Which We Serve*, 10–11
*Ipcress File, The*, 58

Irons, Jeremy, 159–61
*It Always Rains on Sunday*, 14, 44–50

James, Henry, 101–2, 178–9
James, William, 102
Jancsó, Miklós, 106
Jarman, Derek, 1, 3–4, 16, 18, 97
Jennings, Humphrey, 9, 44–5
*JFK*, 130
Johns, Mervyn, 36, 91
Johnson, Celia, 65
Jones, Griffith, 46, 54
Jordan, Neil, 16, 30, 87, 161, 182
*Jour se lève, Le*, 29
Julien, Isaac, 16
Junge, Alfred, 91, 95

Keiller, Patrick, 2–3, 139
Kelly, Grace 23
Kerr, Deborah, 95–6, 101–4
*Kind Hearts and Coronets*, 49–50, 93–4
*Kings of the Road*, 140
Knef, Hildegaard, 59–60
*Knife in the Water*, 119, 152
Knightly, Keira, 93
Knott, Frederic, 22
Komeda, Krzysztof, 116
Krasker, Robert, 45, 48, 52–3, 66
Kubrick, Stanley, 1, 115–16, 141–52, 159
Kuleshov, Lev, 6
Kureishi, Hanif, 16

La Bern, Arthur, 41
*Lady from Shanghai, The*, 74
*Ladykillers, The*, 93–4, 105, 176
*Lady Vanishes, The*, 23, 32–4, 37, 40
Laine, Cleo, 116
*Land and Freedom*, 182
Lang, Fritz, 91
Laurie, John, 76–7
Laverty, Paul, 16, 182
*Lawrence of Arabia*, 3, 64, 69, 78–85, 94, 97, 136
Lean, David, 1, 3, 10–11, 44–6, 64–85, 97, 140, 148, 165–6, 171
Le Carré, John, 58, 62–3, 116
Lee, Bernard, 66
Lee, Christopher, 109
Leigh, Mike, 16, 140
Leigh-Hunt, Barbara, 42
Leone, Sergio, 84
*Life and Death of Colonel Blimp, The*, 84
*Lifeboat*, 23
*Listen to Britain*, 44–5
*Live and Let Die*, 58
Loach, Ken, 16, 181–2
Lockwood, Margaret, 25, 33
*Lodger, The*, 7, 19, 22
*London*, 3–4
*Long Day Closes, The*, 164, 173–7
Lorre, Peter, 101
Losey, Joseph, 1, 18, 115–29, 144, 149, 157
*Lost Highway*, 100
*Lost Weekend, The*, 98
Lumet, Sidney, 58, 62–3, 115

*M*, 101
*McCabe and Mrs Miller*, 109
McCallum, John, 14, 29
McCormack, Leigh, 173–6
McCullin, Don, 130–1
Macdonald, David, 165
Macdonald, Richard, 120
McGowan, Alex, 42
MacGowran, Jack, 105, 152
Mackendrick Alexander, 93–4, 108, 165, 176
Mackenna, Virginia, 100
MacKinnon, Gillies, 16
MacPhail, Angus, 7, 34, 39
McQueen, Steve (actor) , 30
McQueen, Steve (director) , 50, 180–4
*Madeleine*, 64–5, 70–8, 165–6
*Madonna and Child*, 164, 172, 178
Magee, Patrick, 145–6, 149
*Magnificent Ambersons, The*, 176
Malick, Terence, 30, 148
*Man Between, The*, 11, 25, 54–60
Mankiewicz, Joseph, 115
*Man of Iron*, 161
*Man Who Knew Too Much, The* (1956), 22
*Manxman, The*, 5, 12, 14, 16–18
Marks, Leo, 93, 97–101
*Marnie*, 16, 98
Marx, Karl, 125, 128
Mason, James, 14, 29, 59–60, 63, 65

Massey, Anna, 42, 99, 105
*Matter of Life and Death, A*, 88–91, 97–8
Maugham, Robin, 119, 123–4
Maugham, Somerset, 123–4
Maybury, John, 93
Mercer, David, 116, 128–9
Merchant, Vivien, 42, 126
Melville, Jean-Pierre, 38–9
*Michael Collins*, 182
Miles, Sarah, 121
Milland, Ray, 22, 79
Mitchell, Yvonne, 89
*Modesty Blaise*, 144
*Mona Lisa*, 16
Montague, Ivor, 7
Montand, Yves, 128
*Moonlighting*, 115–18, 152, 154, 156, 159–62
Moreau, Jeanne, 118
*Morgan, a Suitable Case for Treatment*, 128
Morris, Oswald, 60, 63
Mortimer, John, 106, 115
Mortimer, Penelope, 106, 115
*Moses and Monotheism*, 87–8
Mosley, Nicholas, 119, 126–7
Moulder-Brown, John, 152–6
*Mountain Eagle, The*, 7
Mulvey, Laura, 99–100
*Murder*, 15
*Muriel*, 126–7
*My Ain Folk*, 164–9
*My Beautiful Laundrette*, 16
*My Childhood*, 164–9
*My Way Home*, 164, 169–70

*Naked*, 12, 140
Naremore, James, 143
*Neon Bible, The*, 177
*Next of Kin, The*, 34–7
Nicholson, Jack, 135–9
Nietzsche, Friedrich, 125, 128
*Night Mail*, 8–11
*Night Train to Munich*, 31, 34, 36, 37
*Nil by Mouth*, 16
Niven, David, 90
*North Sea*, 9
*North by Northwest*, 16, 23, 59
*Notorious*, 67, 70
Novello, Ivor, 19
*Number Seventeen*, 5, 24–6

*Odd Man Out*, 14, 44–53
*Of Human Bondage*, 124
*Of Time and the City*, 164, 166
Oldman, Gary, 16
Olivier, Laurence, 105
Ondra, Anny, 17, 19, 20
O'Neal, Ryan, 148–51
Ophuls, Marcel, 38
Ophuls, Max 171
Orr, John, 2
Orwell, George, 147
O'Toole, Peter, 79–85
*Our Man in Havana*, 31, 57–63, 106

*Painted Veil, The*, 124
*Paradine Case, The*, 66, 71
*Parallax View, The*, 117
Parreno, Philippe, 180
*Passenger, The*, 117, 135–40, 149
*Passionate Friends, The*, 64–70, 73, 77
Pawlikowski, Pawel, 4
Peck, Gregory, 13, 66,
*Peeping Tom*, 14, 43, 79, 97–101, 102, 107–8, 111, 115, 117–18
*Pépé le Moko*, 29
*Performance*, 109, 112–13, 115–16, 124
Petit, Chris, 116–17, 139–40
Philby, Kim, 56
*Piccadilly*, 5, 14–16
Pilbeam, Nova 36
*Pillars of Wisdom, The*, 81
Pinter, Harold, 116, 118–29, 141, 157
Pirandello, Luigi, 24
Pleasence, Donald, 105
*Pleasure Garden, The*, 5
*Point Blank*, 63, 87, 109, 111, 118
Polanski, Roman, 1, 100, 102–5, 115, 141, 152–3, 157
Potente, Franka, 25
Powell, Michael 1, 3, 13, 45, 84, 89–91, 93–101, 107–8, 140, 165, 181–2
Pressburger, Emeric 45, 89–91, 94–7, 181–2
Price, Dennis 49, 93
*Providence*, 116–17, 128–9
*Psycho*, 41, 98, 114

*Quai des Brumes, Le*, 29
*Queen of Spades, The*, 29

*Radio On*, 116–17
Rains, Claude, 66–70
Rattigan, Terence, 30
Rea, Stephen, 87
*Reach for the Sky*, 78
*Rebecca*, 16
*Red Desert, The*, 79–80
Redgrave, Michael, 30, 33, 91, 103
Redgrave, Vanessa, 131–2, 134–5
Reed, Carol, 1, 25, 29, 31–2, 34, 37, 44–63
*Repulsion*, 21, 87, 100–5, 107–8, 115, 116
Resnais, Alain, 69–70, 111, 116, 126–9, 171
Reisz, Karol, 128
Richardson, Ralph, 78
Riley, Sam, 180–2
*Ring, The*, 18
Ritt, Martin, 58, 62–3, 115
Roache, Linus, 178–9
Robbe-Grillet, Alain, 124
Roeg, Nicholas, 1, 3–4, 106, 110–16, 139, 154, 156
*Rope*, 16, 23
Rossellini, Roberto, 168
Rowlands, Gena, 177
*Run Lola, Run!*, 25
*Running Man, The*, 25
Russell, Ken, 1, 97
Ryan, Kathleen, 52

*Sabotage*, 12–13, 21, 36, 41
Sands, Bobby, 180–4
Schneider, Maria, 135–9
Schofield, Paul, 2
Scott, Ridley, 4, 152
*Searchers, The*, 79–80
Selznick, David O., 6, 36
*Servant, The*, 18, 115, 116, 118–26, 149, 157
*Seven Pillars of Wisdom, The*, 81–2, 84
*Seventh Veil, The*, 79
Shaffer, Anthony, 42, 108–9
*Shanghai Express*, 15
Sharif, Omar, 81–3, 85
*Shooting Stars*, 7
Signoret, Simone, 58
Sirk, Douglas, 171, 177
*Shining, The*, 142
*Shout, The*, 116, 154, 156–9
*Silence, The*, 119, 168
Skolimowski, Jerzy, 1, 116, 141, 143, 152–63
Slocombe, Douglas, 45, 48, 120–1
*Small Back Room, The*, 21, 91, 97–8
*So Evil, My Love*, 79
Softley, Iain, 178–9
*Sorrow and the Pity, The*, 38
*Sound Barrier, The*, 64–5, 77–8
*Spellbound*, 13, 21, 23, 98
Spiegel, Sam, 79
*Spy Who Came in from the Cold, The*, 25, 58, 62–3
*Stage Fright*, 31, 40–1
Stander, Lionel, 105
*Star Wars*, 156
Stephens, Robert, 157
Stone, Oliver, 130
*Strike*, 8
Sturges, John, 30
*Success is the Best Revenge*, 116, 153–4, 159, 161–3
*Suspicion*, 21
Szabo, Violet, 97
Szczerbic, Joanna, 157, 161–2

*Tailor of Panama, The*, 58, 63
Thackerey, William, 148–51
*They Made Me a Fugitive*, 14, 46, 54–7
*Third Man, The*, 25, 46–7, 54–60, 66, 79, 117
*39 Steps, The*, 14, 25–6
Thomas, Jeremy, 156
*Time without Pity*, 118
Todd, Ann, 64–79, 118
Todd, Richard, 40
*Tom Jones*, 143–4
Toole, John Kennedy, 177–8
*Touch of Evil*, 57, 66
*Trial, The*, 57
Truffaut, François, 32, 116, 165
*Turn of the Screw, The*, 101
*2001: A Space Odyssey*, 141–2, 143, 144

*Underground*, 7

Valli, Alida, 25
*Varieties of Religious Experience, The*, 182

*Vertigo*, 21, 69, 89, 92, 96, 154
Vertov, Dziga, 6, 8
Visconti, Luchino, 152
Von Sternberg, Joseph, 15, 65

Wajda, Andzrej, 161
Walbrook, Anton, 88–9, 181
*Walkover*, 143
Walsh, Enda, 80
Warner, David, 128–9
*Wasteland, The*, 154, 171
*Waterloo Road*, 45
Watt, Harry, 9
*Waxworks*, 7
*Way Ahead, The*, 31
Welles, Orson, 29, 55–8, 66, 74, 76, 118, 151–2
Wenders, Wim, 60, 117
*Went the Day Well?*, 34–5
Wharton, Edith, 117–19
*Whisky Galore!*, 93–4, 108, 165
*Wicker Man, The*, 108–10, 166
Wilder, Billy, 98
Wilding, Michael, 40
*Wind that Shakes the Barley, The*, 181–2
*Wings of Desire*, 60
*Wings of the Dove, The*, 178–9
Withers, Googie, 48–9
Wollen, Peter, 1–2, 56, 117
Woodward, Edward, 108
Wong, Anna May, 15
Wright, Basil, 9
Wyler, William, 64–5, 76, 115
Wyman, Jane, 40

Yates, Marjorie, 173–6
York, Michael, 125, 159, 161–3
York, Susannah, 157
*Young and Innocent*, 32, 36, 40
Young, Freddie, 62–3, 82

*Zidane: a 21st Century Portrait*, 180